"COVID-19 has given rise to an unprecedented global health and economic crisis. The pandemic, which disproportionately affected the poor, highlights the importance of inclusive and sustainable economic growth, but shifting toward an inclusive and sustainable growth paradigm requires vast resources. This book explores a promising new area of finance—impact finance—which can help the world build back better. Written in crystal clear language that is accessible to general readers, it is a must-read for anyone interested in how impact finance can help unleash private capital for a sustainable future."

Donghyun Park, *Principal Economist, Economic Research and Regional Cooperation Department, Asian Development Bank*

"A sustainable future requires vast investments for environmental and social goals. At the same time, huge amounts of private finance are desperately searching for productive investment opportunities. Therefore, the fundamental challenge facing finance in the 21st century is harnessing and leveraging private capital for green and social investments. Innovative financial instruments such as impact bonds help reconcile private greed with public good. I strongly recommend *Greed Gone Good* for anyone interested in understanding how impact bonds satisfy the profit motive of investors *and* foster a more sustainable society."

Shu Tian, *Economist, Economic Research and Regional Development Department, Asian Development Bank*

Greed Gone Good

Greed Gone Good: A Roadmap to Creating Social and Financial Value brings the how-tos of impact finance to a broad-based audience of investors, from the individual to the institutional. Written in an engaging, jargon-free style and loaded with practical advice, it explores the pitfalls and potential of the burgeoning impact revolution—the increasingly widespread belief that business and financial leaders should weigh social value as well as financial value in all of their decisions, to create both a better business model and a better world.

Cheerleaders have written a number of books advocating the magic of impact finance. *Greed Gone Good* hopes for the magic too, but also believes that an uncritical eye does not effectively advance the cause. We now have 10 years of impact investing history to examine, and not all of it is laudable. We could hold hands and sing Kumbaya in praise of impact finance; or we could employ constructive criticism to figure out what's gone well and what hasn't, and how we should move forward more productively. *Greed Gone Good* focuses on the roadmap—how to reorient and repackage finance and investing in order to deliver on this promise. In particular, it focuses on how to realize the potential of the impact revolution to become a silver bullet against future failures.

Green Gone Good will have widespread appeal to investors ranging from individuals and family offices to the world's largest asset managers and investors.

Jane Elizabeth Hughes is Professor of Practice at Simmons University School of Business, and a former director at Social Finance US. She has served as a consultant to the Asian Development Bank and Inter-American Development Bank, with whom she worked to catalyze the development of Social Bond markets. She has written and lectured extensively on impact investing around the world.

Greed Gone Good

A Roadmap to Creating Social and Financial Value

Jane Elizabeth Hughes

LONDON AND NEW YORK

First published 2022
by Routledge
2 Park Square, Milton Park, Abingdon, Oxon OX14 4RN

and by Routledge
605 Third Avenue, New York, NY 10158

Routledge is an imprint of the Taylor & Francis Group, an Informa business

© 2022 Jane Elizabeth Hughes

The right of Jane Elizabeth Hughes to be identified as author of this work has been asserted by her in accordance with sections 77 and 78 of the Copyright, Designs and Patents Act 1988.

All rights reserved. No part of this book may be reprinted or reproduced or utilised in any form or by any electronic, mechanical, or other means, now known or hereafter invented, including photocopying and recording, or in any information storage or retrieval system, without permission in writing from the publishers.

Trademark notice: Product or corporate names may be trademarks or registered trademarks, and are used only for identification and explanation without intent to infringe.

British Library Cataloguing-in-Publication Data
A catalogue record for this book is available from the British Library

Library of Congress Cataloging-in-Publication Data
Names: Hughes, Jane E. (Jane Elizabeth), author.
Title: Greed gone good: a roadmap to creating social and financial value/Jane Elizabeth Hughes.
Description: Milton Park, Abingdon, Oxon; New York, NY: Routledge, 2022. | Includes bibliographical references and index. |
Identifiers: LCCN 2021008167 (print) | LCCN 2021008168 (ebook) | ISBN 9780367566517 (hardback) | ISBN 9780367568054 (paperback) | ISBN 9781003099376 (ebook)
Subjects: LCSH: Economic development–Finance. | Social responsibility of business. | Sustainable development.
Classification: LCC HD75.8 .H84 2022 (print) | LCC HD75.8 (ebook) | DDC 338.9–dc23
LC record available at https://lccn.loc.gov/2021008167
LC ebook record available at https://lccn.loc.gov/2021008168

ISBN: 978-0-367-56651-7 (hbk)
ISBN: 978-0-367-56805-4 (pbk)
ISBN: 978-1-003-09937-6 (ebk)

Typeset in Bembo
by Newgen Publishing UK

This book is dedicated to my husband of 42 years (but who's counting?). I'm nothing without you.

Contents

Acknowledgments		x
Introduction: greed gone good		1
1	The impact of globalization, poverty, and inequality	8
2	Greed gone bad: a perversion of capitalism	24
3	Greed gone good: reimagining the model	38
4	Investors: the driving force	59
5	Microfinance: the seeds of the impact revolution	78
6	The revolution goes mainstream: equity markets…	96
7	….And impact bonds	112
8	Sustainable banking	134
9	Gender-smart investing: are women the silver bullet?	150
10	The way forward	177
Index		182

Acknowledgments

It takes a village.

I gratefully acknowledge the support of the Taylor & Francis editorial team, especially Rebecca Marsh and Sophie Peoples, in the publication of this book. I also appreciate the excellent research assistance of Madeleine Dixon.

Most of all, I am grateful to my endlessly patient and loving family: Jerry, Alex, Anna, Zack, Cayla, Caroline, Benjamin, and Jilly, who put up with me during the whole process. And an especial thanks to Naomi, Liora, Maya, Gabe, Eden, Ellie, Cassie, and Lev for bringing me joy upon joy even during the grim months of the pandemic.

Introduction
Greed gone good

This movement owes its popularity to the failure of other approaches to development, such as foreign aid. Bottom-line capitalism has brought massive inequity, evident in the class-based and racial overtones of the Hurricane Katrina debacle and the unpleasant reality of global markets exposed in the financial crisis of 2007–2010. And then came COVID-19, which exposed the horrid underbelly of globalization and greed, by hitting poor, underserved, vulnerable, often minority populations with disproportionate ferocity.

There has to be a better way—and there is. The profit incentive is a powerful one, so why not embrace this in our quest for economic and social progress? The concept of ESG-based investing (investing in line with environmental, social, and governance goals) is both an affirmation and a reformation of capitalism.

This book is a roadmap to how we can lure huge gobs of private capital into enterprises that promise both financial and social returns.

> There is a tide in the affairs of men,
> Which, taken at the flood, leads on to fortune.
> (Shakespeare, *Julius Caesar*)

As Shakespeare's Brutus noted, there are moments in time when the world is ripe with opportunity. In the world of finance, great innovations have always arisen from such moments. Financial guidelines and structures were born in the wake of the Great Depression of 1929, paving the way for massive growth and prosperity over the next century. The home mortgage enabled millions of people to become homeowners; the development of syndicated loans and project finance enabled huge development projects from gold mines to the Eiffel Tower.

2 *Introduction*

Sometime around the dawn of the 21st century, another such moment arrived in the financial world as the notion of social, environmental, and governance (ESG) investing (also known as triple bottom line investing—sustainable investing, impact investing, or blended value investing[1]) took hold. As the gatekeepers to finance, lenders and investors are responsible for allocating scarce capital to the most promising sectors. Traditionally, master of business administration (MBA) programs taught that these "promising sectors" were those most likely to maximize shareholder value. Other stakeholders, including government and society, were considered for their nuisance value rather than for their intrinsic worth.

In the past two decades, however, the notion of ESG investing has gained credence, even among the most cynical of managers. Moreover, it is widely recognized that lenders, investors, and business leaders, as the ultimate financial decision-makers, have special responsibilities in this regard. Blended value—which encompasses the social, environmental, governance, and financial performance of a business—will only become more important in a globalized economy marked by scarce and shrinking resources. The COVID-19 pandemic and ensuing economic devastation has highlighted the urgency of ESG investing as a way to build back better.

Among changemakers and investors alike, these ideas are being put into action. In 2020, the Global Impact Investing Network (GIIN) estimated the current ESG-based equity investing market size at $715 billion.[2] Around one-quarter of total assets under management (AUM) are invested for social as well as financial value; and the COVID-19 pandemic has spurred the Social Bonds market to explosive growth in 2020.

Foreign aid: There has to be a better way

The impact movement owes its birth in part to the failure of other approaches. Over the past many decades, foreign aid has been the globally accepted cornerstone policy aimed at poverty alleviation, promotion of Western-style democracy, and disaster relief. Well-intentioned as it may be, the most startling aspect of decades and billions of dollars of development aid is the disappointing results.

In Mexico, for example, the US government has contributed more than $300 million to support criminal justice reform—urgently needed in a country devastated by criminality and corruption. But what has this money bought? According to the *Washington Post* in 2017, mostly chaos. Reporters found that "the most profound overhaul" of Mexico's legal structure in one hundred years, aimed at "restoring order to a country torn apart by drug violence," is instead plagued by unforeseen consequences.

Bickering and confusion reign at each link in the legal chain. Police complain of hours lost on laborious forms; prosecutors blame judges for setting criminals free; judges accuse poorly trained police of botching crime scenes. Powerful drug cartels, meanwhile, are exploiting the weaknesses in the new system and strong-arming authorities with death threats and bribes.[3]

The bottom line? A record high of nearly 35,000 people were murdered in Mexico in 2019.

How about all of the development aid ladled out to post-Soviet Eastern European countries to grease the transition to democracy and capitalism?

After the fall of the Berlin Wall in 1989, the US Agency for International Development (USAID) poured over $20 billion into the region to support economic growth, democracy, and governance. Even more cash rained in from Western European powers and multilateral organizations like the World Bank and International Monetary Fund (IMF).

Again, what did this money buy? Economic growth in a few countries (think of Poland and the Czech Republic) has been impressive. On the other hand, many countries continue to limp along as Soviet-style factories collapsed and foreign investors declined to rush in waving fistfuls of dollars. The ten poorest countries in Europe are all former Soviet republics or clients—Moldova, Ukraine, Kosovo, Albania, Bosnia and Herzegovina, Macedonia, Serbia, Belarus, Montenegro, and Bulgaria. In fact, per capita gross domestic product (GDP) in Moldova, the poorest, was a lowly $3,300 in 2019 compared to Norway's lofty $77,975. This means that Moldovans scrape by on an average of $9 per day, while Norwegians live the good life on $214 per day!

So where *did* all that aid money go? Some of it was frittered away on well-paid Western "experts" who jetted in to the donor countries for a week or two, racked up bills at the best hotels in town, and proposed the same policies for every country regardless of its particular circumstances. Anecdotes about these "experts" abound: One story is that experts arrived in Ukraine to present an employment policy that had simply whited-out "Armenia" and superimposed it with "Ukraine."

And then, of course, there's Afghanistan. An Oxfam study in 2008 panned the huge salaries of "most full time, expatriate consultants, working in private consulting companies, [who] cost 250,000–500,000 USD a year," and estimated that 40% of aid since 2001—around $6 billion—had bounced back to donor countries in the form of corporate profits and consultant salaries.[4] And poverty today is much more widespread than it was immediately after the fall of the Taliban.

Ouch. And we still haven't mentioned Haiti, the poster child for expensive and fruitless, even harmful, foreign aid. Haiti's horrifying magnitude 7.0 earthquake of January 12, 2010 left 220,000 people dead, 300,000 injured, and the poverty-stricken country a mass of rubble and devastation. Well-meaning aid donors rushed in with $13.5 billion in donations and pledges. But while the rubble is cleared and the injured (mostly) repaired, the country remains miserably corrupt, poverty-stricken, and—thanks to UN peacekeepers who spilled their waste into Haiti's largest river—overwhelmed by an unprecedented outbreak of cholera.

One observer explains, "USAID has spent about $1.5 billion since the earthquake. Less than a penny of every dollar goes directly to a Haitian organization." And he adds, "International companies had to fly in, rent hotels and cars, and spend USAID allowances for food and cost-of-living expenses." Danger pay and hardship pay can inflate these consultants' salaries by "more than 50 percent."[5]

I have, of course, cherry-picked the worst possible horror stories of international aid; there are also many good-news stories and many people lifted out of poverty thanks to foreign aid dollars. But aid donors tend not to play well together; this lack of coordination leads to duplication of efforts and spotty results. The high proportion of aid money that actually is absorbed by Western companies and "experts" is appalling; and an influx of foreigners waving checkbooks can also exacerbate local corruption while badly distorting the local economy.

A bald statement that aid hasn't worked is too strong; foreign aid is well-intentioned, and some is even impactful. But it is fair to say that we certainly haven't gotten much bang for our bucks (excepting, of course, the very well-paid international development companies and consultants). There has to be a better way.

And there is our opening.

The better way

> The businessman is only tolerable so long as his gains can be held to bear some relation to what, roughly and in some sense, his activities have contributed to society.
>
> (John Maynard Keynes, 1923)

One of the strongest arguments for an impact-based approach to business and society is that bottom-line capitalism has failed. As the first two decades of the 21st century came to a close, we are unnerved by the rise of authoritarian leaders around the world. Financial markets are shivering in fear of what these autocrats will do with all of their power. Climate change in the form of wildfires, massive floods, and man-eating storms is increasingly evident; and we have been treated to the spectacle of wealthy Asian tourists loading up on $10,000 handbags on the Champs Elysees amid thousands of have-nots rioting in the streets.

And this was before COVID-19! The disease exposed the horrid underbelly of globalization and greed, by hitting poor, underserved, vulnerable, often minority populations with disproportionate ferocity. In the state of Louisiana, for example, where blacks are 32% of the population, they account for an unacceptable 70% of those dead from the disease (as of May 2020).

While the disparity is not quite as vast in other parts of the country, it is patently clear that COVID-19 is taking a massive toll on minority populations in the United States while passing fairly lightly over upper middle-class white populations. Blacks and Latinx tend to have a higher level of underlying, untreated medical conditions; live in closely clustered neighborhoods and homes; have poorer access to health care; work in face-to-face "essential" jobs; and experience high rates of discrimination in the health care system.

And then a grim situation became dire when a white police officer in Minneapolis knelt on the neck of a crying and pleading black man, yet it took officials four days to charge the officer with the victim's death. Black communities nationwide exploded in rage, and US cities were best by riots, looting, and street fighting between police officers and demonstrators, the likes of which had not been seen in more than a generation.

As columnist Thomas Friedman wrote, greed and globalization have broken the world.[6]

In fact, all of these developments highlight the lack of social progress and the failures of the old business model that were already evident even before COVID-19, especially in the class-based and racial overtones of the Hurricane Katrina debacle and the unpleasant reality of global markets exposed in the financial crisis of 2007–2010. A crisis is a terrible thing to waste; and this century has already seen four crises—9/11, Katrina, the financial meltdown, and COVID-19—with another likely to unfold in alarmingly short order.

Underpinning these crises has been an epidemic of blind faith. Blind faith in globalization led to a massive backlash—the election of Donald Trump, the British vote to exit the European Union (Brexit), and French rioting in the streets—as the losers from globalization demand attention for their plight. Blind faith in technology led to massive financial breakdowns from Enron to the financial crisis. And blind faith in free markets paved the way for banks that are too big to fail yet unable to police themselves; financial meltdown; and widespread poverty in the developing world.

Is capitalism the problem? Does a world that is dominated by capitalist markets (the only remaining socialist holdouts are Cuba and North Korea) inevitably engender poverty, inequality, and misery?

Well … not so fast. Let's remember what Churchill is believed to have said about democracy: It's the worst form of government, except for all the others. The same is true of capitalism: It's the worst form of economic framework, except for all the others.

The dismal failure of socialism is evident in the collapse of the Soviet Union, China's choice to largely abandon socialism for free markets, and the death struggles of Cuba and North Korea. There is really no rational argument for socialism as a road to prosperity—history categorically refutes that.

The concept of ESG-based investing is in fact both an affirmation and a reformation of capitalism. The profit incentive is a powerful one, so why not embrace this in our quest for social progress? Why not lure huge gobs of capital into enterprises that promise both financial and social returns? Why not incorporate business notions of efficiency and rigorous measurement of results into the realm of do-gooders?

This book, then, is a call to arms—an urgent plea that we all link arms and take a leap of faith together. Much more than that, it is a roadmap to *how* we can take this leap—and land on our feet. Harkening back to Churchill and Einstein, the impact revolution is a movement to do things differently. And echoing Keynes, it is an affirmation of the power and responsibility of business to do *good* and do *well* at the same time.

Notes

1 ESG (environmental, social, and governance) investing refers to investments that seek both positive financial returns and a positive long-term impact on society and the environment.
2 Dean Hand, Hannah Dithrich, Sophia Sunderji, and Noshin Nova. (June 11, 2020). "2020 Annual Impact Investor Survey." *Global Impact Investing Network.*
3 Partlow, J. (December 29, 2017). "How a US-backed effort to fix Mexico's justice system led to turmoil." The *Washington Post.* Retrieved from: www.washingtonpost.com/graphics/2017/world/torn-apart-by-drug-violence-mexico-aims-to-reform-justice-system/?utm_term=.b325e5cb888e.
4 Bjelica, J. and Ruttig, T. (May 17, 2018). The state of aid and poverty in 2018: A new look at aid effectiveness in Afghanistan. *Afghanistan Analysts Network.* Retrieved from: www.afghanistan-analysts.org/the-state-of-aid-and-poverty-in-2018-a-new-look-at-aid-effectiveness-in-afghanistan/.

5 Knox, R. (January 12, 2015). "5 Years after Haiti's earthquake, where did the $13.5 billion go?" *NPR*. Retrieved from: www.npr.org/sections/goatsandsoda/2015/01/12/376138864/5-years-after-haiti-s-earthquake-why-aren-t-things-better.
6 Friedman, T. (May 30, 2020). "How we broke the world." The *New York Times*. Retrieved from: www.nytimes.com/2020/05/30/opinion/sunday/coronavirus-globalization.html.

1 The impact of globalization, poverty, and inequality

The middle- and lower-income people of rich countries are among the losers from globalization; there is also some evidence that it promotes income inequality. COVID-19 has laid bare the excesses of poverty and inequality worldwide, as the poorest tend to have unequal access to healthcare, clean water and sanitation, stable food supplies, employment, and social safety nets.

But while globalization is deeply flawed, it's still better than the alternatives.

Bears, sumo wrestlers, or sprinters

There's an old Wall Street legend that goes something like this:

Once upon a time there were two bankers fishing in a stream. Suddenly, one looked up and saw a huge bear running toward them. Both bankers took off and started running, but then one stopped and started changing his big wading boots for running shoes. The other one shouted, "Are you crazy? You can't hope to run faster than that bear!"

And the first banker replied, "No, but I can run faster than you!"

The moral of the story is that the global economy is a race in which the slowest runner gets eaten alive.

New York Times columnist Thomas Friedman, one of the premier thinkers on globalization, compares global trends to sports: If the cold war were a sport, he says, it would be sumo wrestling, with two big fat guys in a ring, pushing and shouting, making lots of noise, but with very little real contact.[1]

If globalization were a sport, he adds, it would be the hundred-meter dash, run over and over and over and over and over again.

What is the moral of that story? Events and technology move so quickly in today's globalized world that even the winner can't stop and enjoy it because the race is constantly being rerun.[2]

What is globalization?

So what is this thing called globalization, anyway? And why has so much of the world turned against it?

To you and me, globalization means the McDonaldization of the world—walking down the Champs Elysees in Paris and seeing McDonalds, Subway, Gap, Zara, H&M, and other global brands rather than sweet little French boutiques and patisseries.

Which would you rather have on your romantic trip to the City of Lights? A baguette and a strawberry tart, or a Big Mac with fries?

Most of us, I suspect, would go for the baguette—but globalization has brought the Big Mac, not to mention COVID-19, to every nook and cranny of the globe. And therein lies the rub; we like the benefits of globalization, like getting Vietnamese-made shirts for $9.99 rather than American-made shits for $99.99, for example—but we worry about the McDonaldization effect. And lots of other things too.

There's no doubt that globalization is very real and very dramatic. The numbers tell us that countries have sold stuff to each other in record numbers since the mid-1980s; think of Brazilian-made airplanes flying in Asia, and African-mined tantalum powering your cellphone. Investors also invested massive amounts of money in foreign countries, tempted by the siren song of higher profits and new markets as the former Third World and the former Soviet bloc opened for business.

The meaning of globalization was clearest to me, in fact, when I found myself in Warsaw, Poland, riding in a Toyota car (born in Japan) driven by an Uber driver (Uber is based in San Francisco, California) who was born in Greece, and was using Waze (born in Israel) to navigate. This struck me as a pretty pure reflection of international technology transfer, trade, investment, and immigration—the perfect symbol of globalization. And largely positive.

Or consider the ubiquitous iPhone: It was designed in Palo Alto, but is physically manufactured in a range of countries including China, Japan, and Germany, and marketed worldwide.[3]

Globalization also means the democratization of information flows and technology. Thanks to satellite dishes, the Internet, the TV, and the cellphone, people can now see and hear events and data from all around the globe. In stock, bond, and currency trading rooms, for example, it just takes seconds now for news to be reflected in prices.

Technology, too, has been democratized. Lots of middle school students now have a cell phone—and probably their own day trading accounts, too!

(Not so for the world's poor and vulnerable, of course—but we'll get to that later.)

What is driving us toward a globalized world? The main idea is free market capitalism: The more you let market forces rule and the more you open your economy to free trade and competition, the more efficient and flourishing your economy will be. Moreover, nations tied together by bonds of trade, money, and culture are less likely to destroy each other.

Who likes globalization?

Interestingly, people around the world have a lot of different views on globalization.

A 2018 Pew Research Poll[4] found that most of the world approved of globalization in theory, but many questioned it in practice. Especially in the world's most advanced economies, many doubted that it was good for them personally. Skepticism has been highest in the United States (US), Japan, and some European countries (see, e.g., Brexit)—ironic, considering that these are among the world's most globalized countries.

There's some good news for the pro-globalist camp. In the United States, 74% of people believe that "trade is good," a sentiment espoused by those in advanced economies (87%) and emerging economies (83%).[5]

On the other hand (a phrase that will recur quite a lot in this book), a lot of people in a lot of countries were unsure about the impact of deeper international integration.

- Only in emerging countries did more than half of respondents believe that trade creates jobs (56%), compared to just 47% in advanced economies and 36% in the United States;[6]
- Even fewer agreed that "trade increases wages"—31% in the United States and other advanced economies versus 47% in emerging economies;[7]
- And barely a quarter in advanced economies (28%) believed that trade lowers prices—despite the fact that this is one of economists' main arguments for why nations should trade.[8]

Apparently people's view on trade "seems to reflect a public's general economic mood."[9] Respondents who believe that their economy is doing well tend to have more positive views toward trade than those who believe their economy is doing poorly.[10]

In 2020 (pre-COVID-19), Pew undertook a series of focus groups in the United States and United Kingdom to further unpack people's views toward globalization. Among the most interesting results, "The focus groups confirmed that the story of being 'left behind' remains common."[11] Participants talked about how "the forces of globalization left them rudderless, closing industries, leading people to abandon their homes and harming them economically."[12] The COVID-19 pandemic has certainly underlined the "left behind" theme, as it has devastated the poorest and most vulnerable communities worldwide.

Overall, however, the elites of both advanced and emerging countries tolerate and even embrace globalization, which reflects the overwhelming dominance of one ideological viewpoint from the 1980s through the 2010s. Before then, three ideologies regarding the nature and function of international economics competed for world approval:

- Marxism (in obvious and dramatic decline since the 1980s);
- Economic nationalism, which had dominated international economic relations for many years but was in sharp decline from the 1980s through the 2010s; and
- Liberalism, which underpins globalization—but has come under sharp attack in the past few years.

Indeed, communism dominated large swathes of Europe and Asia through the 1960s—but by 2021, most of the world lives in free to moderately free market-based economies.[13] This reflects the virtual death of communism (except for Cuba and North Korea, which are hardly model economies), and widespread acceptance of free-market capitalism, or liberalism.

At the same time, there has been a growing backlash against globalization in the 21st century. By the 1990s, people were rioting in the streets of Seattle, Washington, D.C., and Genoa against globalization, and this was a significant theme of the Occupy movement that sprang up in 2011. Then anti-globalization rose to new heights in the late twenty-teens, with the British decision to withdraw from the European Union, or Brexit, as well as the election of Donald Trump on a platform that included fiercely anti-globalist themes. Trump, indeed, claimed that globalization has wrecked the US economy, and is responsible for the destruction of working people and the middle class.

No doubt, COVID-19—which spread across an unsuspecting world with the speed of a jetliner—will support and advance this negative point of view in virtually all nations. Yet another Pew poll in July 2020,[14] following the outbreak of COVID-19, found that Americans' views on China have soured considerably. Nearly three-quarters of all Americans polled (73%) viewed China unfavorably, up 26 percentage points since 2018.[15] As Sino–US relations are at the core of a globalized and prosperous world economy, this deterioration marks a critical shift in views on China in particular, and globalization in general.

Globalization: The winners

To some extent, Americans' increasing distrust of China may reflect the fear that China is "winning" the globalization "war," while Americans are on the losing end. This begs the question: Who are the winners and losers from globalization?

According to President Trump, globalization has moved jobs and wealth out of the United States and into Mexico, as well as other overseas countries. Somewhat absurdly, he has accused China of "raping" the United States via its trade and exchange rate policies.[16] He claimed in virtually every campaign speech during his 2015 run for President that global trade makes the wealthy wealthier and the poor poorer; indeed, that it has totally wiped out the middle class.

President Obama, on the other hand, argues that it is impossible to turn back the tide of globalization, and that efforts to do so will make us worse off.[17] The United States can compete and succeed in the 21st century, he believes, so we should embrace the future rather than turn back the tides of time.

Who's right?

Let's start with a discussion of blind faith. As we noted earlier, blind faith in free market capitalism and globalization conquered the world, or at least the world elites, by the 1990s—completely eclipsing prior ideologies of Marxism and economic nationalism. In fact, financial markets beginning in the 1990s were marked by an extraordinary degree of consensus worldwide.

This consensus reflects a shared belief in four basic factors:

- The power of market forces;
- The power of financial models (the more complicated, the better);
- The power of technology (also the more complicated, the better); and
- The power of globalization.

Global political and economic elites agreed that free market orthodoxy, in its most basic sense, was the right and only path to economic salvation. While one may legitimately wonder whether masses of unemployed Greeks agree with this, power brokers around the world were convinced. Vietnam and China moved cautiously but steadfastly toward the development of market economies; even Fidel Castro permitted something of a market to take hold in Cuba.

Not only was there widespread agreement in free markets, these power brokers further believed that quantitative financial models were the path to riches, and that technology would pave this path. Put together, this all added up to an unquestioning faith in globalization, that is, the ability of economic, financial, and political integration to make the world a better place.

As mentioned above, there were some skeptics, even from the beginning. Economists questioned the tactics of the International Monetary Fund (IMF) and World Bank in pushing these beliefs on to developing countries. Social activists questioned the promise of globalization, especially its impact on the world's poorest. But at the same time, there was—and still is—a substantial body of evidence demonstrating that globalization and free market capitalism do benefit countries.

Just not all countries, all of the time.

For proof of its benefits, just look at Ireland. Ireland was widely considered the world's most globalized economy in the early years of the 21st century.[18] And after decades as Europe's sick man, stumbling along at the bottom of the EU rankings, it vaulted to become the Celtic tiger during these years of globalization—the fastest growing economy in the region over the 15 years to 2007.[19]

Indeed, this snapshot illustrates the fact that the world's most globalized economies are also among the world's wealthiest, that is, Singapore, Ireland, Luxembourg, the Netherlands, United Arab Emirates, Belgium, and Bahrain. Interestingly, the world's most globalized economies also include some former Eastern European bloc countries, such as Estonia, which have chosen globalization—quite successfully—as an important element in their drive for economic reform and prosperity in the post-Soviet era.

Perhaps not surprisingly, there is also a high correlation between the world's least globalized economies and the world's poorest, most troubled countries, for example, Somalia, Turkmenistan, and Uzbekistan. Indeed, the UN has found that beginning in the 1990s and lasting until the onset of COVID-19—during a period of fast-paced globalization:[20]

- One billion people were lifted out of extreme poverty;
- The proportion of people living on less than $1.25 per day fell from 33% in 1990 to 12% in 2015;
- The global under-5 mortality rate declined from 90 to 43 deaths per 1,000 live births;
- Millions of young girls are in school now as gender disparity in primary, secondary, and tertiary education has been eliminated in developing countries as a whole;
- The proportion of undernourished people in the developing world fell by almost half;
- China and India were leading contributors to much of this progress, and were also among the world's most enthusiastic globalizers.[21]

While it would be hasty to assume that globalization was responsible for these gains, there is no doubt that it was a contributory factor, especially in China and India.

Even more noticeable is the high correlation between a country's Index of Economic Freedom and its prosperity or standard of living. Indisputably, the countries with the highest levels of economic freedom are also its wealthiest, that is, Hong Kong, Singapore, New Zealand, Switzerland, Australia, Canada, the United Arab Emirates, and Ireland. This list also includes a few countries that have chosen economic freedom as a path to development, such as Estonia and Chile—again, quite successfully.

And once again, the countries with the lowest degree of economic freedom are among the world's poorest and least stable, including substantial pockets of Africa as well as Cuba, Venezuela, and North Korea. Over the past two decades, countries that embraced globalization grew much more rapidly than non-globalizers, and achieved much more impressive results with regard to poverty reduction.

Who else gains from globalization?

Certainly multinational corporations (MNCs) have been winners—and to the extent that many of us are employees and/or stockholders of MNCs, we win too.

I have come to believe that the two biggest winners from globalization are:

- Many people who were dirt-poor three decades ago. This reflects the truly impressive rise of a global middle class, largely reflecting the great march out of poverty in China.
- Many people who were really rich three decades ago. This reflects the equally amazing rise in incomes of the top 1% globally; so the other set of winners is a relatively few people in the already-rich countries, according to a new book by Branko Milanovic.[22]

Gains for MNCs and the wealthy stem from the rapid and inexorable penetration of world-class multinationals into markets around the world. Coca Cola is in 200-plus countries, for example; only 18% of its 2019 unit-case volume sales were in the United States, while China, Brazil, and India together accounted for 31% of worldwide unit case volume.[23]

For Apple, the Americas remain its largest market, but this is declining while China's share has increased rapidly. Again, the majority of Apple sales are outside the United States, and Apple's manufacturing process is entirely dependent on parts, components, and manufacturing in countries like China.[24]

In fact, companies as American as apple pie earn vast chunks of revenue and profit outside of the United States. According to the American Enterprise Institute in mid-2018:[25]

- General Electric earns around 62% of its revenues outside the United States;
- Exxon Mobil: 65%;
- Microsoft: 50%;
- Ford: 40%;
- IBM: 52%;
- Intel: 80%;
- McDonalds: 63%;[26]
- Walmart only earns 25% of its revenues overseas, but 20% of all Walmart stores are now in Mexico, and 54% of its retail stores are outside the United States.[27]

Globalization: The losers

Remember Ireland, our poster child for globalization. The Ireland that became one of the world's most globalized countries, the Celtic tiger with the highest growth rates in Western Europe?

Let's look again at Ireland's growth path, now focusing on the collapse beginning in 2008. Economic expansion seesawed from highs of 7.5%–10% per annum around the turn of the century to an economic contraction of more than 10% in 2008–2010.[28]

What happened?

It turns out that Ireland is also a poster child for the dark side of globalization. Its extreme dependence on the United States, especially high-tech US companies, produced an extreme downturn when the US financial crisis hit, which was exacerbated when MNCs began moving operations to lower-cost European countries like Poland. When the United States caught a cold, Ireland caught pneumonia.

And let's take a second look at the UN's report on progress since the 1990s.[29] On the one hand, overall progress has been extraordinary—no doubt about it.

But on the other hand…progress has been uneven. Extreme poverty remains concentrated in sub-Saharan Africa and southern Asia, where 80% of people in some regions still struggle to survive on less than $1.25 per day. Despite all of the forward movement, some countries and regions remain deeply vulnerable, some even more so than before the 1990s.[30]

Moreover, it's clear that even among many people in the wealthiest countries, anti-globalist political rhetoric has found fertile soil—and for good reason. In a compelling study, *Global Inequality: A New Approach for the Age of Globalization*, Branko Milanovic[31] argues that the losers from globalization are the middle- and lower-income people of the rich countries. These people, he suggests, are leading lives of more insecurity and more worry, especially about the prospects of their children. Globalization has failed to benefit the majority of citizens in the wealthy countries, notably the United States and United Kingdom—which explains the rise of anti-globalization and anti-globalist political movements in these countries.

There's also some evidence that globalization promotes income inequality within countries, even while it's reducing inequality among countries. Within some countries, inequality has worsened as measured by the Gini index. (The index is a score between zero and one; a Gini index of one means a country's entire income goes to one person; a score of zero means incomes are equally divided.)

Inequality in United States, for example, grew by about 20% from 1980 to 2016.[32] On world inequality tables, the United States has a Gini coefficient of about 0.41 along with surprising bedfellows such as Turkmenistan, Tanzania, Malaysia, Kenya, Argentina, and Iran.[33] US inequality increased sharply from 1967 to 2009, perhaps reflecting an increased "college premium"—the value of college degree—as well as a stunning concentration of income at the extreme top end, to the point that the top 1% earners in the United States bring in 20% of the country's income, and the top 0.1% earn an eye-popping 10%.[34]

China, one of the world's fastest globalizing countries over this period, has also shifted from being a moderately unequal economy in 1990 to one of the world's *most unequal* by 2018. Its Gini index rose by 15 points over the same period,[35] probably in part because the coastal areas pulled well ahead of the inland regions. In the world, the Gini index, that is, inequality, has fallen in only a handful of countries during this time period—and there is good evidence that at least some of this is related to globalization.

Here's the reason.

When MNCs come into poor countries, they tend to pay high wages, so globalization tends to boost the wages of skilled workers. As a general rule, globalization thus increases inequality in developing countries because certain regions or groups within the country are much better positioned to take advantage of global integration than others (coastal China, for instance, or English-speakers in India). Like financial leverage, globalization magnifies the damage caused by low skills and low education.

Mexico's northern states, for example, have benefited from globalization because they boast higher levels of infrastructure and human capital than their southern counterparts, along with proximity to the United States. The rural and backward southern regions, on the other hand, remain mired in poverty.

Thus, the debate over globalization's impact on inequality is unresolved, because it has a different impact on different countries, and within countries versus among countries. China is a teachable moment—inequality between China and the rest of the world has declined substantially, but inequality *within* China has jumped.

Taking a broader look at global poverty, we again find that the benefits of globalization are distributed unequally; countries with two billion people (fully 1/3 of the world's population) are in danger of being hopelessly marginalized. Just one indicator tells the story: Around 34% of all global foreign direct investment in 2020 went to just two countries—the United States and China.[36]

Globalization has also brought huge environmental costs and food shortages. As China gets richer, its people want more meat and more cars, which spells higher prices and even shortages for the rest of the world. Indeed, drought in China raised the price of wheat to impossibly high levels for hungry Egyptians—a direct contributor to the outbreak of the "Arab Spring."

And globalization is associated with a boom in busts. More globalized countries are more exposed to international currency and financial crises, which can have a devastating effect on poor and working families.

COVID-19 has exposed the shortcomings of globalization to a horrifying degree. The World Bank believes that 2020 was the first year in which global poverty *rose* in more than two decades, driven by contracting per capita income due to COVID-19. Its economists believe that COVID-19 could, in fact, push as many as 150 million people into extreme poverty around the world by 2021. This means that between 9.1% and 9.4% of the world's population could exist on less than $1.90 per day, much higher than the 7.9% that was predicted pre-COVID-19.[37]

Indeed, COVID-19 has laid bare the excesses of poverty and inequality worldwide. From the United States to the United Kingdom, from Peru to Thailand, the poorest tend to have unequal access to healthcare, clean water and sanitation, stable food supplies, employment, and social safety nets—and as a result—have suffered far more from the pandemic. The pandemic has had a heavily gender-differentiated effect as well, with women more likely to lose their jobs and to be caring for sick relations at home, and with girls more likely not to return to school.

Globalization: The way forward

So what does all of this mean for the future of globalization?

We should start by noting that its most serious and smart critics, like Dani Rodrik and Joseph Stiglitz, are not anti-globalization; their goal is to reform the process so that it plays a more positive role in alleviating poverty, inequality, and environmental degradation.

And it's also worth noting that while markets, models, and globalization are deeply flawed, they're still better than the alternatives. To paraphrase Winston Churchill, free markets and globalization are the worst ideas out there—except for all the other ideas.

Indeed, there's actually evidence that globalization is on the decline in some very important ways. After dramatic growth in world trade during 1985–2007, since 2012 trade volumes have barely kept pace with world growth, and the trend is only growing more pronounced.[38] World trade slipped by about 0.1% in 2019, and is estimated to have plunged by 13%–32% in 2020, according to the World Trade Organization (WTO).[39] Weak growth and further localized outbreaks into 2021 could bring about little improvement.

Why has trade been slowing, even pre-pandemic?

The world's leading economies—the United States, Eurozone, and China—all experienced slower growth overall in the years leading up to the pandemic, so global consumption and investment reflect that slower growth. But there is also some evidence that the slowdown in world trade growth may be more than cyclical. Perhaps most important, some of the world's leading economies are backing away from globalization. A few key indicators:

- The WTO's most recent round of global trade talks, aimed at reducing barriers to trade around the world, ended in failure in 2015.[40]
- Under President Trump, the United States withdrew from the Trans Pacific Partnership, an attempt to forge a regional agreement among the Pacific Rim. The United States launched a mutually destructive trade war with China, and then exacerbated tensions by accusing China of spreading COVID-19 around the world.[41]
- The United Kingdom has withdrawn from the European Union.

Post-COVID-19, de-globalization is likely to accelerate. The speed with which COVID-19 raced around the globe exposed the soft underbelly of globalization: Its ability to spread disaster around the world even more speedily than its ability to spread prosperity around the world. It's unclear when, if ever, travel and trade will return to pre-pandemic levels (my guess is never). Nations are racing to secure supplies of a COVID-19 vaccine, for their own people—which is likely to deepen disparities between wealthy and poor countries, and to further the spread of economic nationalism.

It will take a very long time, generations perhaps, for the world to recover from the trauma of anti-globalist leaders and COVID-19.

Not surprisingly, all of the above are decried by much of the world's elite. In 2016, IMF Managing Director Christine Lagarde worried that "Curbing free trade would be stalling an engine that has brought unprecedented welfare gains around the world over many decades."[42]

Perhaps.

But the bottom line is that the benefits of globalization have accrued disproportionately to the wealthy, while the costs have fallen on displaced workers—and governments have failed to ease their pain. Real incomes rose significantly for most of the world's population between 1988 and 2008, but NOT for most residents of the United States and other developed countries.[43] This probably helps explain why voters in these countries increasingly see themselves as the victims of trade with the developing world, and has led to the current backlash.

Looking forward, economists warn that even if world growth rebounds—and it may never achieve pre-pandemic levels—automation reduces the incentives to invest in low labor cost developing countries, thus eliminating one of the primary reasons for foreign direct investment.

On a more positive note, others suggest that globalization is becoming more about data and less about stuff. They point out that 20th century globalization was defined by rapidly growing trade in goods and investment. Today, growth in global trade and investment has flattened, and looks unlikely to rebound.

So globalization has gone digital; cross-border data flows have grown 45 times in the past decade, and are projected to grow much more and COVID-19 has accelerated the push towards digitization and virtual everything.

Also, as the United States retreats from globalization, China could lead the next phase. It is already moving rapidly to become a leader in clean energy technology and Artificial Intelligence (AI), and is already the world's largest economy by some measures. It is making massive investments in Latin America, Africa, and Eastern Europe, part of an overall increase in South–South investment. As the United States retreats from leading the march toward globalization, China may be picking up the baton.

Finally, it is important not to overstate globalization.

If the world were 100 people…[44]

- There would be 60 Asians, 16 Africans, 14 people from the Americas, and 10 Europeans;
- There would be 31 Christians, 23 Muslims, 15 Hindus, and 7 Buddhists;
- 12 would speak Chinese, 6 would speak Spanish, 5 English, 4 Hindi, 3 Arabic, Bengali, or Portuguese;
- 86 would be able to read and write; 14 would not;
- 40 would have an Internet connection, 7 would have a college degree;
- 78 would have a safe place to shelter, but 22 would not;
- 91 would have access to safe drinking water, but 9 would not;
- 22 would be overweight, 11 would be undernourished, and 1 would be dying of starvation.

Are these figures better than in 1988 or 1998, before the latest great wave of globalization? Absolutely.

But they illustrate the shift of world power away from North America and Europe toward Asia, as well as the existence of deep poverty and disintegration from the global economy among many.

And they also illustrate the unevenness of globalization, which benefits many people some of the time, but certainly not all of the people, all of the time. Its bountiful gifts are a miracle for some, but equally it has bestowed hopelessness and uncertainty on those who are excluded from the global economy.

Still, President Obama is right: We are now part of a globalized economy, for better and for worse. Thus, the way forward is a globalization path that strives to distribute benefits more fairly and more broadly, rather than abandonment of a movement that is both inevitable and infinitely promising.

How do we achieve these goals? This is where ESG-based investing comes in.

Notes

1 Friedman, T. (1999). *The Lexus and the Olive Tree: Understanding Globalization*. Simon & Schuster.
2 Ibid.
3 Kabin, B. (September 11, 2013). "Apple's iPhone: Designed in California but Manufactured Fast All around the World (Infographic). *Entrepreneur.com*. Retrieved from: www.entrepreneur.com/article/228315.
4 Stokes, B. (September 26, 2018). "Americans, Like Many in Other Advanced Economies, Not Convinced of Trade's Benefits." *Pew Research Center*.

Retrieved from: www.pewresearch.org/global/2018/09/26/americans-like-many-in-other-advanced-economies-not-convinced-of-trades-benefits/.
5. Ibid.
6. Ibid.
7. Ibid.
8. Ibid.
9. Ibid.
10. Ibid.
11. Silver, L., Schumacher, S., & Mordecai, M. (October 5, 2020). "In U.S. and UK, Globalization Leaves Some Feeling 'Left Behind' or 'Swept Up.'" *Pew Research Center*. Retrieved from: www.pewresearch.org/2020/10/05/in-u-s-and-uk-globalization-leaves-some-feeling-left-behind-or-swept-up/.
12. Ibid.
13. 2020 Index of Economic Freedom. Retrieved from: www.heritage.org/index/ranking
14. Silver, L., Devlin, K., & Huang, H. (July 30, 2020). "Americans Fault China for Its Role in the Spread of COVID-19." *Pew Research Center*. Retrieved from: www.pewresearch.org/global/2020/07/30/americans-fault-china-for-its-role-in-the-spread-of-covid-19/.
15. Ibid.
16. Diamond, J. (May 2, 2016). "Trump: 'We can't continue to allow China to rape our country." *CNN.com*. Retrieved from: www.cnn.com/2016/05/01/politics/donald-trump-china-rape/index.html.
17. Press Trust of India (August 2, 2016). "Globalisation is here to stay: Obama." *The Business Standard*. Retrieved from: www.business-standard.com/article/pti-stories/globalisation-is-here-to-stay-obama-116080201661_1.html.
18. *The Irish Times* Opinion. (March 13, 2004). "Ireland is world's most globalized country for third year in a row." Retrieved from: www.irishtimes.com/opinion/ireland-is-world-s-most-globalised-country-for-third-year-in-a-row-1.1135380.
19. FitzGerald, G. (July 21, 2007). "What caused the Celtic Tiger phenomenon?" *The Irish Times*. Retrieved from: www.irishtimes.com/opinion/what-caused-the-celtic-tiger-phenomenon-1.950806.
20. United Nations. Millennium Development Goals and Beyond 2015. Retrieved from: www.un.org/millenniumgoals/poverty.shtml#:~:text=The%20target%20of%20reducing%20extreme,of%20extreme%20poverty%20since%201990.&text=At%20the%20global%20level%20more,still%20living%20in%20extreme%20poverty.
21. Ibid.
22. Milanovic, B. (2016). *Global Inequality: A New Approach for the Age of Globalization*. Cambridge MA: Harvard University Press.
23. Coca Cola Company 2019 10-K Filing. Retrieved from: https://investors.coca-colacompany.com/filings-reports/annual-filings-10-k.
24. Kabin, B. September 2013.

22 *The impact of globalization*

25 AEIdeas Blog Post. (June 13, 2018). "Many large US firms sell, hire, and invest more overseas than in US and they have to think globally, not domestically, to survive." *American Enterprise Institute.* Retrieved from: www.aei.org/carpe-diem/many-large-us-corporations-sell-hire-and-invest-more-overseas-than-in-us-and-they-have-to-think-globally-not-domestically-to-survive/.
26 Ibid.
27 Walmart Location Facts. Retrieved from: corporate.walmart.com/our-story/our-locations#:~:text=Today%2C%20Walmart%20operates%20approximately%2011%2C500,million%20in%20the%20U.S.%20alone.
28 The World Bank. GDP growth (annual %) – Ireland. Retrieved from: https://data.worldbank.org/indicator/NY.GDP.MKTP.KD.ZG?locations=IE.
29 United Nations.
30 United Nations.
31 Milanovic.
32 Horowitz, J.M., Igielnik, R., & Kochhaar, R. (January 9, 2020). "Trends in income and wealth inequality." *Pew Research Center.* Retrieved from: www.pewresearch.org/social-trends/2020/01/09/trends-in-income-and-wealth-inequality/.
33 World Bank. Gini index. Retrieved from: data.worldbank.org/indicator/SI.POV.GINI.
34 Stebbins, S. & Comen, E. (July 1, 2020). "How much do you need to make to be in the top 1% in every state? Here's the list." *USA Today.* Retrieved from: www.usatoday.com/story/money/2020/07/01/how-much-you-need-to-make-to-be-in-the-1-in-every-state/112002276/.
35 Jain-Chandra, S. (September 20, 2018). "Chart of the Week: Inequality in China." *IMF Blog.* Retrieved from: blogs.imf.org/2018/09/20/chart-of-the-week-inequality-in-china/.
36 Reuters Staff (January 24, 2021). "China was largest recipient of FDI in 2020." *Reuters.* Retrieved from: https://www.reuters.com/article/us-china-economy-fdi/china-was-largest-recipient-of-fdi-in-2020-report-idUSKBN29T0TC.
37 World Bank (October 7, 2020). "COVID-19 to add as many as 150 million extreme poor by 2021." Retrieved from: www.worldbank.org/en/news/press-release/2020/10/07/covid-19-to-add-as-many-as-150-million-extreme-poor-by-2021.
38 World Trade Organization (April 8, 2020). "Trade set to plunge as COVID-19 pandemic upends global economy." Retrieved from: www.wto.org/english/news_e/pres20_e/pr855_e.htm.
39 Ibid.
40 *The New York Times* Editorial (January 1, 2016). "Global trade after the failure of the Doha Round." *The New York Times.* Retrieved from: www.nytimes.com/2016/01/01/opinion/global-trade-after-the-failure-of-the-doha-round.html.

41 Wiseman, P. (October 27, 2020). "Trump trade policy: 4 years of high drama. Limited results." *AP News*. Retrieved from: apnews.com/article/donald-trump-virus-outbreak-global-trade-trade-policy-mexico-39aadae9a6d18de2b91889f1e552b605.
42 Lawder, D. (September 1, 2016). "IMF urges G20 leaders to boost demand, make case for trade." *Reuters*. Retrieved from: www.reuters.com/article/cbusiness-us-g20-china-imf-idCAKCN11752W.
43 Milanovic, B. (July 1, 2016). "The greatest reshuffle of individual incomes since the Industrial Revolution." *VoxEU*. Retrieved from: https://voxeu.org/article/greatest-reshuffle-individual-incomes-industrial-revolution.
44 Retrieved from: www.100people.org.

2 Greed gone bad
A perversion of capitalism

While there are prime examples of capitalism gone wrong, these cautionary tales should not be read as a rejection of the entire concept. Capitalism does not necessarily imply an abdication of all responsibility except for that to short-term profits and shareholders. This foul twisting of capitalism by such rogue players as Enron, WorldCom, Volkswagen, and Wells Fargo is a gross misinterpretation, not an indictment, of the system. They are brutal examples of what happens when capitalism is distorted by a greed for short-term shareholder value at the expense of all other stakeholders. They are proof that capitalism must be reformed and rechanneled—not that capitalism itself is unacceptable.

In fact, capitalism can also be channeled for good—as the succeeding chapters will demonstrate.

What happened at Enron?

On December 2, 2001, Enron filed for bankruptcy protection under Chapter 11. It was one of the most highly publicized business debacles in history; criminal cases, civil cases, settlements, and even jailings dragged on for years. Twenty years on, it's still instructive to look back on Enron, which can be viewed as a symbol for all that is wrong with a profits-only approach to capitalism.

What happened at Enron?

The rot began to set in early in the 1990s when an ambitious new hire, Jeff Skilling, realized that natural gas was a commodity—just like pork bellies and oil—and could be traded in the same way. Since Enron had been founded nearly a decade earlier as a natural gas company, this realization seemed to pave a pathway to the pile of gold at the end of the rainbow.

Much as Michael Milken had done with junk bonds, Skilling single-handedly created a market to trade natural gas. Not surprisingly,

Enron—with its deep knowledge of the industry—easily dominated the market that it had created. Building on that success, Skilling soon moved up to much more complicated trades in derivatives related to natural gas contracts.

Michael Milken: The Junk Bond King

Michael Milken personified the "Greed is good" era of the 1980s, although it was actually his fellow financier Ivan Boesky who uttered these immortal words (at a college commencement, no less).[1,2]

Michael Milken, and Milken alone, was responsible for Drexel Burnham Lambert's meteoric rise from a third-tier investment bank at the dawn of the 1980s to the very top of the Wall Street stratosphere by the middle of the decade. Forbes reporters called Milken "the man who runs America's economy" in 1984; certainly he was the engine of growth at Drexel.

To a large extent, this outsize praise and position were well-earned. Milken's genius was to realize that junk bonds—high-yield debt issued by high-risk borrowers—often carried less default risk than their hefty interest rates would suggest. In other words, these bonds were substantially underpriced and, thus, highly attractive investment instruments. Inspired by solid academic evidence that he was onto something, Milken single-handedly created a vibrant market for such instruments. Thanks to Milken's junk bonds, many medium-sized but high-potential companies—which would otherwise have foundered due to a lack of funding—suddenly had access to huge pots of capital; and some of these companies became great success stories.

The problem was that Milken turned his brilliant financial powers to the dark side. In October 1988, the SEC filed charges against Milken and others for, among other things, insider trading, stock price manipulation, and defrauding clients. Eventually Milken pleaded guilty to six felonies and paid a fine of $600 million (reportedly keeping an estimated $1 billion in personal and family wealth). He spent 22 months in a minimum-security prison, and emerged as a philanthropist.

Source: Jane Hughes and Scott MacDonald, *Separating Fools From Their Money: A History of American Financial Scandals* (Transaction, 2009).

26 *Greed gone bad: a perversion of capitalism*

But as the 1990s wore on, things started to go sour at Enron. Skilling and other senior managers were under tremendous pressure to deliver profits, each and every quarter. Enron's top management was fiercely ambitious; they aimed to make Enron the world's biggest, greatest company. To support these goals, senior management promised investors 15% earnings growth *every year.*

This was extraordinarily gutsy, even for Enron. By the mid-1990s, its profits derived primarily from Skilling's trading activities. The company revolved around its huge trading operations; Skilling saw Enron's future as its brainpower, not its (boring and old-economy) physical assets like oil pipelines and natural gas plants.

It was a recipe for disaster.

Why? Because trading operations *cannot*, by their very nature, deliver consistent and high profits in every quarter and every year. Markets are risky and capricious; they go up and down and up and down. Wall Street (foolishly) believed in Enron's nonsensical predictions and expected Enron to deliver 15% profits growth every year—but trading simply doesn't work that way. You can't possibly count on steadily increasing earnings in a company whose profits derive from trading. Essentially, Enron was in the business of speculating (also known as gambling), which does not—*cannot*—generate steady earnings growth.

So Enron had to improvise.

At first, its efforts to fill the gap between Wall Street expectations and the reality of trading ran to the usual window-dressing at the end of each quarter—delaying losses, accelerating revenues, playing with the numbers on some assets. It was morally gray, but certainly not unheard-of among envelope-pushing US companies, and generally kosher under generally accepted accounting principles (GAAP). A few journalists wondered aloud if Enron was managing its earnings through aggressive accounting, but no one probed too deeply.

Eventually, this wasn't enough and Enron had to move beyond envelope-pushing. In the waning years of the 1990s, Skilling made his fatal mistake: He decided to move beyond natural gas trading—in which Enron had a massive competitive advantage due to its expertise and holdings in the industry—into trading other commodities. He pushed into trading electric power, broadband, and more, areas where Enron had no natural advantage. Inevitably, trading profits stumbled, and managers came under increasing pressure to manufacture profits.

Enter Andy Fastow, who became the Chief Financial Officer (CFO) in early 1998.

Fastow collaborated with the Chief Executive Officer (CEO) of Skilling and Enron, Kenneth Lay, to present what they wanted the world to see. He created a series of off-balance sheet special-purpose companies and complex financing structures to conceal Enron's real (i.e., wobbly) financial positions.

One former employee put it this way:

> Say you have a dog, but you need to create a duck on the financial statements. Fortunately, there are specific accounting rules for what constitutes a duck: yellow feet, white covering, orange beak. So you take the dog and paint its feet yellow and its fur white and you paste an orange plastic beak on its nose, and then you say to your accountants, 'This is a duck! Don't you agree that it's a duck?' And the accountants say, 'yes, according to the rules, this is a duck.' Everybody knows that it's a dog, not a duck, but that doesn't matter, because you've met the rules for calling it a duck."[3]

While Fastow was "spinning dogs into ducks," he was also feathering his own nest. By mid-2001 he was worth $60 million, most of which came from his private partnerships' dealings with Enron. And Fastow was not alone; between 1998 and 2001, a total of 24 Enron executives and board members sold company stock worth more than $1 billion—while other investors eventually lost around $70 billion.

While insiders were enriching themselves, the company itself was fast sinking under the weight of Skilling's foolhardy electricity and broadband ventures. Fastow worked desperately in the last years of the 1990s, creating hundreds of special-purpose entities to hide company debt.

Enter Sherron Watkins.

Watkins, who became *Time* magazine's person of the year in 2002, was an unlikely hero. Second cousin of the singer Lyle Lovett, she had worked the cash register at her family's grocery store before getting her accounting degree and going to work at Enron.

By mid-2001, Watkins was desperately worried; she wrote prophetically to CEO Ken Lay, "I am incredibly nervous that we will implode in a wave of accounting scandals."[4] Lay obligingly hired a team of lawyers to review her charges—the same law firm that did the legal work to set up the special-purpose entities that she pinpointed. Not surprisingly, the legal eagles reported back that the deals were fine.

As Warren Buffett says, when the tide goes out, you find out who's been swimming naked.

For Enron, the tide went out when the bull stock market ended in spring 2000. Enron's stock price tumbled, and by early 2001 the investment community—suddenly wary of the company after years of fawning adoration—finally took notice of Enron's lack of cash flow, high debt, and overpriced stock. In fact, Wall Street analysts belatedly realized that they couldn't figure out just how Enron made its money.

Skilling resigned abruptly in August, but Ken Lay soldiered on, reassuring employees and investors alike. On September 26, 2001, he told anxious employees that Enron's financial position was stronger than ever.

Even more damning, while Lay and other senior executives quietly dumped their fast-falling stock, employees were told that they couldn't sell their own Enron stock because the company's 401K plan was switching administrators. They had to sit back and watch their life savings crash in value. On October 16, Enron announced a $618 million loss in the third quarter, and the stock price crashed. By the time that the 401K asset freeze ended on November 19, releasing the trapped savings of employees, Enron's stock price had plunged from $32 per share to $9 per share. So when the company collapsed, thousands of employees lost not only their jobs but also their retirement savings.

However, the players were still scheming. In the days leading up to its bankruptcy filing on December 2, Enron quietly paid $56 million to some 500 lucky employees. And the team of six Enron executives who went to New York to handle the bankruptcy filing flew in quiet luxury aboard the $45 million corporate jet and stayed at the Four Seasons hotel.

A massive failure of corporate governance

Who's to blame for this massive failure of corporate governance?

In fact, *all* of the systems that are supposed to support good governance failed, from the Board of Directors to government regulators to lawyers to auditors.

The outside auditors, who are supposed to certify that the company's financial statements were prepared in accordance with GAAP, were Arthur Andersen. The smallest of the Big 5 audit firms, Andersen was under intense pressure to land and keep its corporate clients.

And Enron was a very big fish, paying the firm $52 million in 2000.

Enron's Board of Directors were a well-connected, well-educated group of people charged with the responsibility of ensuring that the company was managed in a prudent and lawful fashion. What exactly were they doing while Rome burned?

In fact, there is significant evidence that the Board was fully informed of Fastow's activities; it even suspended Enron's code of ethics—a truly extraordinary step—to approve the creation of partnerships between Enron and Fastow. Enron directors were very highly paid, and many were not really independent. As one observer noted:

Enron failed because its board failed. Either they knew what was happening with the secret partnerships, conflicts of interest, and the cooking of the books, in which case they are culpable for a sin of commission. Or they were inept, slothful or simply did not understand their role as members of the board of directors at Enron, in which case they are culpable for a sin of omission.[5]

Would you rather be stupid or complicit?

And then there are the bankers. Investment banking analysts who gave Enron's stock such enthusiastic buy recommendations were actually rewarded for their ability to get I-banking business from Enron, not for the track record of their stock analyses. Between 1986 and 2001, the biggest Wall Street firms earned $323 million from Enron for underwriting its stock and bonds; by the late 1990s, Enron was one of the largest payors of investment banking fees in the world.

Obviously, the pressure to keep Enron happy with favorable stock ratings was intense.

Politicians too had reasons to love Enron. The company enjoyed close government connections; Ken Lay was dubbed Kenny Boy by President George H.W. Bush. He was a close friend of the Bush family and the Republican Party, and was seriously considered for a Cabinet post in 2000.

In fact, Enron had extensive ties with the government at multiple levels. Around two-thirds of all congressmen received campaign contributions from the company; the US Trade Representative served on Enron's advisory council; Vice President Dick Cheney met with Enron executives six times in 2001; and Ken Lay himself advised the White House on energy policy. Top officials in both the Clinton and Bush administrations served as bill collectors for Enron, pressuring the Indian government to pay the company dubious fees owed for the reportedly corrupt Dabhol project just south of Mumbai.

The media too fawned over Enron. *CFO* magazine bestowed its CFO Excellence Award on Andy Fastow in 1999. Harvard Business School wrote five highly favorable case studies on the Enron model. *Fortune* magazine named Enron America's Most Innovative Company for 6 years in a row. And *CEO* magazine named Enron's Board of Directors (see above) as one of the top five in corporate America.

Finally, Enron benefited from good luck in the form of a favorable business cycle through the 1990s. Until the tide went out, that is.

And Enron itself? A corporate culture of greed, outsized bonuses, and stock options contributed to a fierce focus on short-term earnings and stock prices. Jeff Skilling liked to say that only money and fear motivate people (management experts would disagree—strongly). Contrast this belief to what the great financier J.P. Morgan said. In banking decisions, Morgan believed, "the first thing is character." "Before money or property?," he was asked. "Before money or property or anything else," he replied. "Money cannot buy it."[6]

Greed gone bad

Enron is a near-perfect example of greed gone wrong. The laser focus on inflating short-term value for shareholders flies in the face of an impact-based approach to business, that is, the belief that financial managers should seek to enrich *all* stakeholders, from employees to the community to society at large.

Consider Enron's impact. Some 4,500 employees, as noted above, lost not just their jobs but their life savings—and "Enron" was hardly a blue-chip entry on a resume in the early 2000s. The vast majority of these employees were innocent victims, completely unaware of the fraud perpetrated by the entitled few at the top.

Investors lost over $60 billion, again the life and retirement savings of many.

Enron affected the entire US economy, as its partners, suppliers, and customers struggled in the wake of its sudden collapse. Other energy companies, banks, insurance companies, and energy customers all saw profits fall and costs rise; uncertainty soared while investments plunged.

Perhaps most alarming, trust in the US financial system cratered, as Enron became a symbol for everything that was wrong with Wall Street and the investment world. Enron became a symbol of crony capitalism, corruption, and self-dealing practices on Wall Street.

And it's not alone.

A short history of greed in US financial markets

Indeed, Enron is only one of the more recent—and most extreme—instances of perverted capitalism in the United States. William Duer, a former delegate to the Continental Congress and a close friend of George Washington—who gave away the bride at Duer's wedding—became American's first financial crook; he died in debtors' prison after causing the Panic of 1792.

Skip ahead 130 years to the 20th century—where to begin? How about the Teapot Dome scandal in 1921–1922? Warren Harding, one of the most pro-business (read pro-crony capitalism) presidents, allowed his greedy, oil industry-connected cabinet secretaries to lease rich oilfields in Wyoming. The leases were sold very quietly and without competitive bidding; one oilman literally put $100,000 in cash into a little black bag and handed it off to the secretary of the interior in a Washington hotel (bribery was much simpler in those days).

Another oilman rewarded the same cabinet secretary with six heifers, a yearling bull, two six-month-old boars, and four sows for his New Mexico ranch.

The latter half of the century saw, in rapid succession, the junk bond and insider trading scandals of the 1980s (remember Gordon Gekko: "Greed is good") and the dawn of the Enron-plus scandal at the turn of the century. And then, of course, came the scandal of the 2008 financial crisis, littered with greedy bankers, investors, and derivatives traders.

So there is nothing new under the sun—except that now the politicians get campaign contributions instead of cows and pigs.

Perhaps the most damning of these recent scandals is the financial panic of 2008. Ever since William Duer, every single financial crisis in the United States has reflected a foolish hope that the basic relationship between risk and return has somehow been overturned—a belief that it's possible to earn outsize returns without taking on outsize risk.

Anyone want to buy a bridge in Brooklyn?

The bankers who loaned gobs of money to Latin America in the 1970s and early 1980s forgot that the reason for sky-high interest rates on this debt was the sky-high risk of the borrowers. Those who poured money into Enron in the late 1990s were anticipating a steady and consistent 15% growth in earnings every year, never mind that this is impossible in a trading company. In the first decade of the 21st century, Wall Street should have had an "aha moment" when banks started offering mortgages with zero percent down to people with no proof of employment.

But no.

And then derivatives trades massively exacerbated an already dubious situation by creating complicated derivatives that derived their value from these shaky mortgages, all packaged together into super-shaky mortgage-backed derivatives. By then, it was a matter of when, not if, this precarious structure would collapse.

When Nick Leeson joined Barings Bank Singapore in 1992, his job was to make risk-free trades between the Singapore and Japanese stock exchanges. He was supposed to take advantage of teeny tiny price differences, which would result in teeny tiny profits per transaction.

> But Leeson had much greater ambitions. Instead of sticking with his boring little trades, he made unauthorized trades in derivatives—which promptly went south on him. Much like the Enron bosses would do a few years later, he created a secret bank account to hide his losses.
>
> Leeson was hailed as a star trader at London bank headquarters, for having single-handedly earned one-fourth of the 1994 profits for the entire firm. No one was curious about how these fantastic profits could result from such a low-risk operation (remember the risk–reward relationship).
>
> In the end, Leeson fled; he left behind a note that simply said, "I'm sorry."
>
> And Barings Bank, a venerable 233-year-old institution and banker to the British royal family, was insolvent; ING assumed its liabilities and took over what was left of the great bank for one measly pound.
>
> Source: *Separating Fools From Their Money*

Collapse it did of course, taking the United States and then the global economy with it. As financial wizard Felix Rohatyn famously said of the derivatives market, 26-year-olds with computers are creating financial hydrogen bombs. In fact, derivatives themselves—like greed itself—are not inherently evil; properly used, they help companies protect themselves against price fluctuation and thus reduce risk. However, when misused, derivatives can indeed be hydrogen bombs.

Conclusion: Capitalism gone good

But should these sorry tales be considered symbols of everything that's wrong with capitalism?

Not so fast.

These are prime examples of capitalism gone wrong, but these cautionary tales should not be read as a rejection of the entire concept.

Finance wizards who seek enormous rewards must, by definition, be running enormous risks.

Finance wizards who put their blind faith in financial models rather than common sense and experience will be disappointed.

And princes of finance who lose their moral compass in pursuit of absurd riches must, inevitably, turn into frogs.

Capitalism does not necessarily imply an abdication of all responsibility except for that to short-term profits and shareholders. This foul twisting of capitalism by such rogue players as Enron, WorldCom, Volkswagen, and Wells Fargo is a gross misinterpretation, not an indictment, of the system. They are brutal examples of what happens when capitalism is distorted by a greed for short-term shareholder value at the expense of all other stakeholders. They are proof that capitalism must be reformed and rechanneled—not that capitalism itself is unacceptable.

In fact, capitalism can also be channeled for good—as the succeeding chapters will demonstrate.

Mini-case: Volkswagen

The story broke in September 2015: "Dieselgate." The US Environmental Protection Agency (EPA) had accused German automaker Volkswagen of cheating its way through emissions testing—and as the news unfolded, it told a story that is regrettably not unfamiliar. In the face of a costly new challenge, Volkswagen had decided to cheat, under the assumption that it was too good, too smart, too resourceful to get caught.

Until it did. And the consequences were ultimately costlier than just playing by the rules from the get-go.

What happened at Volkswagen?

In the mid-2000s, the EPA tightened guidelines on the emissions of diesel engines, as a part of the US's efforts to curb emissions more broadly. For diesel-centric Volkswagen, this meant redesigning its engines to meet these new standards, which would require significant time and resources. At the same time, the automaker was already under pressure as the US auto market was becoming increasingly attracted to electric and generally greener vehicles. By comparison, the appetite for diesel looked to be on decline. The EPA's adoption of new guidelines was just one more setback.

A group of engineers at Volkswagen came up with a solution to both problems that might be celebrated for its genius—if it were not so devious. Rather than redesign and rebuild their engines, a costly and time-consuming undertaking to say the least, Volkswagen installed software into a number of its models that could detect when the vehicle was undergoing an emissions test. Once detected, the "defeat devices"[7] would stifle the car's emissions of nitrogen oxides, thus producing test results showing a level of emissions well within the EPA's guidelines. In reality, under normal conditions the cars emitted up to 40 times more nitrogen oxides than allowed by the EPA, and we now know that some 500,000 cars in the United States and 11 million worldwide had defeat devices installed.

Volkswagen kept it up for several years, selling defeat device-equipped cars from 2009 to 2015, until it was found out by the EPA.

This was no small sham.

Volkswagen took a calculated risk that it would not get caught—but then it did. At a surface level, it is easy to say that the company let greed get the best of itself and made the wrong decision. Environmentally, the toll is clear. And more, one peer-reviewed study also concluded that the scandal led to 59 premature deaths, linked to the excess pollution from these cars.

But that is not where the damage stops. Volkswagen, quite literally, had to pay the consequences. Within days of the news breaking, Volkswagen's stock price dropped by almost 30%; profits through the first quarter of 2016 were down some 20% from the previous year; and as of mid-2020, penalties, fines, and other related costs have totaled more than $33 billion.

But let's imagine the alternative, briefly. Go back to the mid-2000s. What if Volkswagen had built a better engine—a truly green car? With the growing popularity of eco-friendly electric vehicles and the like today, perhaps Volkswagen could have had the opportunity to really stake its claim in the green car space. Imagine that: A scenario where the cars on the road are better for the planet, the company got to avoid paying out such massive fines, *and* there is potential for sales growth and innovation.

Volkswagen stayed in the headlines for weeks, even months, after the news broke. Even in 2020, it is not uncommon to run into an article, new study, or graduate thesis about Dieselgate, a cautionary tale and reminder that the world has not forgotten.

Mini-case: General Motors

Anyone who drives a Pontiac G5, a Chevrolet Cobalt, or another of a handful of General Motors vehicles probably remembers 2014 clearly, though not fondly. It was the year of GM recalls, following the discovery of a fault with the ignition switches in several million vehicles. For scale: *Time* magazine wrote that "The recalled vehicles could wrap around the Earth more than four times."[8]

It happened in waves, with GM's recalls totaling more than 30 million vehicles by the end of 2014, including around 2.6 million that were recalled due to faulty ignition switches. And the fault, sans technical jargon: The affected cars' engines could accidentally shut off while driving, and subsequently their airbags would not deploy in the event of a post-shut off crash. Some 124 people died, and 275 more were injured. GM forfeited $900 million in the face of criminal charges; another $600 million was paid out to compensate victims. What's more: in 2014, GM also spent an estimated $2.8 billion to repair recalled vehicles. In a four-week period following the recall, shareholders lost $3 billion in value.

It has been widely reported that GM CEO Mary Barra used the crisis to revamp the company culture and transform the 100+ year-old auto giant for the future. This new direction included a greater emphasis on ethics and transparency.

Barra is GM's first female CEO, and her career at GM now spans four decades. She formally took on her current role in January 2014, just one month before the first round of recalls went live, and just a few weeks after the knowledge of the faulty ignition switches surfaced internally. Given the timeline, a handful of rumors or, rather, conspiracy theories, suggested that she was a scapegoat; but even if that was the case, she has not let the scandal get the best of her, likely because of her focus on controlling her messaging, remaining transparent, and not denying the consequences of the fault. As a testament to her work at GM, in 2015 Glassdoor reported her 86% approval rating among employees, making her the highest-rated female CEO on the site.

As far as deadly corporate scandals go, GM's ignition switches seem to have spent less time in the news cycle than one might imagine. Without doubt, the story was everywhere when it broke, and again as new information surfaced; but it seems that Barra's transparency throughout the crisis as new information arose may have helped reduce the company's time in the spotlight. In some cases, it may have even turned would-be exposés into articles about leadership.

This is not to say that GM did not take the heat—it absolutely did, and rightly so. But it does suggest that Barra's style may have been the secret to actually getting the flames out in a timely fashion, something leaders in the face of crisis notoriously struggle with. Had she spent the balance of 2014 speaking in cryptic apologies, avoiding regulators, or just denying GM's culpability, this might have been a very different (read: more expensive, long-lasting, and fatal) story.

The moral of the story is that corporate governance matters.

Mini-case: Wells Fargo

After the Financial Crisis of 2008, one of the loudest scandals on Wall Street centers around Wells Fargo. In 2016, it was discovered that the bank was opening new accounts for its clients, without their permission or knowledge. In theory, it was the ultimate cross-sell: remove the costs to acquire a new customer, and even remove the costs of selling the current customers on these new accounts. As many as 3.5 million fraudulent accounts were opened between 2011 and 2016, and the bank collected fees of about $2.4 million over 5 years, which seemed to make it a worthwhile sales effort.

Until they got caught.

When the scandal came to light in September 2016, Wells Fargo was slapped with $185 million in fines from the Consumer Financial Protection Bureau and other regulators. But the price Wells Fargo had to pay for its fraudulent behavior did not stop there.

In addition to the fee-burden of accounts they never signed up for, customers' credit scores also took a hit. As more and more fake accounts surfaced and additional regulatory bodies built their cases, Wells Fargo continued to be in an active crisis mode. In April 2018, CNN called it "Wells Fargo's 20-month nightmare," and followed up in September of that year with the headline, "The two-year Wells Fargo horror story just won't end."[9]

And even in 2020, there has been continued news and added fines. Most recently, in February 2020 Wells Fargo settled with the US Department of Justice to the tune of $3 billion.

The Wells Fargo scandal reads as a textbook case of an unchecked, unhealthy corporate culture. However, that is not the narrative that the public received. Neither culture nor broader strategy was cited as being at the root of the scandal. Instead, this was deemed a matter of bad sales practices. Some 5,300 employees were fired; primarily, these were lower-level employees, fitting Wells Fargo's story that this was the result of poor choices made by a small group of employees, not management.

One of the less surprising aspects of the scandal was the appearance of former Wells Fargo employees speaking out against a toxic work culture. Sales quotas were lofty, if not unreachable (without the aid of fraudulent accounts), and threats of termination for underperformance were abound. Can we really separate this intense pressure from the company-wide culture and management?

The then-CEO John Stumpf stepped down in October of 2016, just about a month after the scandal became public knowledge. He was replaced by then-COO Tim Sloan, who stepped down in March 2019 and during his tenure was never quite able to get the scandal under control or out of the news cycle.

Signs of reform would not arrive until later that year, following the entrance of a new CEO, Charles Scharf, in October 2019. Scharf is an industry veteran, having formerly been at the helm of Visa and BNY Mellon. He approached the seemingly endless impact of the scandal in a way that Stumpf and Sloan could not, due to their insider status as leaders during the height of the scandal.

Instead, Scharf admitted the business was flawed. In March 2020, he told Congress that "[Wells Fargo's] culture was broken."[10] While it has yet to be seen what exactly will come of Scharf's time as Wells Fargo CEO, the first months of his tenure have been promising: He has made the amends and set the goals that Stumpf nor Sloan could not—at least, not without heavy criticism for their role in the scandal in the first place.

Notes

1 Actually, the precise words that Boesky uttered were, "Greed is all right, by the way, greed is healthy…You can be greedy and still feel good about yourself."
2 And I agree that greed can be good, though obviously not in the same way that Boesky meant. Much more on this later…
3 Hughes, J. & MacDonald, S. (2009). *Separating Fools From Their Money: A history of American Financial Scandals* (Transaction, 2009).
4 Ibid.
5 Zandstra, G. (2002). "Enron, board governance and moral failings." *Acton Institute.* Retrieved from: www.acton.org/node/6296.
6 Cain, A. (October 17, 2016). "6 memorable leadership lessons from the financial giant J.P. Morgan." *Business Insider.* Retrieved from: www.businessinsider.com/what-you-can-learn-from-jp-morgan-2016-10.
7 As coined by the US EPA. Such devices were banned under the Clean Air Act of 1970.
8 Linshi, J. (July 1, 2014). "All the cars GM has recalled this year would wrap the earth 4 times." *Time.* Retrieved from: https://time.com/2945867/gm-recalls-facts/.
9 Egan, M. (September 7, 2018). "The two-year Wells Fargo horror story just won't end." *CNN Money.* Retrieved from: https://money.cnn.com/2018/09/07/news/companies/wells-fargo-scandal-two-years/index.html.
10 Merle, R. (March 10, 2020). "Wells Fargo's culture was 'broken,' new CEO tells Congress." *The Washington Post.* Retrieved from: www.washingtonpost.com/business/2020/03/10/wells-fargos-culture-was-broken-new-ceo-tells-lawmakers/.

3 Greed gone good
Reimagining the model

A roadmap for impactful investing is based on the urgency of a new approach, and on the reality that over time, there are no conflicts between financial returns and sustainability. The perception that profits will fall if corporate managers add an environmental, social, and governance (ESG) lens to their decision-making simply is not borne out by facts on the ground. In fact, research shows that ESG funds do not underperform mainstream funds—this is a myth, not a reality.

So how do we channel capitalism into good? In order to make progress toward achieving the UN's Sustainable Development Goals (SDGs) by 2030 (zero poverty, zero hunger, gender equality, environmental action, and more), trillions of dollars of private capital will be needed. And there is a strong business case for supporting the SDGs, as it is in everyone's best interests for developing countries to become stable and prosperous. This then is the core of the new model: Aligning business and social interests so that businesses benefit by doing good; they can do good and do well, simultaneously.

Creating a roadmap

The previous chapters have demonstrated that a bipolar world—in which government and philanthropy tackle social ills and business chases short-term profits—doesn't work. That system is broken. We need to reimagine the model such that business chases long-term prosperity, and in doing so joins in the crusade against social ills.

Traditionalists sometimes argue that low-risk impact-based businesses are unicorns; most impact investing is high-risk and only for the brave or reckless.

Let's take a closer look. Is it risky to include environmental (and social) considerations in financial decisions? That question comes up again and again—but what if, instead, we reexamined the risks of business-as-usual?

How risky is investing in mainstream financial institutions, which paid an eye-popping $300 billion in fines and legal fees for misbehavior related to the financial crisis of 2007–2009? What about investing in Miami real estate, which—thanks to climate change—has a high probability of being accessible only to scuba divers in an alarmingly short period of time?

The fact is that it's not that hard to make a lot of money—see Donald Trump (really, not a political statement; he started off with a whopping chunk of money and support from his father), or Nick Leeson, or Enron. It's much harder to make money *with integrity*.

But also…so much smarter.

Let's think about environment. Is climate change a risk that long-term asset owners such as pension funds and institutional investors should be involved in mitigating? Or is it for the politicians and do-gooders to deal with? To answer this question, let's ask one more: Do long-term investors stand to lose money from climate change?

The answer to that, of course, is an unmitigated *Yes!*—investors face huge climate change-related losses. Not just insurance companies, but bankers and property owners are threatened, as well as anyone who produces or consumes food, travels, drinks water, produces, or uses energy… In short, everyone. (Think COVID-19 on steroids.) So wouldn't it be much riskier to *ignore* environmental sustainability in building portfolios than to include it? Sustainability doesn't mean leaving money on the table; it is quite the opposite!

So let's create a roadmap for the future of impactful investing. A few points to consider are as follows:

- It's urgent. Scientists warn us that climate change could cost hundreds of billions of dollars and many thousands of lives—annually. Without major new initiatives, the damage will shrink the US economy by as much as 10% by the end of the 21st century. One study, for example, found that at least one in eight deaths in India can be attributed to air pollution. These risks and costs will harm virtually every investor on the face of the earth; it's far riskier to ignore climate change than to harness the power of private capital to fight it.
- Over time, there are no conflicts between financial returns and sustainability. Scandinavian financier Mats Andersson told conference attendees in 2019 that he runs two funds, one gender-based and one childhood-focused—and both have outperformed indexes made up of traditional companies. After all, he asks, why should a company bring a product to market that will damage society and/or the environment? (Think cigarettes or coal plants.) That makes no sense; it's an unsustainable strategy. If management takes care of society,

Andersson argues, it takes care of the company too.[1] This line of reasoning teaches that financial-statement-based corporate profits are deceptive because they don't take into account the full costs of the company's activities—that is, its environmental and social impact.
- How's that Fortune 500 doing? Think back to the last month of 2017, when the Dow plunged by 800 points one day, tumbled another 700 the next day before regaining 600, then fell an additional 400 the day after that. Or look at the index in the early months of 2020, when the market reacted to COVID-19 with staggering levels of volatility—triggering a market-wide circuit breaker four times in March alone![2] Is that really how you want your retirement money or your children's college accounts to perform?

So traditional investments aren't exactly low-risk, and certainly don't guarantee consistent profitability. Why not consider ESG-based investments then?
- In fact, it's just not true that social responsibility requires lower profits. The perception that profits will fall if corporate managers add an ESG lens to their decision-making simply is not borne out by any facts on the ground. In fact, research shows that ESG funds do not underperform mainstream funds—this is a myth, not a reality.
- Far from lowering returns, impact investments offer unparalleled opportunity. Throughout the 21st century, pension funds and institutional investors have struggled to produce attractive returns in a very low-interest environment. Impact investments such as "green" funds generally offer higher interest rates because of the short-track-record-higher-risk perception. So why not dive into them?

Channeling capitalism into good

So how *do* we channel capitalism into good? What does that look like in real life?

To understand this pathway, let's backtrack to the Millennium Development Goals (MDGs) established by the 191 member states of the UN in 2000. These were eight goals to be achieved by 2015:

- Eradicate extreme poverty and hunger;
- Achieve universal primary education;
- Promote gender equality and empower women;
- Reduce child mortality;
- Improve maternal health;
- Combat HIV/AIDS, malaria, and other diseases;

- Ensure environmental sustainability;
- Develop a global partnership for development.

It's easy to be cynical about such a pie-in-the-sky list, but in fact massive progress *was* achieved in the two decades leading up to 2015. The number of people living in extreme poverty—less than $1.90 per day—tumbled from 1.9 billion in 1990 to 836 million in 2015; more than 1 billion people were lifted out of harsh poverty!

What else? The primary school education goal was just missed, with the net enrollment rate increasing from 83% in 2000 to 91% in 2016. About two-thirds of developing countries have achieved gender parity in primary education. The child mortality rate has been reduced by more than 50% in the past 25 years, falling from 90 to 43 deaths per 1,000 live births between 1990 and 2015, while global maternal mortality rates have fallen by nearly half.

And a Brookings Institution study found that at least 21 million lives were saved (pre-COVID-19) due to accelerated progress in fighting child mortality, HIV/AIDS, tuberculosis, and maternal mortality (thank you, Bill and Melinda Gates, for championing these causes!).[3]

So the numbers demonstrate that cynicism is unwarranted; enormous strides *have* been made in the global battle against poverty and the many ills associated with poverty.

At the same time, the numbers also demonstrate that there's a lot more work to be done. COVID-19 has reversed some of the pre-2020 progress, as global extreme poverty is expected to rise in 2020 for the first time in two decades due to the economic and social devastation wreaked by the pandemic. According to the World Bank, COVID-19 "compounds the forces of conflict and climate change, which were already slowing poverty reduction progress."[4] The pandemic will push up to 150 million people into extreme poverty in 2020–2021.

As the World Bank further notes, "progress was slowing even before the COVID-19 crisis."[5]

Different countries have followed diverse paths, with a few nations accounting for vast swaths of progress while people in others continue to live lives of quiet desperation. Nearly 60% of the world's extremely poor people live in just five countries (India, Nigeria, Democratic Republic of Congo, Ethiopia, and Bangladesh). At the same time, China and, paradoxically, India, make up the lion's share of progress in fighting extreme poverty—it's estimated that around 300 million people were lifted out of poverty in China alone during this period.

Gender inequality persists; women are more likely than men to live in poverty and to be excluded from the financial system, and we are at a serious disadvantage in labor markets from the United States to sub-Saharan Africa. An unacceptable number of mothers still die during pregnancy or childbirth, as "progress tends to bypass women and those who are lowest on the economic ladder or are otherwise disadvantaged because of their age, disability, or ethnicity"[6] (witness the disparate impact of COVID-19 on people of color in the US).

As the UN reports, about 800 million people still live in desperate poverty, largely due to factors well beyond the UN's reach. Climate and environmental degradation undermines progress, and, as always, it is the poor who suffer the most. For example, around 40% of people in the world lack stable access to clean water, and more than a quarter suffer from food insecurity. This links directly to the fact that poor people are overwhelmingly dependent on subsistence farming, and live in areas highly vulnerable to climate change.

Aside from the (hopefully temporary) impact of COVID-19, conflicts remain the biggest threat to development. The UN reports that there are over 70 million "forcibly displaced people worldwide,"[7] more than half of these coming from the failed countries of Syria, Afghanistan, and South Sudan. It further estimates that 37,000 people per day are forced to flee their homes due to conflict or persecution.[8]

What can private capital do about this?

Funding the Sustainable Development Goals

The next act in the UN's playbook, SDGs were established to build on the MDGs' accomplishments and focus on areas where improvement is still needed in the next 15 years. Seventeen goals include zero poverty and zero hunger, with a greater emphasis on environmental and sustainability goals, and women's empowerment, than under the MDGs.

- SDG 1: No poverty;
- SDG 2: Zero hunger;
- SDG 3: Good health and well-being;
- SDG 4: Quality education;
- SDG 5: Gender equality;
- SDG 6: Clean water and sanitation;
- SDG 7: Affordable and clean energy;
- SDG 8: Decent work and economic growth;
- SDG 9: Industry, innovation, and infrastructure;
- SDG 10: Reduced inequalities;
- SDG 11: Sustainable cities and communities;
- SDG 12: Responsible consumption and production;

- SDG 13: Climate action;
- SDG 14: Life below water;
- SDG 15: Life on land;
- SDG 16: Peace, justice, and strong institutions;
- SDG 17: Partnerships for the goals.

When the SDGs were first agreed in 2015, they were bathed in the glow of worldwide optimism—viewed through the rose-colored glasses of the gains of the previous two decades.

This was before COVID-19 and its accompanying economic depression. Enough has been written about the massive decline in the developing world's prognosis due to COVID-19; a brief glance at Venezuela and India should suffice to describe this.

COVID-19 in Venezuela

One of the world's hardest hit countries has been Venezuela; already battling political unrest, a collapsed healthcare system, hunger, malnutrition, and widespread poverty, the country was ill-prepared for the arrival of COVID-19 and will likely need to rely on external financing to fight the disease within its borders and rebuild its economy. Could impact investing be the way forward?

Prior to COVID-19, Venezuela was in economic distress. In 2019, the International Monetary Fund estimated that Venezuela's GDP fell by 35% and may see another 15% decline in 2020.[9] The country's economy over the last several years has also been characterized by incredibly high inflation, with the IMF also projecting a 15,000% increase in consumer prices in 2020—all while 87% of its population live in poverty,[10] and shortages of food and basic goods are climbing.

While no country in the world was fully prepared for the impact of the COVID-19 pandemic, Venezuela found itself particularly unable to keep up with the rate of infection and economic effects of the virus. In 2019, the Global Health Security Index ranked Venezuela 176 out of 195 countries in its preparedness for a health crisis.[11] With a population of nearly 30 million people, Venezuela's entire healthcare system has only 84 ICU beds and a shortage of both healthcare workers and protective gear for its remaining hospital staff.[12]

Virtually all countries are facing some level of acute stress to their healthcare system and the effects of lockdowns, but for oil-producing countries like Venezuela there is an added level of strain as lockdown efforts, travel bans, and widespread business disruption and financial losses have driven down oil demand—and therefore, prices—to unprecedented lows.

As Venezuela's most important revenue source shrinks, external financing is becoming increasingly important to keep its economy afloat. But with a history of corruption and poor credit, Venezuelan President Nicolás Maduro has struggled to obtain financing to support COVID-19 relief. (The IMF rejected a $5 billion loan request in March 2020.) That leaves a giant space for private impact investors to fill—but these investors would have to be far-seeing indeed, envisioning a future Venezuela returned to good leadership and a promising path forward.

COVID-19 in India

While the Global Health Security Index ranked Venezuela as 176th in the world for its preparedness for a health crisis, India landed in 57th place and was categorized as "More Prepared" for a crisis. Even so, India has seen significant and devastating impacts of the COVID-19 pandemic thus far, with its drastic approach to virus containment efforts driving much economic pain and disruption.

Few countries have handled COVID-19 lockdowns exactly the same way; from the physical span of containment zones to the response to wage losses and everything in between, regulations have varied significantly from country to country, and many governments continue to be relatively dynamic in adjusting their policies as new information surfaces. India's lockdown was not only the largest in the world, containing all 1.3 billion citizens within national borders, but one of the strictest responses with a complete ban on citizens leaving their homes for three weeks, with the exception of essential workers.

Even as the lockdowns ended, India faces the pain of this massive economic disruption. In late 2020, Moody's revised its 2020 GDP forecast for India to −9.6% despite signs of progress in battling the pandemic. For the approximately half of Indian citizens that are living at or below the lower middle income poverty line,[13] the risk of contracting COVID-19 is now running parallel to the preexisting risks of devastation due to poverty and hunger. Data from April 2020 show India's unemployment rate at 23.52%, almost three times greater than what it was in March 2020.[14]

Given India's huge population, wealth of human capital resources, and potential for growth and prosperity, ESG-based companies can view this crisis as an opportunity to support development, mitigate COVID-19 fallout, and pave the way for future profitability. Private capital infusions can turn lemons into lemonade, or challenges into opportunity.

Now the world is viewed through scared eyes peeping out above medical masks, and the global economic outlook has declined precipitously. It seems likely that pre-COVID-19 levels of economic activity will not be achieved for years—if ever—and that there will be a massive, worldwide shakeout of many industries, from mom-and-pop shops that fall at the hands of online behemoth Amazon to the giant airline and hospitality sectors. In this new context of uncertainty and disinvestment, it is impossible to summon pre-crisis levels of optimism for the SDGs.

And yet…it's also possible to see new signs of hope. The financial industry has pioneered innovative new COVID-19 bonds designed to ameliorate the economic damage wrought by the disease, while entrepreneurs are busy at work on Minnie Mouse medical masks for children and designer masks for adults. Restaurants and universities are reimagining themselves as online service delivery organizations; people working from home will revitalize once-exurban areas like Cape Cod, Massachusetts, and the Jersey Shore.

COVID-19 bonds

COVID-19 has shed light on the value of impact investing in a global crisis; in this setting, impact investments not only achieve socially minded results, but also support broader financial recovery by reducing the stress on economies hit hardest by the pandemic. As the pandemic began to spread to more and more countries in early 2020, COVID-19 bonds entered the market as a timely, targeted, and innovative solution to mounting global economic strain. By mid-May, the COVID-19 bond market was worth about $65 billion[15] and showing signs of continued growth.

> In early 2020, the Chinese economy saw a rise of companies issuing bonds in pursuit of the funding to fight the virus and overcome business disruption. Altogether, this drew in more than $30 billion in February,[16] and was followed by the rise of COVID-19-specific impact bonds, issued by a growing list of companies, supranational organizations, and commercial banks. A few of the most notable and earliest bonds to have come out of this time include the following:
>
> *The World Bank's* US dollar-denominated five-year, $8 billion global benchmark bond, the largest of its kind;
>
> *The African Development Bank's* three-year, $3 billion "Fight COVID-19 Social Bond";
>
> *Pfizer's* ten-year, $1.25 billion sustainability bond, the first of its kind in the pharmaceutical industry. The bond's focus is broader, focused on environmental and social impact, the latter of which will include supporting the global response to COVID-19; and
>
> *Bank of America's* four-year, $1 billion bond, the first COVID-19-specific bond issued by an American commercial bank.
>
> In 2019, the vast majority of ESG bonds were "green bonds" focused on environmental sustainability, with only 5% of ESG bonds focused on social issues. The landscape changed dramatically in 2020, with a sevenfold leap in Social Bond issuance and a record total sustainable debt market of $732 billion.[17]
>
> Could the global response to COVID-19 be the catalyst for a new era of impact investing?

So are the SDGs still achievable?

I think not. But that doesn't mean we should throw up our hands and cry, "the sky is falling!" More than ever, this is the moment for private capital to direct its wealth and power to solving the ills outlined in the SDGs. Pre-COVID-19, it was estimated that it would cost $7 trillion *annually* in additional investments to reach the SDG goals; post-COVID-19, that cost is almost certainly higher.

And there is only one place—only one source—for that kind of money: private investors. In 2018, official development aid worldwide totaled $153 billion, and global philanthropy is roughly $500 billion per year. Workers remittances[18] usually run close to another $500 billion per year, playing a significant role in lifting millions out of poverty and contributing to the achievement of the SDGs—but these numbers are collapsing in the era of COVID-19, and are likely to be much lower for at least the next few years.

This is a drop in the bucket. All told, aid, philanthropy, and workers remittances will come to perhaps $1 trillion per year, if we're lucky.

Ay, there's the rub. What about the other $6 trillion needed *annually* to finance the SDGs?

Former UN Secretary Kofi Annan has called on the business community to plug this gap: "I am counting on the private sector to drive success. Now is the time to mobilize the global business community as never before."[19]

And in fact, there is a strong business case for supporting the SDGs. Developing countries will eventually morph into developed countries, with newly prosperous consumers itching to buy everything from designer jeans to washing machines. This is a massive opportunity for private companies to support the development process, which can burnish their reputations as good citizens in these countries while growing revenues along the way.

It's in everyone's best interests for developing countries to become stable and prosperous, after all. According to a McKinsey study, consumers in emerging markets could be worth a whopping $30 trillion by 2025![20] And just think of the gigantic breath of relief that we could all draw when Venezuela becomes a real country once again, replete with natural resources and eager to draw in foreign investors. Isn't it in the best interests of private companies to engage in the process of rehabilitating an impoverished Venezuela?

Connecting capital markets to development

There is a vital need for more innovative finance investments like COVID-19 bonds, which can connect capital markets to the development process in mutually beneficial ways. The global fund management industry managed around $89 trillion in assets in 2019, an ample source of funding for the SDGs. The challenge, then, is how to forge the connection so that around 10% of these assets are directed to global sustainable development.

In fact, several influential studies suggest that many investors are already there. Compared to the overall individual investor population, millennials and women are nearly twice as likely to invest in companies or funds that actively target ESG outcomes; millennials are twice as likely to divest from a company that does not meet sustainable practices! Considering that 460 billionaires will soon hand down more than $2 trillion to their heirs over the next 20 years,[21] and that women already control more than half of the personal wealth in the US,[22] the money needed to close the SDG funding gap should be available.

So the demand is there.

What about supply?

Ay, there's another rub.

Potential investors often argue that there is a lack of well-packaged, high-impact, scalable investment opportunities, particularly in the developing world. Risk is unknown or poorly defined, adding to the uncertainty of such investments. Many are small-sized, leading to unacceptable due diligence costs. You can't push on a string, one frustrated investor told me.

But these investors may be looking in the wrong place.

ESG-based debt issuance reached a record $732 billion in 2020, while ESG-based assets under management (AUM) are around $17 trillion in the United States, one out of every three dollars under professional management. Globally, sustainable investment assets reached an astonishing $40.5 trillion in 2020.

Impact investing offers a valuable alternative to the old ways. Remember Chapter 2 of this book—the old ways brought us Enron, the financial crisis of 2007+, and the COVID-19-induced depression of 2020. Why stick to a model that, demonstrably, *doesn't work?*

Most long-term investors today are locked into this model; 80% of investments are in OECD countries (the 35 most developed in the world), and 80% of investments are in listed companies. But most economic growth—that is, investment opportunities—is happening in the non-OECD world, in China, sub-Saharan Africa, and India. These less mature economies are where the greatest potential lies, but it's not in most Western investors' comfort zone. The greatest opportunities may have shifted from old standards like General Electric and Western Europe to new growth engines in India and China.

Moreover, a depressingly large proportion of the US economy and growth in this century has been based on nonproductive, money-shifting investments like mergers, acquisitions, and trading—what most of Wall Street does. To generate return, investors need to go where everyone else *isn't*, and where *real* productive investment is happening—solar power in Kenya, for example, or girls' education in India. Investors like Mats Andersson would argue that the constraint in the impact investing industry is not in fact a lack of investable projects, but investors' inability to understand that investable projects are different from what they're accustomed to.

It's like the guy looking for his keys under a street light, Andersson concluded. You go over and ask him, where did you drop them? Over there, he says. Then why are you looking here? Because that's where the light is. Investing in traditional companies in rich countries makes about as much sense![23]

Moreover, multilateral agencies and philanthropies like the Rockefeller Foundation have stepped up to help midwife the shift into ESG investments, by helping to de-risk such investments and to raise money themselves from private investors.

The World Bank, for example, is committed to driving private capital into investments that support the SDGs in a variety of ways. The Bank's International Development Association (IDA) has tapped capital markets itself, based on its excellent credit profile and investors' eagerness for IDA debt. According to the IDA, "IDA offers investors a unique opportunity to support developing in the world's low-income countries... As an increasing number of investors look to direct capital to products that fulfill their financial requirements and serve a positive social purpose, IDA is a compelling story."[24]

The Bank also provides guarantees to help de-risk private investments and attract capital to projects expected to generate strong development outcomes. These guarantees can reassure skittish investors and lower required returns by covering contractual, regulatory, currency, and political risks.

Cameroon: Electrification through the Nachtigal Hydropower Project

In today's world, power and electricity are essential—no longer just tools for improving productivity or basic standard of living, but prerequisites for many aspects of life in the 21st century. (COVID-19 massively increased the importance of electricity, as work, education, and life largely shifted to the computer screen.) At the start of the millennium, about 78% of the world's population had access to electricity, and by 2018 the World Bank estimated that figure was approaching 90%. Great progress indeed, but it still leaves some 10% of the global population in the dark. The roadmap to electrification varies greatly in different countries and communities, with unique problems that frankly need unique solutions—namely, unique financing solutions.

Take Cameroon as an example. The Western African country is abundant in natural resources such as oil and timber, yet more than a third of its population is living in poverty. At the same time, about half of its population is living without access to power, and the country as a whole faces high consumer prices for electricity. The government of Cameroon plans to increase access to power to 88% by 2022; to achieve that goal, the country must improve its power generation capacity. Hydropower is central to Cameroon's way forward, through the construction of a 420-megawatt plant that alone would increase the country's generation capacity by about 30%.

The project, however, requires capital and of course comes with risks—made only more complex by the politics of sub-Saharan Africa. The World Bank Group has made financing available for the project, including a €171 million loan guarantee, which allowed "a significant portion of local currency financing with an unprecedented long tenor," as well as €60 million of equity and €130 million of debt financing via the Group's International Finance Corporation (IFC).

Despite efforts by the World Bank to mitigate financing risks, many potential equity investors were still worried. (And as we have seen, mainstream, private investors appear hesitant to reconcile projects such as this with their investing comfort zone.) Enter MIGA, the World Bank Group's Multilateral Investment Guarantee Agency, which supplied two project shareholders with breach of contract insurance at the value of €164.5 million and thus supported further risk mitigation for a project that is both a financial investment for its shareholders and an investment in the longer-term roadmap to Cameroon's electrification and poverty alleviation.[25]

The elephant in the room: Returns

The single greatest misconception about impact investing is the notion that investors have to give up return in order to achieve social good. The bad news is that this belief is widespread; the good news is that it is a *mis*conception.

Investors often fear sub-par returns, and/or a loss of the benefits from diversification resulting from the omission of "sin stocks" (guns, pornography, gambling, and tobacco) from their portfolios. In fact, empirical evidence shows that ESG investments on average perform on-par financially with traditional investments. One meta-study of 2,200 studies in 2015 found that 90% of these studies revealed a non-negative ESG–CFP relationship, where CFP is defined as corporate financial performance.[26]

And the research on diversification is equally reassuring; financial performance data indicate that portfolios do *not* endure higher risk and lower returns by omitting sin stocks.[27] Indeed, there is some reason to believe that companies that are managed ethically are likely to be managed *better* in all categories, resulting in lower risk of major adverse events such as product failures, scandal, lawsuits, and environmental liabilities. One study assessed the performance of global equities after screening stocks for ESG criteria—and found that ESG screening did not have a negative impact on performance, *and* actually improved risk-adjusted returns as compared to the un-screened set.[28] In a similar vein, a Harvard Business School study found that firms that perform well on material sustainability issues outperform those with poor sustainability performance in the stock market.[29]

On the risk front, a 2019 report from Morgan Stanley found that sustainable funds show lower risk in market downturns, experiencing a 20% smaller downside deviation relative to their traditional counterparts.[30] Between March 3 and April 16, 2020, for example, the Dow Jones Sustainability Index returned −8.4%, significantly better than the S&P Global Broad Market index return of −12.4%. While sustainable funds are by no means immune to market volatility, this does bode well for breaking down the belief that sustainable investing is excessively risky.

The financial world buys in

Set to Donovan's classic tune, "Catch the Wind," the TV commercial opens with a sweeping view along blue ocean waters to a graceful wind turbine. It's an ad for Citibank, and a Citibanker explains, "Our mission is to make offshore wind one of the principal new sources of energy." Not every bank wants to get involved in such projects, he says, but Citi "saw the promise of clean energy."

In fact, even before the COVID-19 crisis, numerous world-class companies, from J.P. Morgan Chase to Ikea to General Electric, aired commercials touting their commitment to ESG values. In the months since COVID-19 hit, it sometimes seems as if *most* TV ads are devoted to social messages rather than persuading consumers to buy their products.

In fact, what these commercials tell us is that businesses believe their customers and investors want them to change their ways and incorporate doing good into their business model—why else would they be running these expensive commercials on TV?

And why not? After all, why shouldn't companies design commercials that help lure consumers while at the same time espousing a social mission? Indeed, the fact that companies view such commercials as worthwhile suggests that these companies are not only signing onto the impact revolution, but actually bragging about their social values in addition to their products.

Indeed, nearly 3,000 entities with more than $90 trillion AUM have signed onto the UN's Principles for Responsible Investment (PRI), the world's largest corporate sustainability initiative. PRI signatories are investors and managers who commit to integrating ESG factors into their investment decision-making. At least one study finds that PRI signatories do not significantly improve their ESG scores (sigh, greenwashing again), but the fact that they consider PRI membership a marketing advantage is actually a sign of hope; a sign of recognition that investors care about this stuff. And others cite significant improvements; 70% of asset owner signatories now actively include ESG criteria in choosing investment managers.

Does this mean that everyone has drunk the Koolaid? Absolutely not. But it doesn't really matter; as long as businesses believe that their investors and customers want them to align with social values, the businesses will do the right thing. They don't have to be pure believers; they can be pragmatists and still choose to do the right thing—*for the good of the company.*

This then is the core of the new model: Aligning business and social interests, so that businesses benefit by doing good; they can do good and do well, simultaneously. For example, energy companies can avoid huge reputation and lawsuit risks by building stronger tankers that don't break apart and spill oil into pristine waters, and by investing in renewable energy. Consumer food companies can avoid the same risks by developing healthful, tasty snack foods for children rather than peddling cheese puffs and chocolate-frosted cereal. Bankers can seize the opportunity to acquire new customers by doing business in previously redlined[31] communities, and by jumping into the business of lending to clean-energy entrepreneurs.

How can we put this new model into action? Read on!

Mini-case: Patagonia

Founded in the 1970s, Patagonia, Inc. has become a reference point for sustainable business—and for good reason. The outdoor apparel company has built and maintained a business model that accounts for both its impact on the planet *and* its bottom line. Initially started as a one-man operation producing rock climbing equipment, Patagonia today is nearing $1 billion in sales of outdoor gear, sporting wear, and, more recently, its food line Patagonia Provisions. In 2013, as well, the company launched Tin Shed Ventures, taking a leap into the world of environmentally focused venture capital.

Founder Yvon Chouinard was, and still is, the image of an outdoorsman. An avid rock climber in the 1950s, he initially set out to create high-quality, reliable gear for climbers like himself. Like many of the founders of America's most iconic brands, he did not start out with a vision of where Patagonia would be today, but with a solution to a very real, if niche, problem he was facing. He could not find satisfactory gear in the market, so he set out to produce it himself.

The company is known for putting its mission at the center of every decision, even when doing so does seem to go against the "rules" of typical business. Patagonia's efforts go beyond just having high-quality products that sell for a premium price, by aligning with the growing market of consumers willing to pay more for sustainable products. They do not stop at organic cotton or supply chain transparency. In fact, Patagonia is a registered B Corporation,[32] which reflects its commitment to make a positive impact on the world across all of its business operations. And as a passive part of its financial structure, 1% of Patagonia's sales go to environmental preservation and restoration.[33]

The company has also been known for staying true to its mission in its marketing communications. For example, in 2011, they released a Black Friday ad that drew a lot of attention. The ad featured one of Patagonia's jackets, a standard image for a marketing campaign, accompanied by a clear but unexpected message: "DON'T BUY THIS JACKET." In staying true to their environmental mission, the ad asked consumers if they *really* needed a new jacket and, if not, told them not to buy one just because they wanted it.

To say the least, Patagonia thinks outside the box. And it has paid off.

As mentioned, Patagonia's revenues are reportedly coming close to the $1 billion mark. Its financial results have improved particularly over the past 7 years during Rose Marcario's tenure as CEO.[34] Marcario set out to build a more efficient Patagonia, which she was able to achieve. Since her arrival to the company's C-Suite, profits have at least tripled. And looking at profitability in context, Patagonia stacks up really well against its competitors in the outdoor and athletic apparel space. A 2010 study compared Patagonia's financial results against Colombia Sportswear, V.F. Corporation, Nike, and Timberland. Patagonia's gross profit margin was the highest at 52.6%, with Timberland taking second place nearly five points lower.

Patagonia proves that profitability and keeping true to a deeper mission do not have to be mutually exclusive. In many ways, it demonstrates how possible it is to have the best of both worlds: the mission and culture that typically characterize non-profits, but with the access to capital and freedom to innovate well known by entrepreneurs.

And Patagonia is not alone in this style of operating. Increasingly, for-profit companies are laying down the profitability-above-all-else model in favor of something more balanced, and this is happening in parallel with the rise of new certifications and networks for mission-oriented businesses. This comes at a time when businesses are increasingly aware of issues like climate change and social inequalities—and what those issues mean both morally and with regard to their long-term business continuity. We can't do business in a world facing significant environmental degradation. Supply chains will become increasingly difficult to manage, with resources increasingly scarce.

So, it is just good business to care for the planet. Patagonia recognized that well before the corporate sustainability revolution of the past decade or so, and it has reaped the rewards.

Mini-case: Bombas

One of the core buzzwords of today's world is ESG—environmental, social, and governance. Bombas solves for the "S" in ESG with its own S-word: Socks. The business concept is twofold: Set a new standard for the comfort and performance of socks; and for each pair sold, donate another. Founded in 2013, Bombas is the response to what founders Randy Goldberg and David Heath interpreted as a call to action. The two learned that socks are among the most needed items in homeless shelters, and they did not see an obvious solution to fix that problem. So, they set out to build their own solution.

Let's address the elephant in the room right away. Isn't Bombas just bleeding money by giving away half of its inventory for free? Well, yes and no. The "yes" is relatively obvious: In theory, sure, all else being equal they would be making more money per pair if they were selling two pairs for the price of two, not one. But that's not really the point. This is where the "no" comes in. Their pricing model is not an accident; the pair of donated socks is factored carefully into their profitability. That, and it is reasonable to assume that much of their sales are driven by their overarching mission, and by consumers wanting to do good, in addition to customers wanting their high-quality products. Effectively, buying a pair of Bombas equates to donating a pair to those who need them, which is an attractive selling point for many consumers.

It is important to note, also, that Bombas did not invent the buy-one-give-one model. The model was developed and popularized by TOMS Shoes and has been duplicated by a wide range of brands. Bombas did not go in blind.

Now, are they actually profitable? This one is much simpler: Yes. And they reached that milestone within just 3 years of launching, which is a healthy timeline even for the most traditional startup. At present, Bombas has donated nearly 40 million items, inclusive of socks and a few other apparel categories they have entered into.

Bombas are not your average socks. Their team is committed to innovation and building a better sock, for which they are widely celebrated. This matters for two main reasons: They have a more competitive product in the market, and the people who receive a donated pair of Bombas receive a high-quality item rather than people's castoffs.

The question left unanswered is why Bombas didn't just become a nonprofit. The social mission is there, as is the donation model. But Bombas is part of the rising tide of companies focused on the double- or triple-bottom line. It is a certified B Corporation, in good company with Patagonia and 2,500+ other organizations. This blended structure is increasingly popular, and in Bombas' case it seems to be a major part of their success. For one thing, the for-profit structure allowed Bombas to access a highly coveted form of capital among startups: the founders made a successful pitch on Shark Tank in 2014 and made a deal with the Tank's fashion industry expert, Daymond John, at a $4 million valuation. The appearance on the show also shed a lot of light on the company, increasing the brand's visibility and likely speeding up its race toward profitability.

Thanks to the access to capital and investors afforded by their for-profit status, Bombas also benefits from limitless potential to generate revenue. And if we think back to their fundamental business model, the more revenue they generate, the more they donate.

Notes

1 Mats Andersson. Triple Bottom Line Investing Conference (September 2017). Stockholm, Sweden.
2 The US Securities & Exchange Commission mandated circuit-breakers to prevent a repeat of the October 19, 1987 market crash in which the Dow plunged by nearly 23%. Since then, they were only triggered once before March 2020.
3 John McArthur and Krista Rasmussen. "How successful were the Millennium Development Goals?" (January 11, 2017). *Brookings Institution*. Retrieved from: www.brookings.edu/blog/future-development/2017/01/11/how-successful-were-the-millennium-development-goals/.
4 World Bank Press Release. (October 7, 2020). COVID-19 to Add as Many as 150 Million Extreme Poor by 2021. Retrieved from: www.worldbank.org/en/news/press-release/2020/10/07/covid-19-to-add-as-many-as-150-million-extreme-poor-by-2021.
5 Ibid.

56 *Greed gone good: reimagining the model*

6 United Nations. (2011). *The Millennium Development Goals Report 2011.* Retrieved from: www.un.org/millenniumgoals/pdf/(2011_E)%20MDG%20Report%202011_Book%20LR.pdf.
7 UNHCR. (2019, June 19). "Figures at a glance." *UNHCR The UN Refugee Agency.* Retrieved from: www.unhcr.org/en-us/figures-at-a-glance.html.
8 Ibid.
9 International Monetary Fund. (2020). Real GDP growth [data map]. Retrieved from: www.imf.org/external/datamapper/NGDP_RPCH@WEO/VEN?year=2020.
10 España, L. & Ponce, M. (2018, February). *Encuesta sobre Condiciones de Vida en Venezuela.* ENCOVI. Retrieved from: www.ucab.edu.ve/wp-content/uploads/sites/2/2018/02/ENCOVI-2017-presentación-para-difundir-.pdf.
11 Nuclear Threat Initiative. (2019). 2019 Global Health Security Index. Retrieved from: www.ghsindex.org/wp-content/uploads/2020/04/2019-Global-Health-Security-Index.pdf.
12 International Rescue Committee. (2020, April 9). *COVID-19 in Humanitarian Crises: A Double Emergency.* Retrieved from: www.rescue.org/report/covid-19-humanitarian-crises-double-emergency.
13 The World Bank. (2019, October). Poverty & Equity Brief: South Asia: India [data brief]. Retrieved from: https://databank.worldbank.org/data/download/poverty/33EF03BB-9722-4AE2-ABC7AA2972D68AFE/FM2019/Global_POVEQ_IND.pdf.
14 CMIE. (2020). Unemployment Rate in India [Data set]. Retrieved from: https://unemploymentinindia.cmie.com.
15 Levine, M. (2020, May 15). "Money stuff: Investors feel good about Covid bonds." *Bloomberg.* Retrieved from: www.bloomberg.com/news/newsletters/2020-05-15/money-stuff-investors-feel-good-about-covid-bonds.
16 Wei, Z. and Ng, S. (2020, March 4). "China opens a Coronavirus bond Spigot, and companies rush in." *The Wall Street Journal.* Retrieved from: www.wsj.com/articles/china-opens-a-coronavirus-bond-spigot-and-companies-rush-in-11583323208.
17 Mutua, D.C. (2021, January 11). "Social bonds propel ESG issuance to record $732 billion in 2020." *Bloomberg.* Retrieved from: www.bloomberg.com/news/articles/2021-01-11/social-bonds-propel-esg-issuance-to-record-732-billion-in-2020.
18 Workers remittances are funds sent to families at home by workers overseas. For example, a Filipina restaurant worker in the United States may send money home to help support her family in Manila; or a Bangaldeshi construction worker in Dubai will send money home to his family in Dacca. Workers remittances are a remarkably high source of anti-poverty funds in some countries, accounting to 33% of GDP in Kyrgyzstan and Haiti, for example. This funding source has been hard-hit by the COVID-19 depression.
19 United Nations Secretary-General. (2015, September 26). Secretary-General's remarks at the United Nations Private Sector Forum [as

prepared for delivery]. United Nations. Retrieved from: www.un.org/sg/en/content/sg/statement/2015-09-26/secretary-generals-remarks-united-nations-private-sector-forum.
20 Atsmon,Y., Child, P., Dobbs, R., & Narasimhan, L. (2012). "Winning the $30 trillion decathalon: Going for gold in emerging markets." *McKinsey Quarterly*, 4, 20–35. Retrieved from: www.mckinsey.com/~/media/McKinsey/McKinsey%20Quarterly/Digital%20Newsstand/2012%20Issues%20McKinsey%20Quarterly/Emerging%20markets%20on%20the%20move.ashx.
21 UBS & PwC. (2016). Billionaires report. Retrieved from: www.ubs.com/global/en/wealth-management/uhnw/billionaires-report/new-value/feeling-the-pressure.html.
22 BMO Wealth Institute. (2015, March). Financial concerns of women [US edition]. Retrieved from: www.bmo.com/privatebank/pdf/Q1-2015-Wealth-Institute-Report-Financial-Concerns-of-Women.pdf.
23 Andresson, M.
24 van Trotsenburg, A. (2019, November 5). Impact investing with the World Bank. How to make a difference—the case of IDA [Blog post]. *World Bank Group*. Retrieved from: https://blogs.worldbank.org/voices/impact-investing-world-bank-how-make-difference-case-ida.
25 The World Bank. (2019, February 26). How World Bank Group Collaboration is bringing power to Cameroon. *World Bank Group*. Retrieved from: www.worldbank.org/en/news/feature/2019/02/26/how-world-bank-group-collaboration-bringing-power-cameroon.
26 Friede, G., Busch, T., & Bassen, A. (2015). "ESG and financial performance: aggregated evidence from more than 2000 empirical studies." *Journal of Sustainable Finance & Investment*, 5(4): 210–233, DOI: 10.1080/20430795.2015.1118917
27 Hale, Jon. (2016, November). *Sustainable Investing Research Suggests No Performance Penalty*. Morningstar. Retrieved from: https://video.morningstar.com/ca/170717_SustainableInvesting.pdf.
28 Verheyden, T., Eccles, R.G., & Feiner, A. (2016). ESG for All? The Impact of ESG Screening on Return, Risk, and Diversification. *Journal of Applied Corporate Finance* 28(2): 47–55. doi:10.1111/jacf.12174.
29 Khan, M.N., Serageim, G., & Yoon, A. (2015, March). *Corporate Sustainability: First Evidence on Materiality* (Harvard Business School Working Paper, No. 15–073). Retrieved from: http://nrs.harvard.edu/urn-3:HUL.InstRepos:14369106.
30 Morgan Stanley Institute for Sustainable Investing. (2019, August 6). *Sustainable Reality: Analyzing Risk and Returns of Sustainable Funds*. Retrieved from: www.morganstanley.com/pub/content/dam/msdotcom/ideas/sustainable-investing-offers-financialperformanceloweredrisk/Sustainable_Reality_Analyzing_Risk_and_Returns_of_Sustainable_Funds.pdf.
31 Red-lining is the process by which lenders draw a line around communities where they choose not to do business; these are usually minority, immigrant,

underserved communities that badly need capital. The practice was outlawed more than 50 years ago in the US, but is far from extinct.
32 Certified B corporations are legally required to consider the impact of their decisions on their workers, customers, suppliers, community, and the environment.
33 In fact, Chouinard is a founder of 1% for the Planet, a nonprofit to which companies pledge to allocate 1% of their sales to serving broader environmental goals. Individuals can also pledge to donate 1% of their salary to the cause.
34 Marcario stepped down from her post as CEO in June 2020.

4 Investors
The driving force

Obstacles remain, chief among them a lack of transparency and data on impact as well as lack of knowledge in some corners of the investment community, but the momentum of this movement is indubitable.

Sustainable investing abounds

By 2020, an impressive $31 trillion of assets globally were being managed under sustainable investment strategies, representing *over a quarter of the world's professionally managed assets*.[1] We'll define sustainable/ESG investing as an approach that involves the consideration of ESG factors in the investment process. There are three subsets of this definition:

- *Negative screening*, which excludes investments that are not aligned with the investor's values (e.g., pornography, gambling, weapons, tobacco);
- *Integration*, which incorporates ESG factors into traditional investment analysis; and
- *Impact investing*, which selects investments with the explicit intention of generating both measurable environmental and/or social impact alongside a competitive financial return.

To a remarkable degree, the explosion in the sustainable investing market has been driven by demands from investors. Indeed, consistently across the globe and across asset classes, investors have become increasingly committed to including ESG criteria in their investment decisions. This includes investment in specifically labeled ESG instruments as well as consideration of ESG risk factors in all investment decisions. (In the COVID-19 era, that interest has centered on Social Bonds that are specifically intended to fund work that eases the pain of the pandemic on vulnerable communities worldwide.) While millennials are at the forefront of this movement, more traditional investors including huge institutional asset managers and stolid private equity firms have transitioned from cautious exploration to active participation.

ESG investors have traditionally been viewed as existing on a spectrum, from finance-first (those seeking a purely financial return) to impact-first (those willing to sacrifice financial return for social value.) Increasingly, however, this has become a false dichotomy, as a significant body of research has demonstrated that it should not be necessary to sacrifice finance return for social return.

Over the first half of 2020, $20.9 billion flowed into impact funds—an astounding amount since it was just below the number for all of 2019, which was itself four times the 2018 total! And investors pumped some $500 billion into ESG bonds during 2020. Investors are motivated by environmental concerns, the desire to make an impact with their wealth, and ethical concerns—but also by a growing body of evidence that impact investments actually make financial sense. Obstacles remain, chief among them a lack of transparency and data on impact as well as lack of knowledge in some corners of the investment community, but the momentum of this movement is indubitable.

Retail investors

Although institutional investors still dominate the financial market, there is considerable evidence that retail investors are increasingly committed to putting their money where their mouths are with regard to sustainable investing. Retail investors accounted for 25% of sustainable investing assets in 2018, up from 20% in 2016,[2] and this number continues to climb. According to the Forum for Sustainable and Responsible Investment, total US-based sustainably invested assets under management (AUM) jumped 42% between 2018 and 2020 to $17.1 trillion, accounting for fully 33% of US AUM.[3]

This is largely driven by generational change. Numerous studies confirm that the younger generation, especially millennials and women, are much more committed than their elders to aligning their portfolios with their social values.

Over half of those investors (53%) planning to increase their sustainable investments want to do more to support environmental or sustainable companies, but financial considerations are also important; 38% pointed to "growing evidence that sustainable investments outperform non-sustainable ones as a reason for increasing their exposure."[4]

In August 2020, *The New York Times* reported that impact investments "have significantly outperformed traditional bets during the COVID-19 pandemic. And their returns are enticing hesitant investors to rework their portfolios." Citing research from RBC Capital Markets, the *Times* says that 64% of actively managed ESG funds beat their benchmarks in the first seven months of 2020, versus 49% of traditional funds.[5]

Doing good *and* doing well at the same time—and they said it could never be done! Not too long ago, conventional wisdom held that investors had to sacrifice financial returns in order to achieve social goals. Now that this belief has been largely debunked, the sustainable investment climate has improved dramatically.

That's not to say that old-school naysayers have fallen by the wayside. US financial advisors, for example, tend older and whiter than the general population, and have often proved resistant and uninformed about the updated findings on impact investing. It's also true that financial returns for 2020 were skewed by the poor performance of oil companies, which are generally absent from impact-based portfolios. And some investors remain skittish, worried about the challenges of differentiating between genuine social impact and greenwashing or social washing.

This is not a baseless concern; Sustainable Ventures found that only 36% of "sustainable" or "environmental" funds open to retail investors "invest in businesses that actually provide solutions to the challenges of climate change and resource scarcity," with the rest simply investing in companies with good ESG credentials. "However, these companies' primary activity could be highly varied, and include tech giants, investment banks and internet retailers."[6]

About one-third of retail investors, on the other hand, prefer to invest in companies whose core business focuses on environmental damage mitigation; the same percentage also wish that there were more investment opportunities "in companies that are truly sustainable."[7]

Bond investors too have taken great interest in ESG-linked bonds, especially in the era of COVID-19. Japan's Mitsubishi UFJ Financial Group Inc. is in the process of issuing up to $1.42 billion in corporate bonds for individual investors; this will make Mitsubishi UFJ the first bank to issue COVID-19 bonds for retail rather than institutional investors, a big step forward in the development of the market. The bank noted that this issue is in response to numerous inquiries from retail investors for such investments, so this is likely to be only the first of many ESG-linked bonds that are designed for retail investors.

How to get started

During 2020, the pandemic and Black Lives Matter movement highlighted long-standing inequities as well as the undeniable truth that we ignore these inequities at our peril.

In this environment, larger numbers of retail investors are seeking out investments that will address these challenges while not leaving their retirement funds in tatters.

These investors have a surprising range of choices to enter the sustainable investing space. Exchange-traded funds (ETFs) and index funds probably present the lowest-risk and lowest-effort options, as they provide complete transparency while allowing investors to seek out opportunities that match their social values, such as screening out companies in various industries, advocating for climate change, and investing in companies with good ESG practices.[8]

The Wall Street Journal offers some specific suggestions to help new retail impact investors find a home:

- *Calvert Impact Capital*, which accepts new investments online or by mail starting at $20, or with a $1,000 minimum through a brokerage account or financial advisor. The fund addresses nine impact sectors, including affordable housing and community development, and investors can target their dollars toward specific impact sectors.
- *Calvert Research & Management* (unrelated to the above), one of the oldest and biggest sustainable investing firms in the world, with over $23 billion in AUM. All of its funds are managed according to ESG investing principles. Calvert Equity Fund and Calvert Bond Fund, for example, support underserved communities without sacrificing financial returns.
- *Community Capital Management Inc.*, which offers a fixed-income mutual fund, CRA Qualified Investment Fund, that invests along 18 impact themes. In June, it launched a Minority Cares initiative to attract investments aimed at supporting underserved minority communities.
- *Impact Shares*, which has an ETF, NAACP Minority Endowment, that invests in large and midcap US companies that follow the NAACP's principles of good corporate citizenship.
- *Nuveen*, which actively manages funds that invest primarily in investment-grade fixed-income securities that demonstrate ESG leadership and/or direct and measurable environmental and social impact.[9]

High net worth individuals and family offices

The rich are different, said F. Scott Fitzgerald.

Indeed, this category of investors is different from all others, since it is limited to rich people—the modestly rich, the very rich, and the ultra-rich. It begins with those who are fortunate enough to own at least

$1 million of investable assets, also known as high-net-worth individuals (HNWIs). The United States has the most HNWIs in the world, at nearly 5.3 million; China's share is climbing rapidly. Very-high net worth individuals own more than $5 million in liquid assets, and ultra-high net worth individuals possess a net worth of at least $30 million. Then there is the family office, which handles investment management for a wealthy family, generally one with over $100 million in investable assets, adhering to the traditional goals of growing wealth and passing it down to future generations. Increasingly, though, a third goal may be added to this list: Achieving social impact.

Family offices and HNWIs are leading the charge toward ESG-based investing. This category of investors is especially nimble and adaptable to innovation, since they can make decisions quickly and without layers of bureaucracy (unlike institutional investors or foundations, for example).

A report by Cerulli Associates in late 2019 found that for many family offices, "sustainable has become a core component of their investment process that unites family members around common values and beliefs."[10] Like other impact investors, many family offices started out with negative screening (alcohol, tobacco, etc.) but have since "evolved to offer a wider range of strategies to their clients."[11] This report, like many others, found that younger investors want to align their investments with their personal values—especially socially and environmentally conscious young entrepreneurs.[12] These findings are supported by both anecdotal evidence from the field as well as other studies.

A 2019 survey by PwC found, for example, that "ESG has moved from niche to mainstream"[13] in the family office space. PwC recommends several tactics that family offices can use to shift from a commitment to responsible investment into concrete actions:

- *Adopt the common language*: Many family offices already use the Sustainable Development Goals to provide a blueprint for sustainable investing; this "common global language for responsible investment"[14] helps to shape and communicate investment strategies.
- *Dedicated resource*: Family offices should develop the necessary expertise to enact a responsible investment strategy, perhaps a combination of external advisors and in-house skills development.
- *Monitoring and reporting*: Tracking the performance of an ESG investment strategy is both difficult and crucial; "success relies on family offices understanding why they are monitoring and what decisions will be driven by the results."[15]
- *Valuation of performance*: As usual, defining performance metrics is even more difficult and crucial than monitoring. PwC notes that this is

"an area where family offices can lead the debate and there are several global initiatives seeking to define impact and impact standards in an effort to bring greater consistency and rigor to impact claims."[16]

And a 2019 study by UBS found that over one-third of family offices are now engaged in sustainable investing, with 19% of the average portfolio dedicated to this area; they predict that this average portfolio share will jump to 32% by 2024. While wealthy families have traditionally satisfied their social goals through philanthropy, this view is changing as millennials and women especially play a greater role in investment decisions. The most common goals are "'thematic investing' (e.g., clean energy, gender equality, health care, and water)—which 62% of these family offices indicated they have adopted—and the 'integration of ESG factors into analysis and valuation'—which 46% have adopted."[17] Encouragingly, 85% of impact investments met or exceeded expectations, as the old-school idea that you have to accept lower financial returns in order to engage in sustainable investing fades from memory.

And then there's COVID-19: "The coronavirus crisis may be a turning point for wealthy investors,"[18] according to the *New York Times*. Nancy Pfund, a managing partner and co-founder of DBL Partners, says that:

> Every time something goes wrong in the world, it's a boost to impact investing. There's a generalized frustration that whatever people have been doing for the last X number of years, it's not working… You're seeing people flock to impact investing, and now there are the returns.[19]

Aside from COVID-19, climate change mitigation tends to take center stage in motivating family-based impact investors. Impelled to act by terrifying natural disasters and media attention to the extremes of nature, family-based impact investors have expressed a heightened sense of urgency on environmental protection. Also, as noted in other chapters, it is much easier to measure environmental impact than social impact; hence, family investors feel more certain that their impact investments in this area will actually have impact.

Even for the relatively smaller and nimbler family offices, though, a dive into impact investing may be challenging and time-consuming. The UBS study found that 33% of family office respondents believe that sustainable investments lack both a reliable track record and a ready supply of investable projects, while a quarter worry that these investments will generate lower returns.[20] Also, family office investment teams may be small and lacking in expertise, while the due diligence costs (and learning curve) may be steep. Two leaders in the field, CREO and Cambridge Associates, released a White paper in mid-2019 that suggested the following lessons:

- "*Remember there is a path:* Knowing that many successful investors have traveled the sustainable investing path and overcome pain points can help maintain momentum.
- *Derive value from early efforts:* Early investments allow wealth owners and professionals to gain pattern recognition and an opportunity to reflect on aspects of impact that are unique to sustainable investing.
- *Connect with peers:* Working together provides access to lessons, strategies, ideas, deals, and partners, all of which should help enhance returns and impact.
- *Do not reinvent the wheel:* Several frameworks and toolkits already exist, and although they continue to evolve, there is no reason to create them *de novo* just because an investor is new to the space.
- *Regularly reaffirm the leadership:* Investment decision-makers need regular ongoing affirmation of their long-term investing mandates so they avoid pressure to conform too closely to the market or execute too conservatively.
- *Design durable strategies from the beginning:* Conscious forethought about the future resilience of strategies will help them survive over the long term, and even outlive current principals and investment decision-makers.
- *Create values-based touchstones*: Sustainable investing rests on a long-term values-based commitment to making a positive impact on our planet and people; values-based touchstones are just as important as strategic financial reviews."[21]

Foundation investors

Philanthropic institutions don't bring the mountains of money that institutional investors can, but they punch above their weight as partners and pathfinders in the realm of sustainable investment.

With only $2 trillion in global AUM, endowments and foundations are relatively small players in this field—especially since they traditionally take a finance-first approach to investing. Surprisingly, a foundation that devotes sizeable philanthropic money to the environment, for example, may have an endowment that's heavily invested in energy companies. (In 2007, e.g., the Bill and Melinda Gates Foundation was harshly criticized for its $423 million investment in oil companies.) Or a foundation dedicated to anti-obesity initiatives may be heavily invested in snack food companies.

Like other investors, though, foundations are waking up to the siren call of matching their investment decisions with their grant-making decisions, especially since a 2015 IRS notice that allows US-based private foundations to consider the relationship between investments and the foundation's mission. Mission-related investing, or investing a foundation's endowment in line with its mission, is increasingly popular. Two trailblazers in particular led the way: The Ford Foundation plans to invest up to $1 billion of its $12 billion endowment in mission-related investments by 2027, while the F. B. Heron Foundation now invests 100% of its assets toward its mission.

Perhaps even more important than the money they bring is the role of philanthropies as midwives to impact investing. As the Mission Investors Exchange (MIE) explains, "By providing catalytic, patient capital, they also play a unique role in paving the way for other investors seeking market-rate returns or lower risk." Members of the MIE have participated in these projects, for example:

- Investing in a municipal bond to construct storm water treatment infrastructure for better resiliency to climate change;
- Providing low-interest mortgages for first-time homeowners;
- Screening an investment stock portfolio to support carbon-neutral companies;
- Making a venture capital investment into a drug development company.[22]

Sometimes it's about more than money; sometimes it's about the halo and catalytic effect of thought leaders like the Rockefeller and Ford foundations.

Financial powerhouses: Institutional investors

Huge financial players are like huge battleships; they change course very, very slowly. But even these powerhouses, from pension funds to sovereign wealth funds, are taking an interest in sustainable investing.

Prodded by giants like BlackRock ($7 trillion in assets), other institutional investors are lumbering into this space, for a variety of reasons. As one observer points out:

> Of course, Goldman Sachs' interest in sustainability is not altruistic: It is a reflection of the fact that this is where business is headed – investing for return while not destroying our collective home. Just

witness the growth in managed assets for [the firm's Sustainable Finance Group] – from $550 million when they were acquired, to $6 billion in 2016, $11 billion in 2017, $17 billion in 2018, and north of $55 billion in 2019.[23,24]

This amounts to 7.5% of AUM for Goldman, not a huge sum but still an impressive climb from close to zero just a few years earlier.

Part of the impetus behind institutional investors' growing interest in the field is an easing of concerns about fiduciary responsibility. Once stymied by the old-school belief that fiduciary responsibility meant one thing and one thing only—maximizing short-term financial returns—many professional asset managers now take comfort that the fiduciary aspect has been clarified to empower them to incorporate an ESG lens into their investment decisions.

A Harvard Law School study found that:

> The view that ESG is simply part of fiduciary duty is becoming commonplace, with 46% citing this as a top push factor…Our analysis of respondents driven by fiduciary duty suggests that mitigating ESG investment risks and shaping a sustainable economy are viewed as key responsibilities to their beneficiaries – two different drivers but with the same effect.

The Harvard study found that mitigating ESG risk in the portfolio as well as regulatory shifts are also important, with 46% of respondents viewing ESG as a fiduciary duty, 46% seeking to meet or get ahead of regulations, and 44% wanting to mitigate ESG risks.

On the other hand, respondents in this study also cited the following obstacles:

- Consistency and availability of ESG data (44%);
- Resource constraints and cost implications (43%);
- Lack of expertise (40%);
- Fiduciary duty since ESG investing could compromise the ability to maximize returns (38%);
- Existing regulations (33%).[25]

The position of fiduciary and regulatory issues on both lists—both a push factor and an obstacle—is a noteworthy demonstration of the immaturity of the ESG investment space, and the challenges and opportunities that lie ahead.

Investors in different countries, perhaps unsurprisingly, have trodden different paths toward the impact investing space, as the following examples illustrate:

- France: According to law, investors must explain how they incorporate ESG factors into their investment strategies; thus, a majority of French institutional investors now manage their assets using an ESG lens.
- Japan: While still a relatively small player at just 7% of the global market, this represents considerable growth from less than 1% in 2012.
- Europe versus United States: Europe accounts for about one-half of sustainable assets worldwide, followed closely by the United States at just under 40%.

As of 2018, 75% of sustainable investing assets were owned by institutional investors. However, sustainable investing is still a small fraction of total AUM, and it will take concerted and dedicated action on the part of these great powerhouses to really move the needle.

Venture capital and private equity

Like institutional investors, venture capital and private equity firms (VCPEs) have been relatively sluggish latecomers to the field of ESG investing. What investment has taken place in this sector is almost wholly limited to climate change-based projects, with the industry largely eschewing more complex social investments. This picture is starting to change, largely based on investor and consumer demands, but VCPEs are remarkably reluctant to even inch away from their laser focus on money, money, and more money.

This is surprising because successful VCPEs are really good at innovation and risk-taking. Their business model, in fact, is based on their ability to spot a diamond in the rough; to distinguish money pits from unicorns, and to take big risks along the way. Weaning them away from their devotion to financial returns, and financial returns alone, however, is a challenge.

That said, there is a small but growing group of VCPEs that are either focused on ESG-based returns or at least willing to consider them alongside financial returns. As in much of the ESG industry, the impetus for this comes from limited partners (the investors who commit capital to the fund). And ESG in this context largely refers to climate-based investment, a disappointingly limited approach to sustainable investment.

The 2020 Responsible Investment Report by Private Equity International (PEI) highlights this mixed picture:

- Climate change is a growing focus on PE firms, partly because of pressure from environmental activists and partly because the issue is increasingly obvious to investors (see Australian wildfires).
- Risk management is key; corruption and poor governance, for example, can sharply increase the risk profile of investments.
- "Private equity is in a powerful position to drive change," as one large investor told PEI. They can put pressure on portfolio companies, especially with regard to good corporate governance.
- On the other hand, diversity is rarely a deal-breaker: "LPs are becoming more diversity-conscious, but a lack of gender balance in investment teams is rarely a reason to pull an investment." The data back this up; only 13% of partners in PE firms are women, and just 14% of LPs have turned down an investment due to a lack of diversity at the fund manager level.[26]

Private equity firm TPG was an early leader in this field, launching the Rise Impact Fund in 2016 "to deliver positive and sustainable impact" while creating a "top-performing fund."[27] Bain Capital followed suit with its Double Impact Fund, and KKR created a $1.3 billion impact fund.

How much impact is this creating?

Depressingly, the authors of one study in mid-2020 concluded that "The vast majority of private equity ESG efforts remain nascent and superficial." They noted that less than 10% of private equity firms are signatories to the United Nations Principles of Responsible Investment (PRI), and a very small proportion of those signatories require ESG reports from their portfolio companies—suggesting that the VCPE commitment to ESG is barely skin-deep. According to a PwC 2019 survey, 83% of PE firms responded that they were concerned about climate risk, but only 31% said they had taken action to address this.[28]

A stubborn devotion to financial performance is not the only obstacle to adding an ESG lens to VCPE investment decisions. The tight timeline for most PE investments (the median hold period for a portfolio company is just 4.5 years) does not lend itself very well to sustainability-based initiatives, which tend to be longer term in nature. Moreover, since VCPEs invest in many different companies, sometimes in a range of industries, it can be very difficult to determine which ESG factors are relevant for which businesses, and how to compare ESG performance across different businesses.

Also, VCPE decision-makers usually have extraordinary expertise in financial modelling and analysis—but little to none in ESG analysis. They are accustomed to highly quantified results, which also do not lend itself very well to sustainability projects:

> "For example, how might a [General Partner] measure the return on investment tied to a commitment to diversity? Or how should an analyst determine the financial and reputational value of a crisis averted thanks to an investment in human rights monitoring in an overseas factory?"[29]

The difficult-to-quantify performance metrics for social and environmental projects just don't mesh well with the number-crunching background of VCPE experts.

So it's not surprising that VCPE firms, like other early entrants into ESG investing, are largely limited to the relatively simple environmental space—and even there, they had a rocky start. Starting in the early 2000s, these investors "flocked to invest in renewable technologies – from biofuels to new solar energy generating technologies to new battery chemistries and beyond."

But too many of those investments failed, dampening the appetite of even the most risk-tolerant VCPEs. In the past 2 years, however, interest in the sector has ticked up again. In 2018, global venture capital investment into sustainability-based startups jumped 127% to $9.2 billion—its highest level since 2010. Chinese electric vehicles took almost one-third of all VCPE sustainability investments, but opportunities are also ripe in diverse areas from agriculture to new construction technologies for smart homes and cities.

With their appetites for risk and innovation, their skills in financial assessment and research, and their command over large pools of capital, VCPE investors "have a growing and consequential influence on social and environmental outcomes."[30] The VCPE industry midwifed the birth of the US high-tech industry by taking risks and backing unproven technologies; it could play the same role in creating a more sustainable future.

But they're not there yet.

Faith-based investors

There is a great deal of overlap between faith-based investors and impact investors. Both are determined to use their money to make a better world, and both view financial performance as only one of the factors that they use to make investment decisions.

Islamic investors

As an Islamic text exhorts its readers, "O you who believe! Stand out firmly for justice as witnesses to Allah."

Sustainable investing is a natural adjunct to Islamic finance, given its adherence to religious principles and social welfare. Both begin by excluding investments in certain types of activities or products (pork and alcohol under Sharia law, classic "sin" stocks under ESG-based investing).

But the parallels are deeper than that. A broad theme in Islamic finance is its focus on a socially minded approach to finance that aligns more or less with the logic of sustainable finance, that is, financial results are not the be-all and end-all of business, and should not be prioritized above all else or achieved in ways that are not in the best interests of all stakeholders.

Islamic finance is also an important growth area in parts of the developing world. Malaysia, for example, accounts for more than 25% of the Islamic banking market; over 90% of Muslims in that country engage in *zakat,* or an obligatory payment made annually under Islamic law to be used for charitable and religious purposes. And Indonesia is home to the world's largest Muslim population of more than 230 million people, or 88% of the country.

These countries are waking up to the potential for Islamic finance to achieve social goals. In June 2020, Indonesia raised $2.5 billion from a global *sukuk,* or Sharia-compliant bond, intended to help the government fund the battle against COVID-19. The issue was oversubscribed at 6.7 times its target, reflecting strong investor interest in these instruments. Its success demonstrates the viability of the Islamic finance sector in raising funds to alleviate social ills, particularly in the era of COVID-19.

With the exception of a few oil-rich countries, Muslim countries are among the poorest in the world. Here are some thoughts on how to use Islamic finance to address this challenge:

- Investing in Sharia-based financial inclusion, such as microfinance, since it's well established that giving poor people access to financial services plays a big role in poverty reduction;
- Investing in more resilient communities and people though insurance services and agricultural funding; and
- Investing in infrastructure development.[31]

Islamic investment instruments are not for the faint-hearted though, as they must be very carefully structured. Each instrument must be related to a real, material transaction; and paying or receiving interest is prohibited. A number of viable investment techniques have been developed, however, that broadly adhere to Sharia law and would be applicable for sustainable investing purposes. As a World Bank report noted in 2015, "Given the principles of Islamic finance that support socially inclusive and development promoting activities, the Islamic financial sector has the potential to contribute to the achievement of the Sustainable Development Goals."[32]

Judeo-Christian faith-based investors

Investment in accordance with Judeo-Christian values is also highly analogous to impact investment. The Jewish Talmud, for example, speaks about various sustainable investing truths, such as protecting the environment, treating workers well, keeping communities safe, and supporting Israel—these are as much a part of Jewish tradition as not eating pork or shellfish. And as Pope Francis wrote in his 2015 encyclical letter, "Once more, we need to reject a magical conception of the market."[33] Embracing his hopes for an inclusive and equitable economy, the Pope has called on Catholics to not only do no harm, but do real good, with their money.

These beliefs form the foundation for impactful investing approaches based on all of the world's major religions. JLens, for example, created an investment strategy guided by Jewish values in 2015, and has invested in some of the largest US corporations based on this strategy. (Among their favorite companies are General Mills, Accenture, Marriott, Cisco, Microsoft, and Starbucks.) Amana Funds applies Islamic principles and screens out various forms of interest income, while Ave Maria Mutual Funds screens out "companies engaged in activities that are not pro-life or pro-family."

Faith-based investors are a very small segment of the sustainable investing market, and an even smaller segment of the overall market. And as in all corners of sustainable investing, faith-based investors have to be wary of faith-washing (funds that make their investments seem like they're based on religious principles when they're actually not). Still, these funds have tended to outperform traditional stock indexes over time, and the post-COVID-19 era is likely to see lots of growth in this area.

The bottom-line: Demand from faith-based investors, like investors from every walk of life and every corner of the world, is driving the sustainable investing market to new innovations and explosive growth.

Mini-case: TPG, KKR, and Bain Capital

Impact investing is on the rise across virtually every investment firm today, and TPG, KKR, and Bain Capital have all found themselves leading the charge in the private equity space. Between the three, they hold AUM of about $400 billion and have all recently debuted groundbreaking impact funds.

Their active participation in the impact revolution tells us two important things: (1) This movement is not limited to quirky independent firms or tiny impact investments placed here and there; it is much bigger than that. (2) Impact investing is, simply, financially viable. And, further, we are living in a world wherein it is increasingly necessary to fund projects with a positive social and environmental impact, as the economic impact of the climate crisis and social inequalities become more apparent.

In December 2016, TPG launched the Rise Fund, which raised $2 billion in 2016–2017. After 2 years its launch, TPG set plans for the Rise Fund II, targeting another $2.5 billion. The Rise Fund focuses on supporting business solutions aligned with the UN Sustainable Development Goals. Funds like this one put the firm's strengths—identifying investment opportunities, vetting them, and moving capital efficiently—to use. Here, the vetting process includes targeted ESG criteria; overall, this growing trend in financing shows the relative ease with which the private equity industry can shift into the impact space by leveraging skills and resources it has already cultivated.

The PE sector is especially good at considering the measurement and performance aspect of any good investment: The Rise Funds help develop the Impact Multiple of Money (IMM), which is effectively the Internal Rate of Return (IRR), through the lens of broader impact. In tandem with IRR, then, IMM offers impact investors a full picture of their investment, thus solving for the recurring question in impact investing of what exactly *does* a positive impact look like, and how is it measured? For the Rise Fund, an acceptable IMM is a projected creation of $2.50 in social impact (at minimum) for every $1.00 invested, or an IMM of 2.5 times.

Even beyond its formal establishment of the Rise Fund, TPG has had a reputation for making responsible investments for some time now; in 2013, the firm became a signatory to the UN Principles for Responsible Investment (PRI).

While KKR has had a fairly long-term reputation for responsible investing—the firm is in good company with TPG and became a UN PRI signatory in 2009—it formally opened its impact investing business, Global Impact, in 2018. To date, KKR has invested more than $7 billion in solution-focused businesses, addressing a wide range of social and environmental problems. In February 2020, the firm closed its first Global Impact fund at $1.3 billion, which will allow them to continue allocating capital toward impact-oriented business opportunities. In particular, KKR's approach in the space is to focus on smaller investments (i.e., less than $100 million) to support targeted solutions.

And then there's the granddaddy of them all: In 2017, the venerable (read: stodgy?) Bain Capital closed its debut Double Impact fund at $390 million. The fund aims to seek out and invest in companies that have an impact-centered mission and will perform well, both financially and in terms of measurable environmental and social impact. The year 2019 was particularly strong for the young fund, bringing in performance results that speak about the power and viability of Bain Capital's impact strategy: The portfolio saw 31% revenue growth from 2018 to 2019, 37% EBITDA growth and 25% job growth. And on the environmental front, the portfolio led to a reduction of 24 thousand metric tons of carbon dioxide emissions in 2019 alone.

In 2020, impact investing has seen accelerated growth on the heels of the COVID-19 pandemic. At the same time, the rising tide of civil unrest and the realities of growing climate risk are creating still greater demand for a financial services industry that takes a thoughtful, impact-oriented approach across the board. KKR, TPG, and Bain Capital have provided both the proof of concept and some semblance of a playbook by which to make this happen—and others will take note from them and continue to innovate in the impact economy.

Mini-case: BlackRock

Larry Fink's name tends to come up sooner or later in conversations surrounding impact investing and corporate responsibility. Fink, CEO of the world's largest asset manager BlackRock, continues to receive new praise and backlash alike every time he re-addresses the climate crisis and urges other finance leaders to action.

Fink co-founded BlackRock in 1988, initially under the Blackstone Group, before separating from its parent to run BlackRock independently in the mid-1990s. Today, it is a definitive giant in the industry. It closed the second quarter of 2020 with $7.3 trillion AUM, increasing 7% from the previous quarter during which the appearance of the COVID-19 pandemic struck markets globally. Internally, the firm has been focused on setting, and now achieving, aggressive and wide-reaching goals for reducing its carbon footprint. As of June 2020, BlackRock has achieved its 100% renewable energy goal. The asset manager recognizes that its role in sustainability, both environmental and social, is twofold: In investment stewardship *and* in its corporate operations.

Today, Fink is especially well known for his annual open letter to CEOs. His letters are a call to action on corporate governance, and lecture other CEOs on the responsibility of corporations in mitigating climate risk and achieving global impact goals.

In January 2020, Fink released what was arguably the most drastic letter yet, in terms of its urgency and the fact that it laid out concrete commitments on BlackRock's end. Fink began by citing BlackRock's fiduciary duty—which he sees as include a duty to invest responsibility, as climate risk is by no means exclusive of financial risk.[34] In a world where awareness of climate change is growing rapidly, Fink expressed his belief that "we are on the edge of a fundamental reshaping of finance." At the same time, he wrote in his letter to BlackRock clients to announce the firm's divestment from coal and other investments due to high risks related to sustainability. He closed with a call for greater accountability and transparency in finance, under a broader goal of achieving "a more sustainable and inclusive capitalism."[35]

In the retail investment space, BlackRock is particularly well known for its series of Sustainable ETFs. In fact, it debuted its first sustainable ETF back in 2005, launching the first fund of this kind: the iShares MSCI USA ESG Select ETF (Ticker: SUSA). Over the past 10 years, the fund has had an average annual return of more than 11%, a shining reminder that having a positive impact and gaining healthy financial returns from investments are not mutually exclusive. Today, the firm manages three core styles of sustainable funds—ESG Aware, ESG Advanced, and Thematic—which make it easy for investors to interact with sustainability in their portfolios.

Most exciting, perhaps, is the incontrovertible evidence that BlackRock is financially sound. This is not a company bleeding money in the name of a cause—this is a successful business. During the first few months of 2020, as most of the major players in the financial services industry were hit hard by the COVID-19 pandemic, BlackRock was relatively unscathed compared to a number of its peers; revenue increased by 11% in the first quarter and 4% in the second quarter, year over year. In the market chaos of the pandemic, the iShares series remained attractive to investors, further indicating that the firm's commitment to ESG principles has helped, not hurt, its financial results.

BlackRock is without a doubt a leader in the sustainable investing space—which is an increasingly important fact when we consider its massive scale. The world's largest asset manager is committed to coal divestment; the world's largest asset manager is taking a thorough, firm-wide approach to solving social and environmental problems, because it recognizes both the moral and financial value of reshaping finance today to be more resilient tomorrow.

Notes

1. Kumar, R., Wallace, N., & Funk, C. (January 13, 2020). "Into the mainstream: ESG at the tipping point." *Harvard Law School Forum on Corporate Governance.* Retrieved from: https://corpgov.law.harvard.edu/2020/01/13/into-the-mainstream-esg-at-the-tipping-point/.
2. "2018 Global Sustainable Investment Review." *Global Sustainable Investment Alliance.* Retrieved from: www.gsi-alliance.org/wp-content/uploads/2019/03/GSIR_Review2018.3.28.pdf.
3. Nason, D. (December 21, 2020). "'Sustainable investing' is surging, accounting for 33% of total US assets under management." *CNBC.* Retrieved from: www.cnbc.com/2020/12/21/sustainable-investing-accounts-for-33percent-of-total-us-assets-under-management.html.
4. Morris, C. (September 18, 2018). "Retail investors look to increase exposure to sustainable investments." *Corporate Citizenship Briefing.* Retrieved from: https://ccbriefing.corporate-citizenship.com/2018/09/18/retail-investors-look-to-increase-exposure-to-sustainable-investments/.
5. Sullivan, P. (August 28, 2020). "Investing in social good is finally becoming profitable." *The New York Times.* Retrieved from: www.nytimes.com/2020/08/28/your-money/impact-investing-coronavirus.html?auth=login-email&login=email.
6. Morris, C.
7. Ibid.
8. Ghosh, I. (February 4, 2020). "Visualizing the global rise of sustainable investing." *Visual Capitalist.* Retrieved from: www.visualcapitalist.com/rise-of-sustainable-investing/.
9. Munk, C.W. (August 9, 2020). "Interested in social-impact investing? Here's how to start." *The Wall Street Journal.* Retrieved from: www.wsj.com/articles/interested-in-social-impact-investing-heres-how-to-start-11597019400.
10. "HNW Wants More ESG in Portfolios." (December 11, 2019). *Traders Magazine.* Retrieved from: www.tradersmagazine.com/departments/buyside/hnw-wants-more-esg-in-portfolios/.
11. Ibid.
12. Ibid.
13. "As responsible investment comes of age, family offices should look beyond the label to help families put their wealth to work for social good." *PWC.* Retrieved from: www.pwc.com/gx/en/services/family-business/family-office/responsible-investment-for-family-offices.html.
14. Ibid.
15. Ibid.
16. Ibid.
17. UBS. The Global Family Office Report 2019. Retrieved from: www.ubs.com/global/en/wealth-management/uhnw/global-family-office-report/global-family-office-report-2019.html.

18 Sullivan, P.
19 Ibid.
20 Ibid.
21 "Pathways to sustainable investing: Insights from families and peers." *CREO and Cambridge Associates.* (August 2019). Retrieved from: www.cambridgeassociates.com/insight/pathways-to-sustainable-investing/.
22 "Impact investing by foundations: Key terms in philanthropy." (August 2018). *Mission Investors Organization.* Retrieved from: https://missioninvestors.org/resources/impact-investing-foundations-key-terms-philanthropy.
23 Taylor, C. "Green is good. Is Wall Street's new motto sustainable?" (January 13, 2020). *Reuters.* Retrieved from: www.reuters.com/article/us-money-investing-sustainability/green-is-good-is-wall-streets-new-motto-sustainable-idUSKBN1ZC0Z7.
24 Goldman was famously nicknamed the "vampire squid" in 2009 by journalist Matt Taibbi, with its arms "wrapped around the face of humanity, relentlessly jamming its blood funnel into anything that smells like money." So reputation rehabilitation was long overdue.
25 Kumar et al.
26 "Responsible Investment 2020." *Private Equity International.* Retrieved from: www.privateequityinternational.com/responsible-investment-2020/.
27 https://therisefund.com/.
28 Pucker, K. & Kolsantonis, S. (June 29, 2020). "Private equity makes ESG Promises. But their impact is often superficial." *Institutional Investor.* Retrieved from: www.institutionalinvestor.com/article/b1m8spzx5bp6g7/Private-Equity-Makes-ESG-Promises-But-Their-Impact-Is-Often-Superficial.
29 Ibid.
30 Ibid.
31 Ibid
32 Ahmed, H. & Mohieldin, M. (May 2015). "On the Sustainable Development Goals and the role of Islamic finance." *World Bank Group.* Retrieved from: https://openknowledge.worldbank.org/bitstream/handle/10986/22000/On0the0sustain0e0of0Islamic0finance.pdf?sequence=1&isAllowed=y.
33 Bailey, S.P. (June 18, 2015). "10 key excerpts from Pope Francis's encyclical on the environment." *The Washington Post.* Retrieved from: www.washingtonpost.com/news/acts-of-faith/wp/2015/06/18/10-key-excerpts-from-pope-franciss-encyclical-on-the-environment/.
34 Even outside of Fink's letter, this relationship between responsible investing and fiduciary duty is a point of much debate. The US Department of Labor proposed a rule in June 2020 surrounding fiduciary duty and ESG regulation; the ultimate implications and decision making have yet to be seen.
35 Sorkin, A.R. (January 14, 2020). "BlackRock CEO Larry Fink: climate crisis will reshape finance." *The New York Times.* Retrieved from: www.nytimes.com/2020/01/14/business/dealbook/larry-fink-blackrock-climate-change.html.

5 Microfinance

The seeds of the impact revolution

Microfinance has, however, run into some roadblocks in the 21st century. Some or many microfinance institutions (MFIs) were associated with unethical collection practices, exorbitant interest rates, and mission drift (shifting away from poor borrowers to middle-income borrowers in search of greater profits). The greatest blow to the industry was a dawning realization that microfinance might not produce the social impact that many had anticipated and assumed; on the plus side, this has led to long-needed reform and regulation of the sector.

Still, microfinance has taught us some valuable lessons. It has generated growing acceptance of the idea that the interests of large, for-profit companies can be compatible with the interests of the poor, which forms the very basis of the impact revolution. And it has taught us how to evolve these institutions in ways that can be much more impactful. The next step is to incorporate these lessons into the impact revolution.

Muhammad Yunus: Microfinance is born

The story of microfinance starts with Professor Muhammad Yunus, a professor of economics at Chittagong University in Bangladesh (yes, economic professors *can* be pretty cool!).

Professor Yunus was doing research in the nearby village of Jobra in 1976 when he met a 21-year-old woman named Sufiya Begum. Sufiya was just barely keeping herself and her three children alive by weaving beautiful bamboo stools, and Yunus wondered why such a skilled artisan lived in such abject poverty.

He soon learned the answer: She earned just two cents a day, making it impossible that she or her children would ever escape from poverty.

Why such a low profit? Yunus discovered that the raw material for each stool cost about 22 cents, which Sufiya had to borrow from middlemen.

She then sold the stool back to the middlemen for 24 cents as repayment for the loan, netting a miserable two cents profit for each stool.

Didn't she have any other options? All she needed was 22 cents! Perhaps she could borrow from a moneylender, but he would charge even more—10% per week, or even 10% per day. So Sufiya was essentially a bonded slave to middlemen—for lack of 22 cents.

Muhammad Yunus, in his own words, "got angry." He realized that Sufiya could only escape from this bonded slavery if she could find 22 cents for her bamboo—a 22 cent loan could change her life. He decided to try a small experiment, and lent a total of $27 from his own pocket to 42 people in the village who were dependent on the middlemen, including Sufiya.

The experiment worked—and Yunus became even more angry, furious at economic theories and financial institutions that condemned people like Sufiya to endless poverty. He realized that he needed to create an institutional answer to this trap—essentially, a financial institution that would lend to those at the bottom of the pyramid.

And thus was an industry born. In December 1976, Yunus launched Grameen Bank as a micro-lender in the village of Jobra, lending tiny amounts of money to poor rural people. In his remarkable book recounting these experiences, *Banker to the Poor*, Yunus relates the story of a beggar named Mufiya, who lived a life of semi-starvation and regular beatings by her husband.

Finally, in 1974 the village leader arranged for Mufiya to get a divorce from her abusive husband. She was now free of his beatings, but, starving, wound up on the streets begging for money. An entire day of begging would yield a few ounces of rice, barely enough for her and her three children.

Then Mufiya's life changed in 1979 when she joined Yunus's Grameen Bank and borrowed about $22 to start a bamboo business, which enabled her to feed her family regularly, buy clothing, and own cookware.[1]

To support inexperienced, illiterate former beggars like Mufiya, Yunus decided to do exactly the opposite of traditional banks:

- Instead of one lump sum payment, the borrower would make daily payments, repaying loans fully in 1 year.
- Yunus believed that support groups were crucial to success, so he required that all borrowers join a group in their village.
- He also required all borrowers to deposit 5% of the loan in a group fund, used for interest-free loans in the event of seasonal malnutrition, medical treatment, school supplies, natural disasters, and burials.

For a vulnerable people without insurance or social safety nets, this was a great step forward.
- There was no collateral, and no coercive collections!
- All borrowers agreed to follow the Sixteen Decisions:
  - We shall follow and advance the four principles of Grameen Bank: Discipline, Unity, Courage, and Hard work—in all walks of our lives.
  - Prosperity we shall bring to our families.
  - We shall not live in dilapidated houses. We shall repair our houses and work toward constructing new houses at the earliest.
  - We shall grow vegetables all the year round. We shall eat plenty of them and sell the surplus.
  - During the plantation seasons, we shall plant as many seedlings as possible.
  - We shall plan to keep our families small. We shall minimize our expenditures. We shall look after our health.
  - We shall educate our children and ensure that they can earn to pay for their education.
  - We shall always keep our children and the environment clean.
  - We shall build and use pit-latrines.
  - We shall drink water from tubewells. If it is not available, we shall boil water or use alum.
  - We shall not take any dowry at our sons' weddings, neither shall we give any dowry at our daughters' wedding. We shall keep our center free from the curse of dowry. We shall not practice child marriage.
  - We shall not inflict any injustice on anyone, neither shall we allow anyone to do so.
  - We shall collectively undertake bigger investments for higher incomes.
  - We shall always be ready to help each other. If anyone is in difficulty, we shall all help him or her.
  - If we come to know of any breach of discipline in any center, we shall all go there and help restore discipline.
  - We shall take part in all social activities collectively.

Remarkably, from the point of view of traditional bankers who scorned Yunus's ideas and predicted disaster, the business model succeeded beyond even his wildest dreams. His borrowers repaid their loans 97% of the time, an amazing record—far outpacing the record of those traditional bankers!

So Yunus's operations prospered, and he soon made some critical changes to his initial model. Most importantly, he decided to bank on women.

He had launched operations with a goal of 50% women borrowers—a lofty and controversial goal in a highly patriarchal, conservative society—but he soon realized that even this was not high enough, since money in women's hands transforms lives much faster than money in men's hands. As Yunus learned, and subsequent researchers confirmed, when a destitute woman earns extra income, it goes to the benefit of her children and household. When a destitute man earns extra income, he focuses more attention on himself—so, money entering the household through a woman provides maximal benefit to the family, community, and society.

Increasingly, development specialists endorsed this approach: If the goals of economic development are to improve the standard of living, cut poverty, and reduce inequality, then the do-gooders should work primarily through women. And Yunus did just that; he came to focus his efforts almost exclusively on lending to women.

This approach was not without its naysayers, of course. Opposition came, not unexpectedly, from husbands, religious leaders, and moneylenders—but also from educated civil servants and professionals who objected to this seismic shift in the role of women in society.

Also, as Yunus ramped up his work, some 85% of poor women in rural Bangladesh were illiterate, not to mention rarely free to leave their homes without a husband, which presented serious challenges to his group-based model. He had to come up with a series of tricks and techniques to lure and provide services for women borrowers, without subverting age-old social customs.

Yunus describes early conversations with Jobra women in his book:

> One woman, hiding her face with the end of her sari, said, "Your words frighten us, sir." Another explained that only her husband handled money, and a third suggested giving the loan directly to her husband. "I've never touched any [money] and I don't want to," she said.[2]

Yet again, Yunus patiently persevered. Grameen ("Village") Bank was born and by the end of 1982 it had 28,000 borrowers across Bangladesh. Yunus still faced serious opposition from traditional clergy and bankers, who attributed Grameen's rapid growth to Yunus's personality and his faithful followers—it was a cult of personality, they proclaimed, rather than a new and revolutionary banking model.

Yunus—and others, by this time (parallel initiatives were proceeding apace across the globe in Latin America)—proceeded to prove them wrong. Grameen experienced breathtaking growth, opening one hundred new branches every year in the 1980s. Yunus proved that the

Grameen model worked in other countries, expanding into Malaysia and the Philippines, and in 1996 Grameen extended its one-billionth dollar in loans to one of its two million borrowers; just 2 years later it loaned its two-billionth dollar.

Microfinance goes viral

By the mid-1990s, this once-doubted industry—which began with a spontaneous $27 loan out of an economic professor's pocket—had gone viral. Grameen Bank and Muhammad Yunus won the Nobel Peace Prize in 2006, helping to spread the word, and MFIs popped up in every corner of the globe.

Another pioneering organization, Kiva, has even brought microfinance to the retail investor level. For as little as $25, ordinary (i.e., not super-rich) people can lend small amounts of money to help poor people "start or grow a business, go to school, access clean energy or realize their potential." By mid-2020, Kiva had 3.6 million borrowers and 1.9 million lenders in 77 countries; a 96% loan repayment rate; and $1.45 billion in total loans funded since its founding in 2005. Some 81% of Kiva borrowers are women, and a Kiva loan is funded every two minutes![3]

Grameen itself remained at the head of microfinance revolution. By 2018 it had distributed a whopping $24 billion in collateral-free loans to 9 million borrowers, 97% of whom were women. As its website states, "Grameen Bank's positive impact on its poor and formerly poor borrowers has been documented in many independent studies carried out by external agencies including the World Bank…"[4]

Grameen provides four kinds of loans:

- Income generating loans at 20% interest;
- Housing loans at 8% interest;
- Higher education loans for Grameen Bank members' children at just 5%;
- Struggling Members (beggars) loans at no interest.

It also provides pensions, savings products, and loan insurance in the event of death. And according to an internal survey, 68% of Grameen Bank families have crossed the poverty line, with many more on their way!

Perhaps most remarkable, it achieved this positive impact while earning a profit. Grameen has been profitable in almost every year, partly due to its eye-popping 98% loan repayment rate; it has had only three red-ink years since 1990 and regularly distributes dividends.

The seeds of the impact revolution 83

Grameen Foundation's website features the story of Sophie Kandiel, from a village in central Burkina Faso with only one school and a population of 4,000. Sometimes Sophie had to feed her children "wild leaves flavored with a pinch of salt because that was all she had."

> None of this has deterred Sophie. The mother of nine is determined to make sure all of her children are educated. Access to financial services has been key to her success.
>
> "By law, education is free until age 16 in Burkina Faso. In practice, parents often need to pay for school supplies and other fees and communities are frequently responsible for constructing primary schools and housing for teachers.
>
> "Sophie used to rely entirely on her husband to pay the fees, which often led to the children missing school. Then a few years ago she joined a small savings group with other women in her community through a Grameen Foundation program supported by the Margaret A. Cargill Foundation. With help from Grameen Foundation and the local nonprofit, Organisation des Églises Évangéliques, group members learned new techniques to grow their crops and conserve water and vital business skills to help them earn more from their produce.
>
> "Before long, Sophie took out a loan to start a new business brewing dolo (local beer) to help pay for school. The increased income has also enabled her to diversify her farm, and raise chickens. And, if needed, she can get a loan to help defray educational costs.
>
> "Sophie is also quite pleased that her savings group is contributing 1000 francs ($1.78US) for the annual upkeep of the school's water well. Some groups have also offered dishes for the school cafeteria."[5]

And the website of another leading MFIs, FINCA, tells the story of Jane Nakintu, whose four grandchildren were orphaned by AIDS. Jane took them in, despite numerous challenges. Feeding them required Jane to spend hours over a traditional stone fire in her kitchen, which "would get consumed with thick, black smoke that was unbearable to stand in":

> These days, Jane happily prepares her flavorful meals with her clean cookstove from FINCA's BrightLife program. With a loan from FINCA, she purchased a clean charcoal cookstove in 2017. The cookstove uses almost 60 percent less charcoal than a traditional charcoal stove and takes 50 percent less time to cook. The cookstove

also reduces toxic smoke, keeping Jane's four grandchildren safe from harmful pollution.

Today, her grandchildren eat on time as the cookstove heats up in just minutes.

When it would rain, the grandmother didn't like leaving the house to cook in the wooden shack next door. Her new cookstove is portable so she can cook on the porch with her neighbors or inside the house with her grandchildren. Best of all, she could see what she was cooking. During the evening, the kitchen would get so dark that Jane would use a small flashlight against the hot pot just to see if her meals were properly cooked.

Jane likes her clean cookstove as it is not only keeping her grandchildren healthy but it is saving her money every month.

"The charcoal stove is economical and cost saving," she says. She plans to use her monthly savings from the household innovation to nourish her grandchildren in another way – by purchasing books they can read at home.[6]

Thus, Grameen and others have demonstrated that the model works—a bank can help fight poverty, empower women, and earn a tidy profit at the same time! Not surprisingly, others stampeded into the field in Grameen's footsteps. Globally, microfinance had a credit portfolio of just over $124 billion in 2018, reaching 140 million borrowers—80% of whom are women, and 65% of whom are rural laborers. This gives low-income households access to a range of high-quality and affordable financial services to finance income-producing activities, build homes, and send their children to school. Microloans are used to create microenterprises, and also to fund lumpy household expenses such as education fees, medical costs, weddings, and funerals. And the steady revenue inflows to MFIs mean that the industry is sustainable, rather than reliant on constant infusions of philanthropy.

Microfinance has, importantly, expanded beyond micro-lending to other financial services such as savings and insurance. Most poor people use informal mechanisms to save, putting their money under a mattress (literally) or entrusting it to a village elder to mind. Obviously, these methods are risky. So MFIs now provide a range of financial services including credit, savings, money transfers, insurance, pensions, and other financial products directed at poor and low-income people.

Along with these developments and the proof that microfinance can be self-sustaining, the industry has commercialized. The first MFI to transform itself from a nonprofit organization to a for-profit business was in 1992 in Bolivia, when Banco Sol was created because it couldn't get access to enough capital otherwise. Others have followed in Banco Sol's footsteps, and eventually the inevitable occurred: MFIs became publicly traded financial businesses.

In 2007 Mexico's Banco Compartamos went public in an initial public offering (IPO), when its early investors sold 30% of the company for $450 million. Some criticized the move; Muhammad Yunus himself accused the bank of exploiting the poor for the benefit of private investors, and of abandoning its mission. On the other hand, Banco Compartamos' founders argued that gaining access to public markets was the only way to make the bank a financially sustainable operation, and to tap the funds needed to reach even more needy and vulnerable people.

Then in 2010 India's SKS raised $350 million in another IPO, making its founders Vikram Akula and Vinod Khosh into multimillionaires, and the controversy escalated. Akula explained that raising money from profit-seeking investors is the only way to spread microfinance quickly around the world, and therefore to benefit the poor. But Yunus commented acerbically that if you have profit-seeking investors, eventually you will be more like loan sharks than do-gooders.

The impact of microfinance: Does it work?

Yunus is, in a way, decrying the very core of the impact revolution—the notion that it is possible, even desirable, to earn profits alongside benefits for society. The Bible may even agree with him: "You shall not…place a stumbling block before the blind…," it tells us; that is, don't exploit someone else's bad fortune for your own benefit.

Microfinance serves as a good litmus test for the impact revolution hypothesis: Does it prove, or disprove, the core idea that profit-seeking and do-gooding can peacefully coexist within the same institution? The cheerleaders believe that the success of microfinance proves the concept of using profit-seeking businesses to create good. The naysayers, on the other hand, argue that it proves the *impossibility* of chasing both profits and social good without sacrificing one or the other.

Who is right?

Soon after the SKS IPO, the microfinance world imploded and for a time it seemed that the cheerleaders had been roundly defeated by facts on the ground. But let's go back even further, to the beginning of our microfinance story: What happened to Sufiya Begum?

As you recall, Yunus's first borrower Sufiya Begum had been locked in abject poverty for lack of 22 cents to buy raw material for a bamboo stool—until Yunus came along. So in 2010, some journalists went back to

Jobra to find Sufiya and/or her descendants; their findings were featured in the controversial (and depressing) documentary "The Micro Debt." According to journalist Tom Heinemann, Sufiya died in abject poverty in 1998, and her sad fate echoed the failure of microfinance to produce meaningful positive change for a great many of its borrowers.

Deepening the mystery, other videos were posted online after the documentary appeared, apparently indicating that Sufiya was alive and well in 2010. The bottom line? Nobody knows *what* happened to Sufiya Begum. And in a way, this is a great metaphor for the debate over microfinance that continues to rage today: For all the billions of dollars and the incredible volume of research, nobody really knows what the true impact of microfinance has been.

A fierce backlash against microfinance exploded in response to a crisis in Andhra Pradesh, India in mid-2010. Remember SKS, the MFI that IPO-ed earlier that year and made its founder, Vikram Akula, a multimillionaire. Well, by late 2011 Akula was forced to step down amid a wave of fury stemming from farmer suicides in Andhra Pradesh that were linked to the practices of SKS. SKS, it was charged, had been overly aggressive in both lending and collecting money, directly leading to the surge of suicides.

Other microfinance crises also emerged in Bosnia, Nicaragua, and Morocco. In mid-2008, the microfinance sector in Nicaragua was shaken by the emergence of a movement called "Movimiento No Pago," which produced violent protests and forced MFI branches to close. This movement too was sparked by farmers and spread quickly; total borrowers in the industry dropped by about 100,000, or one-third of the total.

And then there's the Pakistan microfinance crisis of 2010, which began with massive floods that eventually submerged almost one-fifth of the country's total land area. Women were especially hard-hit, as agriculture was devastated and even those with other skills like sewing and crafts "lost their tools, raw materials, work spaces, and clients… Basically, the borrowers, most of them being women, lost all means of repayment of their existing loans as they lost their means of livelihood."[7] And just when more microloans were urgently needed to get people back on their feet again, the funds were unavailable due to MFIs' inability to collect on outstanding debts.

The microfinance sector in Bosnia too suffered severe reverses in 2009 as a result of high indebtedness among borrowers plus the effects of the global financial crisis. A flood of competing MFIs had led to over-borrowing, which in turn (inevitably) led to repayment shortfalls. Controversy, scandal, and accusations abounded.

These events unleashed an outpouring of criticism from politicians and social activists, first in India and then worldwide, taking square aim at the microfinance sector. They pointed out that some MFIs earned record profits while charging poor women interest rates of 30%–65% per annum (sometimes even higher). Since repayment rates in microfinance are remarkably high at over 95%, these critics argued, the risk of lending is quite low—and so, what accounts for the usurious interest rates? How is this not exploitation?

On a broader scale, the 2010 Indian crisis provoked a broad debate about the role of for-profit firms in the microfinance industry. Muhammad Yunus, the father of the industry, was himself forced out of Grameen Bank in disgrace (though this appears to be a politically motivated act rather than a real blow against microfinance itself). The Prime Minister of Bangladesh, who may have been threatened by Yunus's fame and popularity, accused micro-lenders of "sucking blood from the poor in the name of poverty alleviation," and governments rushed to impose regulations and interest rate caps on the sector.

Other, more dispassionate, critics noted a number of challenges to the industry. Some or many MFIs were associated with unethical collection practices, exorbitant interest rates, and mission drift (shifting away from poor borrowers to middle-income borrowers in search of greater profits). Many microfinance borrowers were overly indebted, and frequently borrowed from multiple MFIs to pay back earlier loans (rather cleverly creating mini-Ponzi schemes in the process).

The greatest blow to the industry, however, was a dawning realization that microfinance might not produce the social impact that many had anticipated and assumed. (Yunus himself had predicted that microfinance would relegate poverty to museums by 2030.) New and more rigorous studies than those done by the MFIs themselves showed limited benefits for microfinance borrowers (remember the unknown fate of Sufiya Begum and her family). Some studies found that credit can be as dangerous and addictive as a drug and that it could be exploitative and do more harm than good.

Indeed, it is well established that in some cases microfinance contributes to over-borrowing, and therefore to greater long-term poverty. One expert commented that Indian households in 2009 had been "carpet-bombed" by MFIs, leading to extreme over-indebtedness.[8] The problem is akin to that of college freshmen in America being bombarded by "free" credit card offers; this easy access to credit has led many a wide-eyed 18-year-old to a lifetime of indebtedness. In summary, poor and vulnerable people should not be brought into the financial world without safeguards, protections, and education.

Lamia Karim, in her powerful book *Microfinance and Its Discontents*, took direct and compelling aim at the industry. She has some pretty sobering objections to MF:

- *Economic shaming becomes a form of collateral.* Grameen and other large MFIs, she points out, demand no collateral yet boast a 98% loan recovery rate. Is this too good to be true? There is a complex story behind this recovery rate, she argues, because the MFIs create an "economy of shame" in which rural women—whose honor is a cornerstone of community life—are shamed/coerced by their fellow villagers into repaying their loans at any cost.
- *While women are official borrowers of money, their husbands are often the users.* Karim and others have documented the tendency for men to control the use of funds, even though their wives are responsible for repayment. Perhaps related to this, a large number of funds are NOT invested in productive activity; rather, they are used for personal consumption, paying back old loans, paying dowries, and money lending. One borrower's husband told Karim: "We took a cow loan. 50% will be spent to pay off old debts, 50% invested in money lending. If a manager comes to see our cow, we can always borrow from neighbors."[9]
- *MFIs become a shadow government with no accountability to citizens of the country.* These powerful institutions provide essential services and employment in the rural economy of many countries—which is certainly much needed—but in the process have become almost a shadow state, accountable neither to people nor regulators. Shouldn't development efforts be focused on strengthening democratically elected governments instead?
- *Most research on microfinance is hopelessly skewed.* Karim argues that much of this "research" is essentially a form of policy advocacy; Grameen, for example, has claimed that 50% of its borrowers graduated from poverty, but no other studies have been able to support this claim.[10]

Karim has not been the only one to challenge the foundations of microfinance.

A year of microcredit probably doesn't help poor people as much as a year of girls' primary education, it's been pointed out—so why are 60% of impact investing portfolios invested in microfinance?[11] In fact, the popularity of microfinance takes scarce resources (both philanthropic and profit-seeking) away from other sectors, like health and education.

Moreover, all of the money and human capital pouring into microfinance may be just displacing more effective anti-poverty measures.

For example, in 2008 Grameen Healthcare formed a joint venture with Veolia, a French water company, to sell low-price, arsenic-free water to people in rural Bangladesh. (Some 60% of the groundwater in Bangladesh is said to be contaminated with arsenic.)

Even the Grinch couldn't disapprove of this venture—or could he?

Here's the problem: Water is a public good; everyone on the planet should have free access to safe and plentiful water. So shouldn't the solution to Bangladesh's water problem be a concerted governmental effort to provide this public good to all its citizens, rather than a private, nongovernmental effort to sell water, no matter how low the price? Is this, possibly, an example of Karim's "shadow government" argument?

In fact, one can play dueling studies until the end of time. A mainstream consensus has emerged that microfinance can, under the right circumstances, help launch small businesses, ratchet up women's socioeconomic status, and improve social indicators such as health, school, fertility, and violence against women. But the key conclusion—that microfinance reduces poverty—is still questionable. The most highly credible study, done in 2010 by MIT's Poverty Action Lab, found some increase in durable goods spending as a result of microfinance, but, critically, no major impact on measures of health, education, and women's decision-making power.[12] And there's no compelling, definitive evidence that microfinance has led to sustained poverty reduction anywhere.

Lessons from the microfinance sector

Whoa! Whiplash! First we hear that microfinance can end poverty forever, then we hear that its downside may outweigh its benefits. What now? Should I pull my money out of Kiva and forget about this impact investing nonsense?

But it's not time to despair. Microfinance has taught itself—and us—some very valuable lessons that are being put into action to reform the sector, as well as the broader field of impact investing.

For one thing, there's been phenomenal growth in the microfinance industry in the 21st century, linking together nongovernmental organizations, multinational corporations, philanthropies, and big institutional investors. These players are betting on the tremendous potential of the industry, and its ability to make profits or at least break even, while helping the poor—a win-win scenario for all. Microfinance has generated growing acceptance of the idea that the interests of large, for-profit companies can be compatible with the interests of the poor, which forms the very basis of the impact revolution. And the industry's setbacks in 2010 brought much-needed government regulation and new governance standards to the field.

Even more auspicious, mounting evidence that microfinance can't cure poverty on its own is pushing the industry in new, and more promising, directions. In truth, micro-lenders—and micro-borrowers—often need *less* money, not more. Poor people have special and compelling financial needs. They're much more likely to send a family member abroad to work, for example, so they need reliable and legal systems for workers to send their money back home to the family. (Just look at the mushrooming construction sites in Dubai and see how many countries those workers spring from.) So money transfer services are a priority.

Also, poor families' income and spending flows are *much* more unpredictable and precarious than for middle- and upper-income families. One poor harvest, a late monsoon season, drought, natural disasters, or the illness of a wage earner can send the fortunes of a poor family into an unending and catastrophic downward spiral. For poor people, income is not just low but highly vulnerable and variable. This suggests that risk management—that is, insurance and savings—may be even more important than access to microcredit. Until the past decade, MFIs focused almost solely on micro-lending, but now, increasingly and much to the good, they are refocusing their work on providing savings and insurance products for their customers (who need these products much more than they need more debt).

Furthermore, poor people need education and financial literacy to go along with their newfound access to financial services. It's been argued that microfinance is essentially an exploitative and unequal relationship between a sophisticated set of bankers with heady quantitative skills and an uneducated, financially illiterate set of customers.

Can we really expect to give illiterate women with no land and a lifetime of wounds a small loan, and expect them all to blossom into successful entrepreneurs?

Accordingly, many MFIs are embracing the notion that microfinance works best when combined with larger programs for economic development and education. Poor people, they have discovered, need not just access to capital but advice, support, and links to markets for their goods.

Better regulation and standards new emphasis on savings and insurance rather than lending, education and development support along with financial access—is this enough to cure the microfinance industry of its past ills and lead to more unequivocally positive outcomes?

In other words, does microfinance still have a shot at curing poverty?

Well…it won't cure poverty all by itself—but it *can* help. Two decades into the 21st century, nearly two billion people around the world do not have access to any financial services at all (other than village moneylenders, which really doesn't count). At least 200,000 micro, small, and medium-sized enterprises in emerging markets have no or insufficient access to credit; there is a staggering financial gap of $2.2 trillion between what these businesses need and the amount of credit available. And not surprisingly, women are much more likely to be locked out of financial services than men.

This matters because financial inclusion is a necessary and *addressable* component of poverty eradication. The World Bank, for example, places great emphasis on financial inclusion; its mandate is to end extreme poverty, and experts believe that this will not happen unless and until women have access to jobs, education, and financial services. There is broad and significant evidence that access to financial services supports poor households, communities, and countries in the quest for social and economic well-being.

Perhaps the greatest gift from the microfinance sector to the broader impact investing sector is a set of lessons learned:

1. It is possible to generate profits and benefit society at the same time; the impact revolution hypothesis appears to be valid!
2. Yes, women are pivotal in the process of economic development—another hypothesis proved.
3. On the other hand (this is why God gave economists two hands, after all), poverty reduction is hard. It's complex, multipronged, and really *hard*. We need not one silver bullet, but a dozen.
4. Regulations and standards have to keep up with brilliant innovations like microfinance. While Grameen never preyed on its borrowers or levied exorbitant fees and interest rates, other MFIs did. It took the crisis in Andhra Pradesh to really underscore the need for industry guidelines, even policing.
5. And finally, don't over-hype! The microfinance journey is truly whiplash at its worst: We've stumbled from the hope that poverty would be gone by 2030, to the crippling fear that microfinance doesn't reduce poverty at all, to the eventual belief that microfinance is important in the poverty alleviation process, but that lots of other things have to go right as well.

The next step, then, is to incorporate these lessons into the impact revolution—though it's too late, at least, for one of them. Hype and hyperbole already mark the young field of impact investing; is whiplash sure to follow?

Mini-case: Banco Compartamos

Though its roots are in tiny loans and grassroots efforts to inspire economic opportunity in underserved areas, the microfinance space is closing in on something that resonates with mainstream finance. But can and does this shift actually co-exist with the truly positive social impact of these loans? Can we, and how should we, build a microfinance industry that is genuinely supportive of borrowers while still remaining attractive enough to commercial-scale investors to keep the pool of capital consistently replenished? How do we manage risk while maintaining an appropriate awareness that most investment risk in this space is directly tied to borrowers' lives and livelihoods?

Admittedly, the debate is still raging, though the controversy of two major voyages into the world of commercialized microfinance has really opened up the discussion, for better or worse.

Let's start with the initial public offering (IPO) of Mexico's Banco Compartamos, a then-17-year-old MFI (in English, Compartamos translates to "let's share," embracing its idealistic founders' commitment to reducing financial inequities).

By 2007, the bank had more than 600,000 customers and had formally become a licensed full-service bank. In April 2007, Banco Compartamos filed for its IPO, raising $468 million—making it the first Mexican MFI to take this route. It was priced at the equivalent of $3.65 per share, with a market valuation of more than $1.5 billion.

At a basic level, the logic of commercializing the microfinance industry probably *does* make sense: By widening the pool of capital so that more money can be lent out, more individuals and communities can obtain greater economic prosperity. Indeed, this is the very core of sustainability for the microfinance industry, with sustainability here meaning the ability to keep on lending without philanthropic support. And by this measure, the Banco Compartamos IPO was deemed a success by many, at least in the beginning.

But going public also meant adding a stronger layer of financial responsibility to shareholders and a for-profit operating structure into the mix. Banco Compartamos is a clear example of how this can go wrong; in this case, according to detractors, early shareholders got rich—at the expense of borrowers. And interest rates remain (unconscionably?) high; Gentera charged an average interest rate of 65% in 2015.[13]

This is at the root of criticism of the IPO, arguing that Banco Compartamos' focus on commercial profitability defeats the microfinance mission of serving poor people.

This view, however, ignores the complexities of Banco Compartamos' reality. For one thing, the early shareholders who "got rich" were not greedy Wall Street money-grabbers, but nonprofit organizations poised to use this money to help seed younger and needier MFIs. And for another, the bank's founders and senior executives remain deeply committed to its mission of expanding financial inclusion to the underserved, particularly poor women who would otherwise have no access to safe lending, deposit, and insurance services. According to one independent report in 2016, "Compartamos has been a leader in the consistently growing microfinance sector with high levels of profitability, consistent asset quality and adherence to best practices."[14]

Gentera, the holding company created in 2013 to include Banco Compartamos, now serves around 3.8 million clients; women comprise 88% of clients in Mexico and Peru, and 100% in Guatemala; and the default rate is less than 3%. The organization promotes a "savings culture," financial education, and insurance services, which are critical to empowering and supporting vulnerable women. It has 22,000 employees, and was number two of the Great Places to Work survey in Mexico in 2019. Gentera has remained consistently profitable, although ROA declined from 2017 to 2019; and profits may turn to losses in 2020 due to the fallout from the COVID-19 pandemic.[15]

On balance, it seems that Gentera's commitment to its mission has held true, while its ability to raise funds on public capital markets helps make that mission sustainable.

Mini-case: SKS

After 3 years Banco Compartamos went public, and nearly 10,000 miles across the world in India, what was then SKS Microfinance[16] filed for its own IPO. SKS was the largest player in the robust but crowded Indian microfinance sector, which was estimated to have nearly 23 million clients in 2009, just prior to SKS's IPO in 2010.

The offering raised $350 million, pricing the shares at the equivalent of $13.10. The SKS IPO was the financial image of success; its $1.5 billion valuation was over 6.7 times the company's book value, more than twice the standard for other banks and financial institutions in emerging markets. It was especially a success for founder Vikram Akula, who had already sold some shares to earn millions; he was now a many-times-over multimillionaire.

Barely a year later, in late 2011, Akula was forced to step down from the bank he had founded in disgrace. Crisis suddenly engulfed the state of Andhra Pradesh, bringing much of India's microfinance industry—especially SKS—down with it. Borrowers had become heavily overindebted, and critics charged that SKS and other MFIs were too aggressive in their collection policies, sparking mass misery and even a spate of suicide among farmers.

Indeed, the SKS crisis was only part of a broader movement. As more MFI's headed toward a focus on commercial success and IPOs, a backlash quickly set in. Local politicians in Andhra Pradesh began a campaign against MFIs, arguing that it hurt rather than benefited the poor. The state government quickly issued an ordinance making the microfinance business almost impossible to conduct; collections plummeted to barely 20% and the SKS share price tumbled 88% from the heady days of its IPO.

But here's the problem: Pre-crisis SKS was successful from the perspective of its shareholders, and by traditional means of measuring success—means that are disconnected from the borrowers and the broader social mission of SKS. The institution was criticized for profiting from poverty, not unlike the criticism of Banco Compartamos.

It's unclear how much SKS contributed to its own woes, but it does appear that amid the competition and rush to profitability in the Indian microfinance industry, there *was* an alarming pattern of abuses and exploitative behavior. Unlike Banco Compartamos, the Indian microfinance crisis underlines the danger of a focus on commercial success in this industry, where duty to shareholders runs the risk of outweighing the MFI's responsibility to support the borrowers' economic prosperity. This is not just a hypothetical risk; it *happened* in India in the years leading up to the 2010 crisis. At an HBS conference in 2012, Akula himself admitted, "Professor Yunus was right… Bringing private capital into social enterprise was much harder than I anticipated."[17]

But the opportunity lies in the aftermath of the crisis, when reasonable regulations began to take shape and the microfinance industry began to learn from its excesses and mistakes. The Indian microfinance space has stabilized and recovered, while SKS itself returned to profitability in mid-2012. It seems likely that the bad press and heavy criticism dealt to Banco Compartamos and SKS Microfinance, among others, following their IPOs may help shift the trajectory of the microfinance space away from a model that supports shareholder interest over borrowers, in favor of a model that meets somewhere in the middle.

Notes

1. Yunus, M. (1999). *Banker to the Poor.* New York: PublicAffairs.
2. Ibid.
3. www.kiva.org.
4. www.grameen.com.
5. https://grameeenfoundation.org/impact/personal-stories/sophie-kandiel.
6. FINCA. (2018, August 15). For Her Grandchildren. Retrieved from: https://finca.org/client/grandmother-clean-cookstove/.
7. Six microfinance crises that the sector does not want to remember. (2011, April 22). *Microfinance Focus.* Retrieved from: www.microfinancefocus.com/6-microfinance-crises-sector-does-not-want-remember.
8. Gokhale, K. (August 13, 2009). "A Global Surge in Tiny Loans Spurs Credit Bubble in a Slum." *The Wall Street Journal.* Retrieved from: www.wsj.com/articles/SB125012112518027581.
9. Karim, L. (2011). *Microfinance and Its Discontents: Women in Debt in Bangladesh.* Minneapolis: University of Minnesota Press.
10. Ibid.
11. The quick answer: Because microfinance is more reliably profitable and less risky than other impact investments—see Chapter 6.
12. Banerjee, A., Kinnan, C., Duflo, E., Glennerster, R., & Breza, E. "Measuring the impact of microfinance in Hyderabad, India." *Poverty Action Lab.* Retrieved from: www.povertyactionlab.org/evaluation/measuring-impact-microfinance-hyderabad-india.
13. Rocha, A.R., Ponce, L.A.B., & Zepeda, M.C. (2019). "Difference in the interest rates of microfinance institutions in some markets economies: an HLM approach." *Estudios Economicos (Mexico, D.F.)*, vol. 34, no. 2, 2019. Retrieved from: www.redalyc.org/jatsRepo/597/59762642004/html/index.html.
14. Final Report: Study on Microcredit Interest Rates in Mexico. (May 2017). *Triple Jump.* Retrieved from: https://triplejump.eu/wp-content/uploads/2018/03/Study-on-Microcredit-Interest-Rates-in-Mexico.pdf.
15. www.gentera.com.mx.
16. In 2016, it was renamed Bahrat Financial Inclusion.
17. Thirani, N. "'Yunus Was Right,' SKS Microfinance Founder Says." (February 27, 2012). *The New York Times.* Retrieved from: https://india.blogs.nytimes.com/2012/02/27/yunus-was-right-sks-microfinance-founder-says/#:~:text=Akula%20also%20told%20conference%20attendees,statement%20from%20conference%20organizers%20said.

6 The revolution goes mainstream
Equity markets...

According to Sir Ronald Cohen, impact investing is the next venture capital (VC). Like the early days of VC, impact investing is a new recipe for financial innovation: These investors want to solve social and environmental problems while *at the same time* generating financial returns for themselves and their families. It's a hybrid of philanthropy and investing in some ways: Philanthropy is pure charitable giving to reduce poverty and misery, while investment is driven by returns. Impact investing blends the two together. Some of our favorite for-profit, impact-based firms that you may be familiar with include Zipcar, Honest Tea, Etsy, Bomba's, and Patagonia (famous for its "don't buy this jacket" ad campaign).

Impact investments, with the overall goal of reducing poverty and countering climate change, are in fact mostly directed toward a few sectors: Microfinance, of course; energy green-tech ventures; and housing. This narrow focus reflects the youth and inefficiency of the field, and the difficulty of putting its concepts into action. There's a paucity of companies and projects that can use investors' funds to demonstrate positive impact alongside profits. Much of the progress in this field, then, is likely to be made by traditional, well-established companies that are learning to embrace the concept of impactful decision-making as part of their overall corporate strategy.

Impact equity: From cookstoves to Amazon

When we think of impact equity investing, we may think of social enterprises that provide solar panels in Kenya, or clean cookstoves in India.

But in fact, ESG-based equity investments can be great or small, in Manhattan or Mumbai. Impact equity runs the gamut from investments by large companies like Amazon or Royal Dutch Shell to young, small companies in Rwanda or Peru. In fact, some of the most important works in this area is being done by big, mainstream firms—which may prove to be the most impactful in the end, since that's where the deep pockets are.

This suggests that it is not always possible, or necessary, to differentiate between companies that are truly dedicated to impact, and impact work done by large for-profit companies. Amazon, for example, has launched a $2 billion VC fund focused on tech investments to address the impact of climate change; the aim is to help Amazon and other companies reach "net zero" carbon emissions by 2040.

So does that make Amazon an impact investing firm?

Not so fast…let's take a deeper dive into these murky waters.

The promise of impact investing

If Muhammad Yunus was the father of microfinance, Sir Ronald Cohen is the fairy godfather of impact investing. He was also a parent of VC, having co-founded and led what many consider the first VC firm in Europe, Apax Partners. By the time Cohen retired from the firm in 2005, Apax had invested more than 12 billion euros in more than 500 deals.[1]

So when Ronald Cohen opines that impact investing is the next VC, we should listen very, very carefully. That 2005 "retirement" proved to be only a career change; he's devoted his second career to birthing and growing the field of impact investment—with impressive results.

And if this young field is looking for a role model, it could hardly do any better than VC. VC firms provide very early, relatively modest amounts of money to precocious startups that are barely in toddlerhood, yet are believed to have oodles of long-term potential. In venture capitalists' favorite analogy, they swing hard, and occasionally hit a home run; those home runs include some of today's giants, including Uber, Amazon, Facebook, Alibaba, Google, Genentech, Workday, and Apple. And the VC market itself has ballooned, with over $254 billion in new deals in 2018 alone.

So if impact investing follows anything like the trajectory of VC, it has a remarkable path ahead of it—and we should all be fighting for places on the bandwagon.

But Cohen goes even bigger than that. The impact revolution that's taking place today, he believes, is similar to the tech revolution that has changed all our lives; it's going to be that big. (Remember trying to meet a friend at a concert without cellphones. Or arguing with a used car salesman without access to a computer.) Today's impact investing market reminds Cohen of the early days of the tech revolution, as well as the VC market. Both began with a handful of small entrepreneurs, who proved that small companies could create great value—and both helped these entrepreneurs to change our lives forever.[2]

What is impact investing?

But let's not get ahead of ourselves; first let's agree on what exactly impact investing *means*. Definitions can be deadly dull, like the first lines of a book that begins "John Doe was born..." (to wit: the first sentence of *Great Expectations*). We don't need to reach for the Cliff Notes yet, though, since defining impact investment is actually sort of a parlor game.

In fact, let's start with what it's *not*. Impact investing is *not* socially responsible investment (SRI), a 20th century term that feels pretty old-fashioned in the days of the Impact Revolution. SRI managers put together investment portfolios that screen *out* certain types of companies—usually those engaged in pornography, tobacco, alcohol, natural resource extraction, or guns. Screening-out took on something of a nasty whiff, as it became clear that this would lead investors to exclude some of the world's most profitable (e.g., oil) companies from their investment portfolios—and thus would decrease returns.

Impact investing is also most decidedly *not* philanthropy, because capital is supplied by investors rather than donors. When investors write a check, they expect to get much more than a thank-you letter and warm fuzzy feeling; they expect to get their money back, with some interest or dividend payments as the cherry on top. And it's different from pure investment like VC, since impact investors want to bring about positive social change; venture capitalists just want to get rich.

So impact investing is a new mixture: These investors want to solve social and environmental problems while *at the same time* generating financial returns for themselves and their families. It's a hybrid of philanthropy and investing in some ways: Philanthropy is pure charitable giving to reduce poverty and misery, while investment is driven by returns. Impact investing blends the two together.

So here goes with that definition: Impact investments are direct investments into companies and funds, made with the *intent* of generating positive social and environmental impact, *and* for financial returns.

This definition may sound as dull as the first page of *Great Expectations* (sorry; not a Dickens fan), but it actually represents a massive disruption of the business world, which is built on the premise that for-profit investments should seek only to generate financial return, while social problems should be addressed by philanthropist do-gooders and the government. In a sense, this is a fundamentally optimistic disruption, based on the belief that businesses can play a huge and positive role in promoting the common good.

Light-bulb moments

What if a friend came to you with this business idea: Let's provide life insurance for people who are living with AIDS or are HIV-positive! Wouldn't most of us think our friend had a screw loose? Is this the worst business idea *ever*—insuring people with a life-threatening disease?

But that's exactly what Leapfrog Investments, a visionary "profit with purpose" private equity firm, did in its first deal in 2009. Leapfrog bought a $6.7 million stake in AllLife, a South African company that provides life insurance to the nearly 20% of South African people who are living with HIV or AIDS. But there is a condition, which transforms this puzzling deal into pure genius: AllLife's insured customers get health care support and regular blood tests to prove that they are taking life-saving drugs to tame the disease.

And there's the lightbulb moment! AllLife provides insurance to those who are shunned by ordinary insurance companies; its customers live longer and healthier lives because they're incentivized to stick with what is sometimes a grueling drug regimen; and AllLife profits because its customers live longer. Profit with purpose, financial and social value—it's the perfect model for an impact investment. And it worked; AllLife now covers 100,000 people and has expanded its insurance services to people living with diabetes.

Then there's the story of Dial 1298 for Ambulance, an emergency medical service formed by five friends in Mumbai after Shaffi Mather's mother experienced a life-threatening emergency in the middle of the night, and there was no 911 service for her terrified son to call. As Ben Schiller wrote in 2014:

> In 2004, Sweta Mangal, Naresh Jain, Manish Sacheti, Shaffi Mather, and Ravi Krishna started with two ambulances and a hunch that there was a need for better ways to get people to hospital. They developed a sliding-scale business model. People going to public hospitals would pay little or nothing. Richer people going to private hospitals would pay full fare. Other costs would be met through advertising on the vehicles, and outside private support.
>
> Initially, the startup received grant money and some technical assistance from ambulance operators in New York and London. But the service was soon profitable in its own right, such was the need.

Indians don't have 911-like services, and more often than not the poor take a cab or private car if they need to get to the emergency room. In 2007, Dial 1298 for Ambulance got $1.5 million in philanthropic financing from the Acumen Fund to continue its expansion, then commercial investment from Envision Healthcare, one of the world's largest ambulance providers. Today, Dial 1298 has served 2.4 million people. It operates 800 ambulances in huge states like Kerala, Punjab and Maharashtra. And last year it had revenues of $20 million.[3]

Like Dial 1298, the impact investing market has experienced impressive growth since the term was first coined in 2007. According to the Global Impact Investing Network (GIIN), itself a young but increasingly authoritative organization, market size in 2020 was around $715 billion. J.P. Morgan's experts, no fuzzy tree-huggers either but even more bullish, believe that market size could hit $1 trillion in the next few years.

Surveys consistently found that fund managers and investors too are optimistic about the potential of the market, although many warn that it is still in its infancy. They expect impact investments to make up 5%–10% of the portfolios of high-net-worth individuals (translation: rich people) and institutional investors within a short period of time. GIIN's annual conference in late 2018 drew more than 1300 attendees, and the guest list proved beyond any doubt that the field had spread from a "small group of quirky people" according to one speaker, to every major financial organization in the world today.

As demonstrated in Chapter 4, market growth is largely bottom-up: Customers and asset owners are demanding impact investment products, and impelling financial institutions to provide them. As Sir Ronald Cohen correctly notes, people are voting with their feet away from companies with bad values; investors are challenging their pension funds and asset managers to construct portfolios that do good and do well at the same time.

And investors are drawn to the field not just because they want their money to support their social values, but because, on the financial side, impact investments are not well correlated with market-based investments and thus can help to lower risk and raise the returns on a portfolio.

English, please? If you strip away the jargon, this means that when the Dow plunges by 800 points in an hour and investors break out into a cold sweat, the value of the impact-based companies that they invested in will *not* swoon with the Dow—a piece of good news on a bad-news day. One investor told me that his "aha moment" came when he realized that after the 2008 financial market crash, the microfinance debt that he had invested in was the top-performing asset in his portfolio! That financial crash convinced a lot of investors that traditional financial markets did a very poor job of understanding and managing risk; perhaps companies that think about *all* stakeholders rather than the short-term bottom line would do better.

These results are underscored by the market's wild ride in 2020. According to *The New York Times*, "impact investments…have significantly outperformed traditional bets during the COVID-19 pandemic. And their returns are enticing hesitant investors to rework their portfolios." For the first seven months of the year, 64% of actively managed ESG investment funds beat their benchmarks versus 49% of traditional funds. (And the S&P Global Clean Energy Index, which covers 30 big utilities and green-tech stocks, is up 37% over the past 2 years, compared with 18% for the S&P 500.) Every time the markets run into headwinds, according to one leading investor, "it's a boost for impact investing."[4]

Fun fact: Forty trillion dollars in wealth are expected to move to millennials and women over the next generation. This is a very good thing for the impact investing market, because:

- *Millennials* will inherit around $12 trillion in assets over the next 10 years, and studies consistently report that millennials have a very strong desire to match their investments with their social values, much more so than their parents and grandparents. According to a survey by Spectrem Group, 53% of millennials make investment decisions based on social factors.[5]
- *Women* are expected to inherit 70% of transferrable wealth over the next two generations—and women invest differently from men. According to one expert:

  Women investors in general, and Generation X and Millennial women in particular, tend to take a more holistic approach to investing, concerned about investments that support their values as much as they are about financial returns. They're looking for investment options that make an impact on what they believe in. Impact investments provide viable options for women striving to make a positive social or environmental impact with their investment dollars.[6]

So with massive chunks of investable wealth passing to women and millennials, and with many of these investors committed to investing for good as well as for profit, the future of impact investing is rosy indeed.

Some of our favorite impact-based firms

Here's a sampling of some favorite, for-profit, impact-based firms that you may be familiar with:

- Zipcar, a sustainable car sharing network;
- Honest Tea, which produces iced tea with an ethical supply chain;
- Etsy, an online marketplace where people around the world connect to buy and sell unique, artisan-produced goods;
- d. light, which designs, manufactures, and distributes solar light and power products throughout the developing world;
- Tom's Shoes, whose slogan reads "We've always been in business to improve lives." Since 2006, the company has given nearly 100 million pairs of shoes to people in need; now, for every $3 they make, they give $1 away.
- Bomba's, which notes that socks are the #1 most requested clothing item in homeless shelters. For every pair of socks purchased, it donates one pair of socks (and now, other clothing items). As of late 2020, 43.9 million items had been donated!
- Patagonia: Famous for its "don't buy this jacket" ad campaign, Patagonia is "in business to save our home planet" through environmental activism, donations, and sustainable business practices.

On the other hand…

Are these feel-good social enterprises the faces of the future? Or are they the outliers?

What is the reality of this young and precocious field? Even using the rosy J.P. Morgan forecast of a $1 trillion impact investing market size of $1 trillion, PwC puts the size of the total investment market worldwide (assets under management [AUM], to be technical about it) at $111 trillion. You don't need to reach for a calculator to see that impact investing's share of all investments, then, is less than 1%. Ouch.

So let's take a closer look at what this market consists of, and what are the obstacles to its growth.

Impact investments, with the overall goal of reducing poverty and countering climate change, are in fact mostly directed toward a few sectors: microfinance, of course; energy green-tech ventures; and housing. Other, smaller, sectors include clean water, agriculture, health (especially maternal health), and education. Non-microfinance investments generally go to companies that are early, small, but relatively complex social enterprises with revenues in the low millions range. These firms need *patient* capital—investors who are willing to wait for their money, and are willing to take risks along the way.

This is because impact investing, aside from the well-established sector of microfinance, is *hard*. There are no easy financial returns; rather, there is typically a long, hard road to any returns at all. Home runs are scarce.

For one thing, social enterprises (i.e., firms that pursue social as well as financial objectives) typically take longer to grow than mainstream businesses. They may operate in sectors with untested business models (can you really make money selling to poor people?), and they may require substantial advice and support in addition to capital. And local partners can be sketchy: Another investor told me, with a rueful grin, that he had invested in a social enterprise in West Africa that provided solar energy for poor rural households; his partner embezzled the money and took off for the Caribbean. "Corruption in Africa exhausted me," he concluded.

When it works, it's beautiful—remember AllLife in South Africa. But when it doesn't work, it's a world of pain.

Here's the rub: Despite all of the question marks surrounding the impact of microfinance (see preceding chapter), more than 60% of impact investing money still goes to microfinance. Why? Common sense alone tells us that education, especially educating girls, is worth more to society than lending more money to poor women. But microfinance is highly developed—it's been around since the early 1980s—increasingly well-regulated and well-governed, and produces pretty reliable profits when done right.

On the other hand, finding companies in emerging markets that promise to do well and do good—and have even the most rudimentary evidence that they're capable of achieving this feat—is not too far removed from finding a clean public toilet in Manhattan (don't get me started)—difficult, if not impossible. So impact investors keep funding microfinance, even though they know perfectly well that it's not the best use of their money.

Quite simply, the constraint in this sector is not supply of funds—remember all those millennials and women—it's on the *demand* side, where there's a paucity of companies and projects that can use investors' funds to demonstrate positive impact alongside profits. AllLife and Dial 1298, it turns out, are rare birds indeed.

So what exactly is holding this market back from explosive growth?

- *It has no track record.* Investors, financial analysts, and bankers like to have some kind of historical track record, so they can understand or at least guesstimate what the future path of their investments might be. If Coca-Cola wanted to introduce Peppermint Coke (yuck), it could base its sales estimates on how well other Coke products did, for example. If Cheerios wanted to invest in Molasses Cheerios (double yuck), it could check out the record of Honey Nut Cheerios. And so on. But the impact investment market is both very small and very young, and most investments are private; so there simply isn't a public, reliable, and definitive track record on which an investor could base estimates of future performance.

- *Mission drift is a constant worry.* As we noticed in the preceding chapter, in its drive to achieve commercial viability and rake in the funds via IPOs, microfinance has become highly susceptible to mission drift. Some MFIs have directed their lending toward middle-income rather than poor people to raise profits; others have used coercive lending and collection practices in pursuit of the same. It could even be argued that the prominence of microfinance in impact investors' portfolios is in itself a form of mission drift; the investors know it's not the best use of their money, but the return is relatively reliable.
- *Can we measure social impact?* Again, microfinance taught us a valuable lesson: Everyone in the field assumed that lending small amounts of money to poor women would result in social progress—and industry-funded "research" supported this assumption—but in fact nobody's really sure how much social impact all this micro-lending has wrought. We can measure profits quite easily, of course, and cash flows, and other financial indicators. But how do you measure the value of sending more girls to primary school, or preventing thousands of cases of malaria, or providing safe housing to the homeless? How do we know which investment is likely to be more impactful, if we can't reliably measure impact? How does an investor know that her money is really helping society?
- *There aren't any real market mechanisms.* Think about mainstream financial markets: They boast rating agencies to help investors understand how risky a potential investment is. They have clearinghouses to help handle the money, and regulators and standard setters to keep the market safe and orderly (at least in theory). They have a standard, universally accepted set of accounting standards for measuring financial results. The impact investing market has the GIIN, a strong and growing organization—but it's just a clearinghouse for ideas and nothing more.
- *You can't push on a string.* As already noted, the real constraint on market growth is a lack of investment opportunities in targeted countries and sectors. There is a desperate need for talented entrepreneurs and social enterprises with the ability to absorb what would be quite a large chunk of capital for these small operators. An analyst with one

major impact-investing fund told me that over a ten-year period the firm looked at more than 5,000 social ventures—and deemed just 57 of them investment-ready. Many young social enterprises in emerging market countries lack even the most rudimentary requirements for outside capital: Financial statements, experienced management, and a system for assessing social impact. And that's without even taking into account the ordinary risks of working in emerging countries, from corruption to limited respect for the rule of law, to political upheaval.

The result of all these obstacles is that the market is extremely inefficient—which, as any business neophyte knows, means higher risks. For the impact investor, this also means high startup costs because of expensive due diligence. (Translation: It takes just as much time and energy to analyze a $100,000 investment as a $10 million investment—for much less payback.) The investment is likely to be highly illiquid for a very long period of time; as one wag has it, emerging markets are markets you cannot emerge from in an emergency. And at the core of it all is the nagging fear that the investment will not, in fact, support social progress since we can't accurately measure impact.

And there's one more question to consider, potentially the most problematic since it challenges the core assumption of impact investing. Those who invest for blended social and financial impact are using business methods to tackle social and environmental problems. This seems like a smart move, since the power of business to innovate and to drive progress is absolutely undeniable—just think Google, or Apple, or General Electric (in its better days).

But impact investing is different from inventing computers or the light bulb or the Internet. By definition, impact investors are directing their money toward the world's most vulnerable and marginalized people—people who often can't read and write, let alone understand financial risks and variables.

So is profiting from this investment opportunity exploitative?

And to the extent that impact investors provide what should be public goods, such as clean water, health care, and education, are they undercutting the functions of government, or becoming shadow, unelected, undemocratic governments, as Lamia Karim has argued?

Here are the core questions:

1 Who oversees and regulates these investors?
2 Shouldn't government be providing these services?
3 Is it possible that impact investors are profiting from the misery of vulnerable people?

At some point, all impact investors wrestle with these questions—and if they haven't, then they should.

The new venture capital?

Deep and searching questions like those above do not mean that we should consign impact investing to the rubbish heap; rather, they mean that we're on a steep learning curve, with these and lots more questions to resolve:

- *How much profit is enough?* This is one of the most contentious issues to address, since it goes right to the heart of the exploitation question. Most of us probably have a visceral reaction that interest rates of 50%–100% charged by MFIs are simply too high; it reeks of exploitation. But what's the right number? Should impact investors expect to earn a market return on their money, that is, the same profit as they would earn by investing in a portfolio of NYSE-listed companies? Over time, you should expect to earn a return on your stock market investments of around 7%, so is that what you should earn on a portfolio of impact investments? Or should your return on the impact portfolio be even higher, since it carries more risk than standard investments?

    The fact is that investors approach these questions with a range of philosophies. Some studies suggest that more than half of all impact investors would sacrifice some level of financial return in order to produce meaningful social impact. (This may suffer from what I call the PBS effect, though; lots of people tell pollsters that they watch sheep-shearing documentaries on PBS, when in fact they spend all their time glued to *Naked and Afraid*.) Others believe that impact investments should deliver returns in line with the market; otherwise investors will be reluctant to commit large sums of money. And in the middle are those who believe that a certain threshold of return is necessary to entice a critical mass of funds into the market, but it's fine for returns to hover somewhat below the traditional market.

    A lot of this debate rests on the critical question of whether a trade-off between financial and social returns is inevitable. We can certainly think of some examples where it is: It's more costly to build a clean energy plant than to produce energy from an old coal plant. And a hybrid car can be 20% more expensive than the same car powered by a gasoline engine. When we factor in the long-term impact of those carbon emissions, of course, the arithmetic changes—so to some extent, the answer to the trade-off question depends on the time horizon.

But it's also true that there simply isn't any answer to the question—the truth is that we just don't know. There's no historical track record for impact investing; also, the field is still in a steep learning curve phase so future investments will almost certainly perform much better than in the past. Our only clue comes from the field of socially responsible investing (SRI), since SRI funds have been around for quite a while, and their performance has been the topic of quite a few dissertations and studies.

Unlike microfinance, here we don't have to worry about dueling studies. A large body of research convincingly tells us that SRI investors do not—repeat, *do not*—have to sacrifice financial returns in order to align their investments with their social values. Some studies even suggest that socially minded investment portfolios actually outperform traditional portfolios, supporting the notion that corporate managers who care about society are better corporate managers all around.

These findings don't translate perfectly to impact investing, which can involve putting money into small, young companies in very imperfect countries—but they are encouraging. So let's tackle some outstanding questions to provide a roadmap for the future of this nascent industry:

- *What kind of businesses should be targeted?* This relates to the additionality principle; impact investors should not be redundant. These funds should not go to sectors where there's already a lot of money flowing from government, development banks, philanthropists, and private investors. So providing telecommunications in Africa—while undoubtedly good for society—doesn't need impact investment, because private telecoms companies are already all over it. Neither do well-publicized diseases like HIV and malaria; worthy causes they certainly are, but they get plenty of attention already from organizations like the Bill and Melinda Gates Foundation.

  Thus, impact investors should, ideally, focus on undercapitalized areas like the provision of basic services to the poor and poorest. It's only fair to point out, though, that some sectors are capital-starved for a very good reason—because it's really hard to make a profit in that field. It's a puzzlement, as the King told Anna in *The King and I*.
- *What geographies should be targeted?* Again, we don't want to trip over investors and philanthropists who are already in high gear in a region. Thousands of aid organizations flooded Haiti following the devastating 2010 earthquake, with the best of intentions but deeply unimpressive results. Their failure to coordinate effectively with each other

and with the government led to duplication of many efforts, and the squandering of millions of dollars. Impact investors, ideally, should be committed to the poorest regions of the world, not those that are easiest to operate in and where everyone else is already competing for the best investment opportunities. Reflecting this concern, one prominent aid group in the United Kingdom rewrote its policies a few years ago so that 75% of funds would go to low-income countries (and 50% to Africa)—thus limiting investments to Eastern Europe and middle income, relatively low-risk countries like Brazil and India.

- *What should impact investors bring to the table?* As the question implies, they need to bring more than money. Remember that one of the lessons from microfinance is that the recipients of money need support and education rather than just a wad of cash. Impact investors have to be prepared to provide assistance for the entrepreneurs they're backing, including help in creating reporting systems for both financial and social impact.

Impact for Africa's "Silent Killer"

Who knew that inhaling smoke from indoor cookstoves is more lethal than malaria? It's true; according to *The New York Times*, "ailments related to smoke from cooking, including cataracts, heart disease and respiratory ailments…in many countries kill more people than malaria, HIV and tuberculosis combined."

Budding social entrepreneur Eric Reynolds visited villagers in Rwanda and saw this for himself. "There is nothing in the house that causes as much suffering as cooking," he told the *Times*. "It's dirty. It's smoky. Momma is there with the baby on her back, and both are coughing… I could see that this was a time bomb."

So Reynolds launched Imyenyeri, a social enterprise that would distribute new, clean-burning stoves for free, while selling wood pellets using a clever barter system—rural villagers would gather sticks; Imyenyeri would trade pellets for the sticks, and then use the sticks to make the pellets, which it sells back to the villagers.

Today, Imyenyeri has 5,000 customers in Rwanda, including a camp for refugees from the neighboring Democratic Republic of Congo. It still needs large capital infusions to scale up its efforts to all of Rwanda and beyond—and Reynolds is counting on impact investors to make this happen. "Profit feeds impact at scale," he says.[7]

A great concept, but will it work?

Enter the dinosaurs

By the impact investing definition that I've been using, of course, Amazon is *not* an impact investment since its corporate mission is profit-driven, not impact-driven. Some activists would laugh at the very notion, pointing to the company's occasionally spotty record on labor and consumer protections.

And yet, Amazon—like many other mainstream companies—is increasingly committed to including impact in its decision-making process. And where the impact revolution meets the deep pockets, the result is progress *at scale*, rather than one cookstove at a time.

This upends our notion of impact investing, of course. If it's possible to consider huge behemoths like Amazon, and even huge dinosaurs like Wall Street banks, as organizations with the potential to drive positive impact, then what's next? Does this expand the definition of impact investing until it implodes, like a birthday balloon inflated to bursting?

In fact, Sir Ronald Cohen himself embraces the notion of corporate impact. In a recent interview with *Barron's*, he commented:

> Corporations are aware now because of the rebellion, the social inequality, the protests about environmental damage. They have begun to realize that it will affect their sales and their profits. Many companies that didn't embrace technology were left behind by nimbler competitors who designed more disruptive, more effective business models. The same will happen to companies that don't manage their impact properly, that don't address the conflicts their business models pose between profits and impact. The market capitalization of [oil producers] has fallen sharply. Companies are beginning to realize that ignoring the arrival of impact will hold the same risks as ignoring the arrival of technology.

Cohen added, "The advantage now is to companies that achieve a proper balance between risk, return, and impact." He cites Tesla as a "new disruptive company…which aims to optimize risk, return, and impact by reducing emissions from cars."[8] And it seems that the market doesn't disagree; Tesla's valuation in late 2020 at $459 billion was greater than nearly the entire established auto industry (Ford, GM, and Fiat Chrysler together were valued at just $128 billion).

Note, by the way, that Cohen is *not* talking about "corporate social responsibility" (CSR), which generally refers to philanthropic and charitable undertakings by a for-profit company. It's great when BankAmerica cuts a check to the Boston Ballet, but this does not incorporate doing good into the bank's DNA, that is, its corporate strategy.

Supporting charities and local communities through charitable giving may help burnish a company's reputation and get tax deductions—and even do good for the community.

But that is *not* impactful investment—in fact, it's not investment at all. Impactful investment would be when BankAmerica launches lending programs as part of its corporate portfolio for underserved or minority communities, or chooses to lend to an electric car company rather than a coal company.

Examples abound of traditional, well-established companies that are learning to embrace the concept of impactful decision-making as part of their overall corporate strategy:

- In July 2020, France's Danone published its earnings per share weighted by environmental impact.
- At Procter & Gamble's annual meeting in October 2020, two-thirds of shareholders voted against management because of deforestation concerns.
- Giant investment manager BlackRock ($7.8 trillion of AUM) plans to push investee companies for greater ethnic and gender diversity in their boards and workforces, and will vote against directors who fail to take action on this.
- State Street Global Advisors ($3 trillion of AUM) said in August 2020 that it too will ask companies about their metrics and goals for boosting racial diversity.
- Nasdaq plans to require most companies listed on its US exchange to include at least one director who identifies as female and one who identifies as an underrepresented minority of LGBTQ.
- Prudential has committed more than $1 billion over the past decade into a variety of projects as part of its commitment to revitalizing the city of Newark, New Jersey.
- Goldman Sachs has said that it will no longer take a company public in the United States and Europe if it lacks a director who is either female or diverse.

No one in their right mind could accuse Goldman or State Street of being an impact-based enterprise. And yet…companies like this may prove to be the most impactful over the long run. Prodded by their customers, investors, and consciences, huge corporate entities have the scale and power to generate real progress—both in their backyards and around the world. And these examples suggest that the differentiation between companies that are truly dedicated to impact, and impact work by large for-profit companies, may be irrelevant and distracting. Impact is impact, no matter who achieves it.

This suggests that it is possible to create an impact-based equity portfolio that includes smallish social enterprises as well as some of the world's largest companies—dramatically expanding the scope and potential of the space.

In the end, all investments have impact—both positive and negative. So it makes a lot of sense to focus investment policy on seeking out those companies and projects that simultaneously pursue positive social/environmental impact alongside financial returns. What doesn't make sense is to ignore impact and do things in the old-fashioned way, that is, *not* to harness the power of money and investors to make the world a better place for all.

Notes

1 Cox, L. (July 30, 2018). "From refugee to venture capitalist to social impact pioneer." *Forbes*. Retrieved from: www.forbes.com/sites/sorensonimpact/2018/07/30/from-refugee-to-venture-capitalist-to-social-impact-pioneer/?sh=902bf9d68863.
2 Cohen, R. & William A. Sahlman. (January 17, 2013). "Social impact investing will be the new venture capital." *Harvard Business Review*. Retrieved from: https://hbr.org/2013/01/social-impact-investing-will-b.
3 Schiller, B. (August 20, 2014). "What's the future for impact investing?" *Fast Company*. Retrieved from: www.fastcompany.com/3032493/whats-the-future-for-impact-investing.
4 Sullivan, P. (August 29, 2020). "Investing in social good is finally becoming profitable." *The New York Times*. Retrieved from: www.nytimes.com/2020/08/28/your-money/impact-investing-coronavirus.html.
5 www.investopedia.com/articles/financial-advisors/111315/socially-responsible-investing-how-millennials-are-driving-it.asp.
6 www.investopedia.com/advisor-network/articles/women-can-change-future-impact-investing/.
7 Goodman, P.S. (December 9, 2018). "A low-cost fix for Africa's silent killer." *The New York Times*.
8 Norton, L.P. (November 27, 2020). "Companies that fail to measure impact will be left behind, this investor warns." *Barrons*. Retrieved from: www.barrons.com/articles/tesla-deftly-balances-risk-return-and-impact-says-this-venture-capitalist-51606491301.

7 . ...And impact bonds

The International Capital Market Association has defined three categories of environmental, social, and governance (ESG) bonds: Green Bonds (environmental projects), Social Bonds (social projects), and Sustainability Bonds (green and social projects). The Green Bond market was the first to take off due to investor demand and because environmental outcomes are more easily quantifiable than social outcomes. During 2020, however, the Social Bond market took a giant leap forward as hundreds of billions of dollars in bonds were issued to combat the pernicious impact of the COVID-19 pandemic. Other types of ESG-linked bonds, such as catastrophe or disaster bonds, pay-for-success instruments, and diaspora bonds, are a much smaller segment of the market.

A robust Social Bond market will help to address huge economic and social development needs in the wake of the pandemic; mapping these bonds to the UN Sustainable Development Goals (SDGs) has been especially popular. Philanthropic foundations, multilateral institutions, and financial institutions can help to overcome obstacles, mitigate risks, and build on the momentum of 2020 in the Social Bond market.

Bonds versus equity: And the winner is...

As the previous chapter demonstrated, much conversation about impact investing focuses on equity, that is, investing in companies that seek ESG improvements alongside financial returns. An impact investing firm may put its money into a social enterprise that provides clean water in sub-Saharan Africa, for example, or housing for the homeless in Manchester, England.

But by numbers, equity investments—buying an ownership share in a company—are actually the runt of the financial markets. In 2020, the total size of global equity markets was $32.5 trillion versus $128 trillion in global bond markets. This suggests that equity investment is likely to be dwarfed by the amount of money going into fixed-income instruments,[1] that is, bonds, in the impact investment landscape as well.

A quick rehash of Finance 101: Essentially, firms can raise funds in two ways: debt or equity. Debt means borrowing money from investors in international capital markets, usually in the form of long-term instruments called bonds. The bonds usually pay interest every year, and are eventually paid back in full by the borrowing company. Firms raise equity, by contrast, by selling *ownership shares* to external investors, who become part-owners of the firm rather than lenders to the firm. These investors never get their money back unless they sell the shares to other investors; they may receive dividends periodically, or they may just benefit from the rising value of the share price (think Amazon or Tesla).

In fact, debt markets in general are now the principal source of external financing for US companies. Partly because it costs much less to issue bonds than to issue equity (equity issues result in very, very fat bonuses for Wall Street investment bankers), bond issues have far outstripped equity issues in recent years.

Also, other classes of borrowers—governments and supranational institutions like the World Bank—can *only* raise money by issuing bonds. They can't sell equity (imagine a world in which the US government sells off part of Seattle, or New Jersey, in order to pay its bills), so these borrowers swell the size of the bond market and are increasingly turning to ESG-based bonds.

Indeed, bonds have the potential to be powerful pillars of the impact revolution—especially because fixed-income investments tend to attract investors with long time horizons, which is especially well-suited to the impact space. Climate change, for instance, is a long-term problem; but many investors tend to plan over a shorter time horizon. ESG bonds fill this need to connect investors with long-term sustainability projects.

ESG bonds: Historical and market context

And this movement is well underway: Bond markets have increasingly embraced investor demand for ESG-linked instruments. Global ESG bond issuance jumped 52% to $321 billion in 2019, and slightly surpassed $500 billion in 2020 as bonds to address the pernicious effects of the COVID-19 pandemic proliferated; outstanding ESG bonds passed the $1 trillion threshold in the middle of 2020.

These promising developments in the arena of sustainable finance have been accompanied by widespread confusion about terminology and guidelines among participants, ranging from market experts to retail investors. For example, some use the terms "Green Bonds," "sustainable," "social impact," and "social" bonds interchangeably despite significant differences between them. It is challenging to talk about precise definitions of the various ESG bond instruments because there is no single market consensus; and where there is consensus, it tends to vary by region.

Definition debates rage on (and would put most of us to sleep). Perhaps viewing with alarm the potentially hazardous proliferation of ill-defined and ill-governed ESG bond instruments, in 2014 the International Capital Market Association (ICMA) issued the first version of the Green Bond Principles, followed by the Social Bond Principles and Sustainability Bond Principles in 2017 (with the Social Bond Principles most recently updated in June 2020). The ICMA approach is market-based rather than one of exhaustive definitions and taxonomies, reflecting the lack of consensus noted above. The publication of these principles is an encouraging development, to be sure, but the principles are still voluntary and pretty vague.

ICMA has defined three categories of ESG bonds, and we will adhere to the ICMA guidelines, as follows:

- *Green Bonds* raise capital for projects with environmental benefits. This category includes blue bonds, which are focused on sustainable use of ocean resources to keep waters healthy, productive, and cool (in every sense of the word).
- *Social Bonds* raise funds for projects with positive social outcomes, such as improving food security and access to education, health care, and financial services.
- *Sustainability Bonds* direct their proceeds to a combination of both green and social projects.[2]

Blue Bonds for Blue Waters

Ocean-bound and ocean-bred, fishermen have been trolling the beautiful waters of the Seychelles for longer than anyone can remember, way before the tourists started to arrive. But climate change, depleted fish stocks, and polluted oceans pose an existential threat to the Seychelles, whose entire way of life rests on the twin pillars of fishing and tourists. Now, the Seychelles is also famous for introducing the world's "first sovereign blue bond" to maintain the beauty and purity of its oceans.

Says Seychelles Vice President Vincent Meriton:

> Through the blue bond and other project support, we aim to show how fisheries, as an ocean economy that is already well developed, can shift from business-as-usual to more responsible fishing and management practices that align with the core principles of a Blue Economy.[3]

The $15 million, 10-year bond benefited from World Bank support, including a $5 million guarantee that helped entice investors to the project. Since then, the Nordic Investment Bank issued a Nordic-Baltic Blue Bond, raising money for wastewater treatment and prevention of water pollution, and the World Bank sold $10 million of blue bonds to address plastic waste pollution in oceans.

Oceans are vital to the economic and social well-being of the world; blue bonds offer the opportunity to tap into private capital markets to protect this extraordinary resource.

Green Bonds

The first ever Green Bond was issued by the European Investment Bank in 2007 as a "Climate Awareness Bond" for stimulating investment by institutional investors. The World Bank soon followed with the world's first labeled Green Bond in 2008, setting the stage for today's expanding and diversifying market in ESG bonds. Soon other issuers, mainly multilateral lending organizations such as the Asian Development Bank and World Bank, joined this market with inaugural Green Bonds of their own. The first US issuer to use this term was the Commonwealth of Massachusetts, which sold $100 million of Green Bonds in 2013 and another $1 billion in 2017 to fund water infrastructure throughout the state.

Market issuance of Green Bonds has expanded rapidly from 2013, as the market tripled by outstanding face value each year. In 2017, the market went indisputably mainstream when the giant asset manager BlackRock launched its Green Bond Index Fund in response to investor demand for these investments in the fixed-income space. In October 2017, the market expanded to poorer corners of the world when the World Bank helped Fiji issue the first sovereign Green Bond from a developing country, raising about $50 million. And in early 2019, Indonesia issued the world's first sovereign green *sukuk* bond, that is, a financial instrument designed in accordance with Islamic law, to the tune of $1.25 billion.

Dedicated Green Bond funds are now widely available to investors in regions around the world, and annual issuance of Green Bonds grew to more than 3% of all global debt issuance in 2019, making these instruments an increasing component of mainstream portfolios as well.

In 2019, total Green Bond issuance surged to a record $255 billion, dominating the ESG bond market (as usual). Issuers and investors alike love Green Bonds, especially since research indicates that companies and governments that borrow via these instruments can save some money. Analysts are trying to precisely measure "the greenium," that is, how much extra investors will pay for Green Bonds compared to conventional bonds. While the exact number is still elusive, it's clear that companies and governments selling Green Bonds can "meaningfully lower borrowing costs."[4]

A few fun facts from 2019:

- The Green Bond field in 2019 was dominated by clean energy projects, low-carbon buildings and transport, water and land use, and waste.
- The United States was the largest Green Bond issuer ($51.3 billion) in 2019, followed by China ($31.3 billion) and France ($30.1 billion).
- The biggest single deal was a $6.7 billion Climate Bond issued by the Netherlands.
- Fannie Mae was the world's largest issuer of Green Bonds, selling $28 billion to back buyers of green-certified apartment buildings.

Green Bonds in the corporate mainstream

In early 2016, Apple once again flexed its innovative muscles to become the tech industry's first issuer of Green Bonds. In a deal managed by investment banking giants Goldman Sachs, Bank of America Merrill Lynch, Deutsche Bank, and J.P. Morgan, the tech giant issued $1.5 billion and earned Environmental Finance's 2016 Corporate Green Bond of the Year award. Proceeds will go to renewable energy like solar and wind projects, energy-efficient facility upgrades, water efficiency, and R&D into "greener materials."

And where Apple goes, others will follow. Just a few months later, Starbucks issued $500 million in Green Bonds to be used, in part, to support farmers who grow and harvest crops according to sustainability guidelines. The Starbucks offering was wildly popular, bringing in new investors and earning high marks from sustainability analysts.

Even so, the Green Bond investment market suffers from some of the constraints of the equity impact investing market, especially one: You can't push on a string. Incredibly—but auspiciously—there aren't enough Green Bond instruments around to satisfy investor demand for the things; supply can't keep up with demand. Most Green Bond issues, like the Starbucks deal, are oversubscribed (meaning that there are more eager investors than there are Green Bonds to go around).

Social Bonds

Social Bonds were long the poor stepchild of the ESG bond market, lagging far behind the Green Bond market. But the Social Bond market experienced remarkable growth in 2020, as total issuance increased more than sevenfold from 2019's $18.2 billion to $149.4 billion. If the current level of growth and market diversification seen in 2020 continues in future years, then it is possible that the Social Bond market will follow the Green Bond market's development pattern in a reinforcing and sustainable cycle of issuance and investment.

COVID-19 Social Bonds

In 2020, a new subset of Social Bonds, referred to as COVID-19 bonds, emerged to finance activities that mitigate the economic fallout from the pandemic. This development has ushered in a new era of explosive growth for ESG-linked bonds in general, and Social Bonds in particular.

Case study: Philippines COVID-19 Response Bond

In August 2020, the Bank of the Philippine Islands issued a COVID-19 Action Response Bond to stimulate economic recovery by supporting micro-, small-, and medium-sized enterprises (MSMEs). The country was slammed by the pandemic, with gross domestic product shrinking by as much as 10% in 2020, the worst performance in the region. The Philippines had the second highest

> COVID-19 caseload in Southeast Asia; even worse, the pandemic may have pushed 2.7 million more people into poverty.[5]
> MSMEs are the lynchpin of the Philippines economy, accounting for 99.5% of businesses in the country and employing 63% of workers—so raising funds to support MSMEs is deeply impactful.
> The issue was notable on several levels:
>
> - Investors loved it; the $443 million bond was oversubscribed sevenfold, and attracted a diverse pool of institutional and retail investors.
> - The bond featured SDG linkages: SDG 8 (decent work and economic growth), SDG 9 (industry, innovation, and infrastructure), and SDG 10 (reduced inequalities).
> - It was compliant with the Social Bond standards developed by the Southeast Asian region.

The COVID-19 crisis has refocused public and private sector attention worldwide on social challenges such as unequal access to healthcare, the vulnerability of marginalized populations to systemic shocks, and the urgent need for private sector involvement to address these challenges. The pandemic has highlighted specific areas that can be addressed by Social Bonds, from medical research and production to SME financing for struggling businesses, and to revitalizing rural areas to accommodate an expected increase in remote working.

Indeed, the COVID-19 impact is expanding and giving new meaning to the Social Bond format. There really has been a surprising amount of good innovation; the movement goes far beyond financing for vaccines and masks. Thus, activists, stockholders, and employees alike are pushing corporations into adding a social and environmental lens to their business strategy, products, and services. Investors are demanding concrete action and verifiable results, and they are increasingly checking that corporate actions and behavior during the crisis are aligned with their ESG and corporate social responsibility principles.

The COVID-19 pandemic poses a unique threat to progress on human development indicators such as poverty and inequality. But like all challenges, the pandemic also contains an embedded opportunity: to accelerate and mainstream the use of blended finance instruments like Social Bonds. It has provided a cohesive and powerful organizing theme for Social Bonds, much as climate change did for Green Bonds, where there was not a well-defined common theme pre-pandemic. Accordingly, the pandemic has dramatically changed the landscape of the ESG bond market, increasing issuer and investor interest in Social Bonds relative to Green Bonds. The fearsome impact of the pandemic on health and economies worldwide has focused attention on innovative financial instruments that target both social and financial returns simultaneously—in other words, Social Bonds. Moreover, COVID-19 has suddenly generated a large supply of financing needs and a large pool of social assets and projects that can be financed by Social Bonds.

Pre-pandemic, the main factor that constrained ESG bond issuance was not the demand side, but the supply side. Corporate issuers like banks and nonfinancial issuers have to find assets on their balance sheets or eligible projects that meet the issuing principles, which is considerably easier for green projects (typically things) than for social projects (typically people). In this context, COVID-19 may be seen as the "global climate change for Social Bonds," because it is a big global issue that grabs attention and, crucially, is investable. The Social Bond concept has found new meaning as an optimal framework for raising funds to mitigate the devastating economic impact of COVID-19. Thus, this is very much the right time and right place for such financial innovation to thrive.

In response to the fast-growing COVID-19 bond market, on June 10, 2020, the ICMA expanded its list of eligible projects and target communities included in the Social Bond Principles (SBP).

June 2020 update to the International Capital Market Association Social Bond Principles

Social project categories include, but are not limited to, providing and/or promoting:

- Affordable basic infrastructure (e.g., clean drinking water, sewers, sanitation, transport, and energy);
- Access to essential services (e.g., education and vocational training, health care, financing, and financial services);
- Affordable housing;
- Employment generation and programs designed to prevent and/or alleviate unemployment stemming from socioeconomic crises, including through the potential effect of financing micro, small, and medium-sized enterprises;

- Food security and sustainable food systems (e.g., physical, social, and economic access to safe, nutritious, and sufficient food that meets dietary needs and requirements); resilient agricultural practices; reduction of food loss and waste; and improved productivity of small-scale producers; and
- Socioeconomic advancement and empowerment (e.g., equitable access to and control over assets, services, resources, and opportunities; and equitable participation and integration into the market and society, including the reduction of income inequality).

Target populations include, but are not limited to, the following:

- Those living below the poverty line;
- Excluded and/or marginalized populations and/or communities;
- People with disabilities;
- Migrants and/or displaced persons;
- The undereducated;
- The underserved (owing to a lack of quality access to essential goods and services);
- The unemployed;
- Women and/or sexual and gender minorities; and
- Aging populations and vulnerable youth.

Source: International Capital Market Association Social Bond Principles.

Green Bonds versus Social Bonds

In the world of ESG bonds, the Green Bond market was the first to take off. However, in the era of COVID-19, Social Bonds are quickly proving to be the right innovation at the right moment in time.

Green Bonds probably owe their early lead in the issuance count to two factors: investor demand and the relative ease of impact measurement. Issuers have learned that "greening" their bond issue adds to its perceived value in the eyes of many investors without increasing risk. Moreover, impact measurement for Green Bonds can be relatively straightforward and based on a quantifiable and generally standardized set of data, such as the reduction of carbon dioxide equivalent emissions in metric tons, or the number of kilowatt-hours of renewable energy generated. This increases investor certainty that their funds are actually helping to achieve real environmental improvements in a verifiable way, rather than just "greenwashing" (i.e., making a project look more environmentally sound than it actually is).

Accordingly, some institutional investors have established dedicated Green Bond portfolios, responding to studies finding that a solid—and increasing—majority of investors want their portfolios to contribute to the battle against climate change.

ESG bonds: All colors of the rainbow

While the ESG bond market is dominated by Green, Social, and Sustainability Bonds, other categories of ESG bonds have popped up as well, which are discussed next.

Disaster bonds

Catastrophe or disaster bonds, sometimes nicknamed cat bonds, are used to transfer risk from an insurance company to investors. Why does this advance social well-being, you may well ask? Doesn't this just benefit a private insurance company?

Well, no. There are two problems with leaving all this risk in the hands of a private insurer. First, these insurers can simply refuse to insure properties and homeowners at high risk of major disasters—a category that is rapidly expanding to include all of southern Florida and coastal New England, for example. Second, in the event of a major disaster hitting, say, an urban area with loads of high-value properties (Miami, anyone?), the private insurer may simply be unable to cover the damages.

This explains why the first cat bond was created in the mid-1990s after the twin natural disasters of Hurricane Andrew and the Northridge, California earthquake; the purpose is to set aside the proceeds of the bond to help pay for future disaster claims, if needed. Since these bonds are pretty risky (especially as climate change cranks up the risk of major natural catastrophes almost daily), they may pay a pretty hefty interest rate and have a term of only a few years.

The World Bank has been a leader in the cat bond field for poorer countries; it first issued a cat bond to cover earthquake and hurricane risks for 16 Caribbean countries in 2007, and since then has provided drought insurance to Malawi, and weather and commodity price insurance to Uruguay. The Bank facilitated the issuance of cat bonds for Mexico and the Philippines in August 2017; three weeks later, Mexico received a $150 million payout following the powerful 8.2 magnitude earthquake. And in December 2017, the province of Davao del Sur in the Philippines received about $1.6 million following Typhoon Vinta. In 2020, cat bond issuance hit a record of over $10 billion, bringing total market size to over $40 billion.

The good news for investors in these instruments: If no disaster occurs during the term of the bond, the insurance company would pay interest and principal back to the investors.

The bad news: If a catastrophe does occur, then the investors can forget about getting their money back (let alone any interest), and the insurance company would use the funds to pay victims of the catastrophe. In that event, the investor essentially becomes a charitable donor rather than investor—but for an awfully good cause. Cat bonds also have the advantage of offering high yields (remember all that risk) to investors, and of being completely unlinked from traditional markets like the New York Stock Exchange. Back to our Finance 101 rehash again: Anything that improves diversification for the investor is good.

Natural disasters like hurricanes, wildfires or earthquakes are horrific for anyone who suffers through them, of course. But their impact is dramatically *worse* for poor people and poor countries than for the comfortable middle classes of the world. It's estimated that global economic losses from disasters are now over $300 billion per year, of which 75% is attributed to extreme weather events. Also, disasters force some 26 million people into poverty each year.

Here's the problem: An earthquake that might kill dozens, even hundreds, in the United States could take the lives of *hundreds of thousands* in the developing world due to inadequate preparation and insurance, dismal health care facilities, lack of emergency services, shoddy building, and much more. It's estimated that Mongolia, for example, lost 20% of its economy to natural disasters in the period 1980–2015.

So there is a place for cat bonds in the catalogue of impact: They provide some much-needed protection for the most vulnerable among us.

Diaspora bonds

Diaspora bonds support pretty much the same groups. These nifty little instruments are usually issued by a country to tap into its own diaspora—that is, its people and their descendants who live abroad but maintain a close attachment with their country of origin. Developing countries can use Diaspora bonds to tap into the wealth that these people have accumulated, and put their funds to good use in the home country. According to one World Bank expert, Diaspora bonds could generate about $50 billion a year for developing countries, partly helping to offset a pandemic-related plunge in foreign direct investment in 2020–2021.[6]

The State of Israel has made great use of these instruments, raising more than $40 billion in Israel bonds since 1951 from Jews scattered in all corners of the earth. India, which also has a relatively well-off and loyal community worldwide, has raised $11 billion through three Diaspora bonds; Nigeria issued its first Diaspora bond for $300 million in 2017, which was oversubscribed by 130%; Rwanda, Haiti, and Kenya have all expressed interest in creating their own Diaspora bonds.

The proceeds of these bonds can be used to fund social progress via infrastructure, education, and health in the home country—with the government paying interest and principal back to its loyal investors. Their beauty lies in their investors' patriotism; the bonds can get away with paying lower interest rates to loyal expats, a sort of patriotic discount for the country. Diaspora bonds are often long-term and carry pretty low yields, so this can be a very stable source of funds for underfinanced developing countries.

On the other hand, these instruments—like all other impact bonds—are hardly perfect. Ethiopia, for example, tried but failed to issue a Diaspora bond a few years ago; no matter how much its emigres loved their home country, they didn't trust the government to use their money in good ways. High corruption levels in many developing countries feed fears that the proceeds of these—or any—bonds will disappear into the hands of dirty politicians rather than serve the people left behind. The result is that many emerging market countries simply can't access funds in this way, at least not until corruption is under control.

And if we knew how to make that happen, we would deserve the Nobel Peace Prize for the entire 21st century.

Pay-for-success (PFS) instruments

In line with the growth of ESG bonds thus far in the 21st century, another set of financial instruments has emerged that is based on the principle of pay-for-success: social impact bonds (SIBs), development impact bonds (DIBs), and sustainability-linked bonds (SLBs). Not to be confused with the above discussion on ESG-linked bonds, SIBs and DIBs are a very small and different set of instruments, which are not really bonds at all. Rather, they are public–private partnerships based on an agreement that investors will receive a return of their principal plus some financial return, *if and only if* the project achieves a predetermined rate of success on social and/or environmental goals.

These are best understood as pay-for-success projects, where success is defined as the achievement of socially beneficial goals such as improved early childhood health or higher employment rates among at-risk youth. In a SIB, government is the outcomes funder who repays investors when success is achieved; in a DIB, the outcomes funder is a nongovernmental entity such as a philanthropic organization or multilateral development bank.

Case Study: Educate Girls Development Impact Bond—Rajasthan, India

This project was funded by India's first Development Impact Bond (DIB) and was led by Educate Girls, an NGO working to improve enrollment of girls in public schools in Rajasthan, as well as their learning outcomes. In rural areas of Rajasthan, which are dominated by subsistence agriculture, about 10% of girls aged 11–14 do not attend school, mainly because they are needed to add to family income or care for siblings. The quality of girls' education in these areas is also a concern, as the female literacy rate (in 2011) was just 52%, compared to 79% for men and the national average of 65% for women.

When the three-year project concluded, the outside evaluator found that there was reason to celebrate: The project exceeded the pre-agreed performance metrics on both enrollment and learning outcomes, giving investors a modest financial return and enabling Educate Girls to substantially scale up its funding and impact. The pay-for-success-based DIB structure enabled project leaders to adjust their methods in real time, and improve efficiency through active performance management.[7]

Despite its good intentions, however, it is hard to hold up the Educate Girls DIB as a funding structure worthy of emulation. Development of the project began in 2013, but complex negotiations and calculations with the various players meant that the program did not actually launch until 2015; remarkably, the direct project budget of $270,000 was less than the evaluation cost of $300,000. (Of course, this direct budget number omits the thousands of man-hours required by the lengthy development process.) Total costs, including management expenses and funds to publicly communicate the results, were estimated at about $1 million.

> Even more disappointing, the DIB did not bring new, or private, capital to the project. It merely passed money from one philanthropy to another—the upfront investor was UBS Optimus Foundation, which was repaid by the outcome payor, the Children's Investment Fund Foundation. Also, the evaluation results prove only that the Educate Girls intervention method was a success, not that the DIB financing mechanism added value to the project. In fact, the complexity and long lead time demanded by this process suggest that its benefits did not exceed its costs.
>
> The value of the project, however, is still significant. It underlined the need for quality girls' education in poor, rural areas of Asia; it introduced better teacher training and management in order to manage education quality, and it included real-time assessment to enable real-time performance improvement. This creates an opportunity to scale up this type of project using private capital throughout the region.

The first SIB was launched in the United Kingdom in 2010 to great fanfare; after 10 years of much-hyped growth, total issuance through the end of 2020 was still pretty paltry at about $420 million. SIBs and DIBs suffer from many deficiencies, including (1) a dependence on philanthropy to fund outsize project development costs, (2) complexity, (3) small size, (4) the potential for adverse consequences, and (5) a spotty track record. As a result, SIBs are really not a viable sustainable finance instrument at scale for the developing world.

Table 7.1 Social impact bonds versus environmental, social, and governance bonds

SIBs	ESG Bonds
Not true bonds	Bonds
Based on PFS	Not usually PFS
Variable return	Fixed income
May have guarantee of principal	Usually no guarantees
Impact-first investors	Mainstream investors
Long development time	Quick issuance
$420 million in issuance in 10 years	$500 billion in issuance in 2020

Urgent need for a robust social bond market

Economic development needs

Even before the COVID-19 pandemic, the UN estimated that meeting the 17 SDGs would require global investments of $5 trillion–7 trillion per annum through 2030, implying that there is a huge funding gap that only the public and private sectors working together can fill.

The pandemic has upended those estimates. Based on its October 2020 estimate, the International Monetary Fund (IMF) expects a 4.4% contraction in global gross domestic product in 2020, even after accounting for the announcement of trillions of dollars in economic stimulus measures from governments. The IMF anticipates that the pandemic will leave medium-term scars as well, warning that "the cumulative loss in [global] output relative to the pre-pandemic projected path is projected to grow from $11 trillion over 2020–2021 to $28 trillion over 2020–2025," which represents a "severe setback to the improvement in average living standards across all country groups."

The need to shore up their sagging economies will take an especially heavy toll on the budgets of developing economies. According to the IMF, these countries will add 5.5 percentage points of GDP to their fiscal deficits and 6.8 percentage points to their public debt levels in 2020.[8]

Social development needs

The COVID-19 pandemic threatens to erase many of the hard-won gains in social indicators of development in the developing world. Gig workers and those in the informal economy, for example, have been hard-hit by the lockdown as street vendors and small and medium-sized enterprises (SMEs) struggle to survive. The all-important tourism industry has staggered under the blow of the pandemic—down 88%–100% in developing Asia at the height of the crisis—while global manufacturing also slowed due to declining demand and supply chain disruptions. This is why financing for SMEs affected by COVID-19 has been such a large part of Social Bond issuance to date.

As fiscal revenues collapse and crisis-response spending and debt grow, public resources that can be allocated to long-term issues like climate change and education are shrinking. Thus, there is an enormous funding gap that Social Bonds can fill.

The COVID-19 pandemic has also exposed the depth and importance of the digital divide. Broadband access for disadvantaged populations (or the lack thereof) has always been one of the use-of-proceeds areas for Social

Bonds, but the COVID-19 crisis has made this need much more immediate and pressing. Addressing this issue is likely to become even more imperative as some of the shift to more virtual education and work is likely to become permanent—a compelling illustration of how Social Bonds have been given new meaning and urgency by the COVID-19 crisis.

Funding gap

With just 10 years remaining to achieve the ambitious SDGs, developing economies face a severe funding gap that is being exacerbated by the pandemic. Even more worrisome, much of the private sector investment in developing economies focuses on middle- and high-income emerging markets, leaving lower-income economies even farther from reaching their goals.

As noted above, the UN Conference on Trade and Development estimates that $5–7 trillion per annum will be required to achieve the SDGs by 2030, including $3.3–4.5 trillion in developing economies. This leaves an annual funding shortfall of around $2.5 trillion globally. Funds are desperately needed for power, transport, digital infrastructure, climate change mitigation, health care, education, food security, water and sanitation, and more. A 2014 Ceres report warned that the world needs to invest an additional $1 trillion per year for the next 36 years to avoid the worst effects of climate change alone.[9] With official development assistance at perhaps $150 billion per year and workers' remittances at around $450 billion, the need for private capital to fill this gap is both obvious and dramatic.

And then COVID-19 arrived, with devastating effects on public sector finances and a sharp deterioration in living conditions for the most vulnerable communities around the world. This pandemic's impact is a double-edged sword: It has both enlarged the funding gap and made more urgent the need for private capital to address these challenges.

Why Social Bonds?

In terms of the broader financial landscape, Social Bonds are an attractive instrument for helping to close the funding gap by financing social investments. Since the issuer of a Social Bond commits to measuring and reporting its impact, the quality of project outcomes is likely to be more enhanced due to this greater scrutiny. This aspect of Social Bonds is particularly valuable for the not-for-profit (e.g., public sector and multilateral) issuers whose missions tend to be most aligned to social financing needs—and who are the most active issuers of Social Bonds.

Social Bonds present a unique opportunity for better governance in bond markets, since issuance of these bonds goes hand-in-hand with disclosure of corporate or government activities and use of proceeds. As a result, issuers and investors can see a clearer linkage between funding and use of the money—a significant effect in the developing market context where a lack of transparency can be problematic. Thus, Social Bonds can create a direct impact such as improved healthcare or education, while also creating an indirect impact through increased transparency.

As noted above, the COVID-19 pandemic has given rise to a dramatic increase in Social Bond issuance worldwide. It is not clear yet whether Social Bond issuance will slacken as the immediate shock of the pandemic eases, or whether the pipeline is still quite full; but nonetheless, 2020 was a record year for Social Bonds.

Investors

To a large extent, investor demand has been the driving force behind growth in the ESG bond market. Consistently and across the globe, investors are increasingly committed to including ESG criteria in their investment decisions. This includes investment in specifically labeled ESG bonds, as well as consideration of ESG risk factors in all investment decisions. In the COVID-19 era, that interest has centered more and more on Social Bonds that are specifically intended to ease the pain of the pandemic on vulnerable communities worldwide.

A BNP Paribas Asset Management investor survey from June 2020 found that 23% of respondents believe that ESG has become more important as a result of the pandemic. Perhaps most interesting from the survey was the following: "Social issues were considered far more important post- than pre-pandemic; half of respondents saw social issues as important before the crisis, compared with 70% today." Moreover, 79% of respondents "expect social issues to have a positive long-term impact on both investment performance and risk management."[10] This suggests a major increase in sophistication among investors, upending the traditional (and largely disproven) belief that investors must sacrifice financial returns to achieve social goals.

Investors in ESG bonds may have two reasons to include ESG in their investment management process: The values rationale and the value rationale. The values rationale is grounded in moral judgment: Individuals are the ultimate owners of most investable assets so they should be invested in ways that make society better off. Not investing in companies that pollute or that produce harmful products creates an incentive for these companies to change their behavior or risk being cut off from investment capital. The value rationale argues that ESG factors are potential risks to investment portfolios. Integrating ESG analysis into the investment process provides a better assessment of the expected return of an investment and, thus, will generate superior investment returns.

Investors are well aware of the many scandals that have embroiled some businesses—accounting fraud, bribery, money laundering, and environmental disasters—and they choose to avoid these companies for the good of society and the good of their portfolio returns. The ESG approach also improves diversification within portfolios, thus lowering risk while increasing returns.

Mapping bonds to the Sustainable Development Goals

Remember the UN's call to action in the Chapter 1: They developed a group of SDGs to guide and impel private investments for social and environmental solutions. Now, many impact bond issuers specifically tie their bonds to SDGs in an effort to define the social impact of these instruments. For example, in February 2018, a Swedish insurance company, Folksam, partnered with the World Bank on a $350 million bond that focused on four SDGs: Good Health and Well Being (SDG 3), Gender Equality (SDG 5), Responsible Consumption and Production (SDG 12) and Climate Action (SDG 13).

And then there are vaccine bonds, which help make vaccines available to the 71 poorest countries in the world—and which are aligned with SDG 17 (the need for stronger commitment to partnership and cooperation to achieve sustainable development). The International Finance Facility for Immunization, launched in 2006, provides funds by issuing vaccine bonds backed by wealthy donor countries. The facility expects to disburse $1.3 billion for vaccines over the 2016–2020 period to Gavi, the Vaccine Alliance, which has prevented more than ten million deaths since its founding in 2000.

The World Bank has even issued a global pandemic bond, raising funds from socially minded investors to be channeled to developing countries facing the risk of a pandemic. It was designed to prevent another Ebola crisis, and was the first time that pandemic risk in low-income countries was transferred to the financial markets.

Saving lives…protecting refugees…battling climate change—is there anything these wondrous ESG bonds can't do?

Overcoming obstacles to social bond market growth

While the need for Social Bond market growth is obvious and imperative, there are significant obstacles to market growth that must be addressed. It is generally agreed that the greatest obstacles to growth in the Social

Bond space are the lack of clarity about measuring and assessing impact, as well as a supply-side shortage. More precisely, there has not yet been a coalescing around standardization in the measurement of impact, which is extremely difficult to do because Social Bond projects and assets are by their very nature much more diverse than Green Bond projects and assets. While the ICMA framework is a step forward, it falls well short of a standardized set of metrics that would enable comparison of impact performance across instruments. Surveys find that asset owners and managers view social impact as the most difficult sector to analyze—compared with, for example, environmental impact; hence, finding solutions to this issue would vastly open up the field.

Without this clarity, the risk of social washing, or overstating the social value of a bond, is very real, and investors are keenly aware of this risk. Indeed, even before the emergence of COVID-19 bonds, many market participants worried about "rainbow bonds" in which all matter of labels might go hand-in-hand with greenwashing or social washing.

But the advent of COVID-19 brings an opportunity to turn this into a virtuous cycle, as attention is high and focused, and the need for financing is immense.

Financial advisors, in particular, may be an obstacle to market growth, as they are often poorly informed on this sector and may believe that ESG investments detract from returns. They may also think that ESG applies largely to the equity sector; therefore, they may be resistant to driving their clients into socially responsible, fixed-income investments.

Also, many sovereigns and corporates that would like to participate in the Social Bond market—and probably will in the future—do not yet have Social Bond frameworks in place. It takes time, money, and manpower to develop ICMA-compliant issuance procedures, all of which may be limited resources in some parts of developing Asia. The due diligence required to become ICMA-compliant is significant and thus an obstacle to participation in this market. Sovereigns and corporates alike often have to get departments and ministries that are typically siloed from each other to join together, which is a challenge; but once achieved, it can result in better long-term collaboration.

Of course, with every challenge comes an opportunity, and there is certainly a broad opportunity for market participants to develop this holy grail: a widely accepted, standardized set of metrics to assess social impact. Various bodies—from the Sustainability Accounting Standards Board to European authorities—are pursuing a system of standardized reporting to include social impact. There is, however, a continuing debate in the market between the right mix of regulatory oversight versus market-principles-based oversight.

Fortunately, noninvestment actors—including philanthropic foundations, multilateral institutions, and financial institutions—can help to overcome these obstacles, mitigate these risks, and continue to build on the momentum of 2020 in the Social Bond market. It is crucial that an ecosystem comes into existence, especially in Asia, to support and educate potential market participants.

The way forward

There is undoubtedly an urgent and compelling case for the development of a robust ESG bond market. Harnessing the power of private capital to address critical social needs is an opportunity for both issuers and investors to address these needs in a financial context. While the pandemic will fade away, one lasting impact may well be its catalytic effect on the development of ESG bonds, particularly Social Bonds, worldwide. Much as the beautifully clear skies and air during the stringent lockdowns of early 2020 illustrated the environmental damage being wrought by business and industry, the pandemic has also highlighted the peril of ignoring social risks in our investment decisions.

Even before the pandemic hit, a report by the Business and Sustainable Development Commission estimated that achieving the SDGs could unlock $12 trillion of market opportunities in food and agriculture, cities, energy and materials, and health and well-being, while also creating 380 million new jobs by 2030.[11]

So we know that achieving the SDGs makes business sense. This means that financial instruments aimed at pursuing social as well as financial value can play a critical role in fostering growth and progress in the developing world.

Interest in investing in bonds that pursue ESG goals alongside financial returns was already mounting before the onset of the COVID-19 pandemic. However, much of this interest focused on instruments that addressed climate change and environmental concerns, while Social Bonds lagged well behind. Then the pandemic refocused both issuers and investors on the urgent need for innovative financial instruments such as Social Bonds to address the social challenges that have become so much more pressing in the era of COVID-19.

An overly narrow focus on COVID-19-specific issues for Social Bond issuers, of course, will eventually be a dead-end. So how should issuers and investors leverage the increased market awareness of social factors for sustainability projects beyond climate change?

Every actor in the ecosystem has a role to play. Governments, supranationals, and philanthropic institutions can all support the development of this market, offering technical assistance, guarantees of capital, education, thought leadership, and a supportive regulatory environment. Issuers can seek out social investment opportunities and put into place the scaffolding for Social Bond issues that can be quickly erected and completed in accordance with ICMA guidelines. And investors, who are the key to making this work, should seek out well-constructed and well-documented Social Bond investments while remaining ever vigilant for social washing.

The overall ESG bond market is still small at about 5% of the total global bond market. But the pandemic has proven the concept and value of ESG Bonds to address social challenges and achieve the SDGs. This provides a solid basis for the market to continue its path toward maturity in the post-pandemic environment.

Momentum in the impact revolution is strong, and probably strongest in the bond sector.

Notes

1 A fixed-income instrument is one that delivers a fixed income (surprise, surprise), that is, annual or semi-annual interest payments that are fixed in advance. So a $1000 3% bond will provide $30 in interest to the investor every year over the life of the bond.
2 www.icmagroup.org.
3 The World Bank. (October 29, 2018). *Seychelles Achieves World First with Sovereign Blue Bond.* World Bank Group. Retrieved from: www.worldbank.org/en/news/feature/2018/10/29/seychelles-achieves-world-first-with-sovereign-blue-bond#:~:text=October%2029%2C%202018%20%2D%20Famous%20for,world's%20first%20sovereign%20blue%20bond.
4 Wirz, M. (December 17, 2020). "Why Going Green Saves Bond Borrowers Money." *The Wall Street Journal.*. Retrieved from: www.wsj.com/articles/why-going-green-saves-bond-borrowers-money-11608201002#:~:text=A%20growing%20body%20of%20research,save%20a%20bit%20of%20money.&text=While%20a%20broad%20bond%20market,projects%20at%20even%20lower%20rates.
5 Reuters Staff. (December 8, 2020). "World Bank sees strong Philippine economic rebound, COVID-19 resurgence a risk." Retrieved from: www.reuters.com/article/worldbank-philippnes-economy/world-bank-sees-strong-philippine-economic-rebound-covid-19-resurgence-a-risk-idUSL4N2IO12C.
6 Shalal, A. & Arnold, T. (April 24, 2020). "Pandemic could fuel demand for 'diaspora' bonds, says World Bank*Reuters*. Retrieved from: www.reuters.com/article/us-health-coronavirus-diaspora-bonds/pandemic-could-fuel-demand-for-diaspora-bonds-says-world-bank-idUSKCN22635H.
7 Bogglid-Jones, I. & Gustafsson-Wright, E. (July 13, 2018). "World's first development impact bond for education shows successful achievement of

outcomes in its final year." *Brookings*. Retrieved from: www.brookings.edu/blog/education-plus-development/2018/07/13/worlds-first-development-impact-bond-for-education-shows-successful-achievement-of-outcomes-in-its-final-year/.

8 Gopinath, G. (October 13, 2020). "A long, uneven and uncertain ascent." *IMF Blogs*. Retrieved from: https://blogs.imf.org/2020/10/13/a-long-uneven-and-uncertain-ascent/#:~:text=After%20the%20rebound%20in%202021,28%20trillion%20over%202020%E2%80%9325.

9 "Investing in the Clean Trillion: Closing the Clean Energy Investment Gap." (January 15, 2014). *Ceres*. Retrieved from: www.ceres.org/resources/reports/investing-clean-trillion-closing-clean-energy-investment-gap.

10 "BNP Paribas Asset Management survey shows COVID-19 prompts rise in social considerations within investment decision-making." (July 13, 2020). *BNP Paribas Asset Management*. Retrieved from: https://mediaroom-en.bnpparibas-am.com/news/bnp-paribas-asset-management-survey-shows-covid-19-prompts-rise-in-social-considerations-within-investment-decision-making-8e57-0fb7a.html.

11 "Press Release: Sustainable business can unlock at least US$12 trillion in new market value, and repair economic system." (January 16, 2017). *Business Commission*. Retrieved from: http://businesscommission.org/news/release-sustainable-business-can-unlock-at-least-us-12-trillion-in-new-market-value-and-repair-economic-system.

8 Sustainable banking

The Equator Principles (EPs) became the first real foray of banks into sustainable finance—a huge step forward from charitable giving, but still a mechanism for risk mitigation rather than business opportunity. After the EPs, the next big step for banks was the realization that a sustainable approach to finance offered business opportunities, not just risk mitigation. Largely driven by consumer demand and awareness of reputation risks, more banks are positioning themselves as responsible partners in the drive for improved environmental, social, and governance (ESG) impact.

The latecomers: Banks

Banks have been latecomers to the world of sustainable finance. Rather than driving progress, the banking industry has been something of a laggard, having tended to view ESG issues through the lens of risk management rather than opportunity. (Who will sue us? How much will the settlement cost? Will our reputation be dinged?)

But a slow change of heart in the banking industry has been underway for the past decade or so, and is likely to accelerate in the aftermath of COVID-19 and worldwide demands for a more equitable and fair economic model. This has been a two-phase process: First, banks came to realize that the reputational, litigation, and financial risks of lending to eco-unfriendly, socially destructive, and poorly governed projects were substantial. And then, belatedly, it dawned on bankers that there were benefits and opportunities in lending to ESG-positive projects. The conversion is far from complete, but it is happening.

Project finance: Opportunity and risk

Banks first dipped their toes into the waters of sustainability in the area of project finance. Project finance (PF) is the exact opposite of microfinance;

it refers to some of the biggest, most expensive, and most transformative projects in the world—especially the developing world. PF is used for infrastructure and natural resource projects such as power, roads, ports, and mining, so these tend to be the projects with the largest ESG implications in a bank's portfolio.[1]

The precise definition of PF is that it's used to finance economically separate capital investment projects, in which the project cash flows are used to service the debt. If this definition sounds dull, in fact PF is anything but dull. It can be the Wild West of finance, covering massive and hugely complex investments in long-lived physical assets that are central to the field of sustainable development. The Suez Canal drew on PF in 1858; the Eiffel Tower too in the late 1880s; and the 120 billion yen financing for Universal Studios Japan in 1998 was the largest PF deal ever in that country.

Because PF deals are usually very long term (extending over decades, perhaps) and huge, they carry inordinate risks. There's resource risk, meaning that the minerals or oil simply won't be there in the amounts expected. There's completion risk—it may take longer or cost much more money than expected to complete the project, not at all unlikely in a deep jungle or stormy ocean. (The final cost of the Chunnel between the United Kingdom and France was 80% higher than originally planned, for example; the cost overruns on the Big Dig in Boston were almost 200%.) Market risk refers to the fear that demand or prices for the product will fall, which is exactly what happened to expensive oil projects when prices plunged in 2019–2020.

Operating risks cover the likelihood that even after the project is completed, it will struggle with labor, transportation, breakdowns, or other problems. There's also political and regulatory risk, that is, the risk that government and/or regulators will take actions that will harm the project.

And then there's *force majeure*, which can best be described as acts of God: Adverse events that are neither predictable nor preventable. These range from warfare to extreme weather to COVID-19, a massive *force majeure* event that shut down the world economy to an extent that no one could have predicted or protected against.

Perhaps the biggest risk of all, however, is the possibility of adverse ESG impact. Huge infrastructure projects inevitably displace people and communities; they can have massive environmental effects; and they produce sudden and unprecedented inflows of cash—a recipe for mismanagement and corruption.

Despite the high level of risk inherent in PF, it exploded in the 1980s with huge infrastructure projects in both the developed and developing worlds. Massive growth reflects the privatization of state-owned companies, deregulation of key industrial sectors, globalization, and depletion of natural resources that forces firms to search in increasingly remote and risky—that is, expensive—locations to find more reserves.

According to Thomson Reuters, global PF loans in 2018 rose to a record $283 billion from 871 deals, up 22% from 2017. The power sector remained the most active, accounting for nearly half of the market activity.

As the PF sector has racked up huge numbers and built huge amounts of infrastructure, it has also become increasingly controversial. Activists opposed to projects that fail to take account of ESG principles have figured out that targeting the banks that financed these projects can be very effective. Banks, after all, are founded on nothing but reputation and trust—when the public's faith in the bank fails, so can the bank itself.

Since a lack of infrastructure can be a key obstacle to development, it might be surmised that PF supports development in poor countries and should be welcomed. And indeed, this is often the case. Studies have found that there is a multiplier effect to infrastructure spending, which contributes to higher economic growth and employment. Potential investors in India long bemoaned the lack of reliable electricity, while investors in Africa are stymied by the lack of usable roads. According to McKinsey, Brazilian "development is constrained by narrow roads, a lack of railways in the new agricultural frontiers, and bottlenecked ports...."[2]

It's been estimated that the developing world will need $24 trillion in infrastructure through 2030 to jump-start economic progress, which implies a sharp increase in PF to fund these projects.

But while PF helps to meet critical infrastructure needs, it also raises critical ESG issues.

The Chad–Cameroon pipeline

One of the most egregious examples of this ESG disconnect is the Chad–Cameroon pipeline. In February 1996, a consortium of oil companies began serious work with the two countries' governments to extract oil from (landlocked) Chad, and to build a pipeline through Cameroon to bring the oil to the open sea. ExxonMobil, the leading shareholder with a 40% ownership share, had a stated commitment to environmental responsibility—but a "tainted environmental record due to the Exxon Valdez oil spill in 1989," which dumped 11 million gallons of oil "along the pristine Alaskan coastline."

The oil companies' governmental partners were even more badly tainted. One political analyst described Chad's President Idriss Deby as "a warlord…few credible analysts would argue that Deby is anything other

Sustainable banking 137

than an African strongman, whose weapons purchases dwarf levels of social spending in one of the world's poorest countries, where incidents of political violence continue." Cameroon, with a corruption perceptions ranking of 99 out of 99, was considered highly corrupt, and Chad was not much better.

Yet both countries were among the poorest on the face of the earth, and the oil development project was their only viable path to economic progress. So a project finance deal was put together that included commercial banks and the World Bank's International Finance Corporation, and provided $1.4 billion of PF debt to finance the pipeline. The plan was that the government of Chad would follow a Revenue Management Plan (RMP) to force it to use the windfall from the pipeline appropriately—to support economic progress for its people rather than enriching public officials.

From the outset, this deal was dogged by fierce opposition. The Environmental Defense Fund criticized the World Bank for participating, and other environmental groups "pointed to deforestation and oil spills as serious risks." Social activists, not to be outdone, criticized the project's planned resettlement and compensation of indigenous people living in the area. And pretty much all critics warned that the Chad government would not abide by the terms of the RMP.

Tragically, the critics had it right. While the project generated revenues aplenty during the high oil price years of the early 21st century, corrupt officials squirreled away big chunks of the proceeds for their own enrichment, or used the money to purchase weapons. A post-mortem review by the World Bank (which dropped out of the project in 2008) found that the goals of helping Chad reduce poverty and improve governance were not met; despite generating higher government revenues, there was no evidence of human development progress—and a substantial worsening of corruption.[3]

Many other projects followed the trajectory of the Chad–Cameroon pipeline. As PF projects exacerbated environmental devastation, corruption, and the destruction of indigenous people's habitats and way of life, it became a wake-up call for banks. Nongovernmental organizations (NGOs) and civil society organizations increasingly targeted the private financial institutions involved with PF. As these confrontations grew noisier and more public, banks became aware of the reputation, litigation, and credit risks associated with PF for controversial projects. When bankers realized that the poor ESG performance of their clients was a threat to the banks' own bottom line, they began to look more closely at these issues.

Until the chorus of criticism became too big to ignore, banks' approach to sustainability was pretty meek: Introducing paper recycling programs, or letting bankers swing hammers one day a year to build a house for Habitat for Humanity. Most banks also had philanthropic arms, which served to burnish their reputations while supporting high-prestige organizations like the symphony or ballet.

But it's hard to see any of this as hugely impactful. Completely absent was any sense that banks could incorporate ESG principles *into their core business* to create financial value; at most, sustainability issues were the province of their philanthropic activities and risk managers.

The Equator Principles: Still risk mitigation

The EPs became the first real foray of banks into sustainable finance—a huge step forward from charitable giving, but still a mechanism for risk mitigation rather than business opportunity.

Reacting to the chorus of criticism described above, in June 2003 ten leading international financial institutions adopted the EPs, a voluntary commitment that they would use clear, responsible, and consistent rules for managing the environmental and social risks that inevitably arise from project financing. The EPs have gone through several strategic reviews and revisions since then, most notably in July 2020; and there are now just over 100 signatories in 38 countries.

So what have the EPs wrought?

The guidelines apply to all global PF projects with total costs above $10 million, and are estimated to cover 80% of international PF in emerging markets. The provisions include a commitment that the borrower will conduct a social and environmental impact assessment, that projects in developing countries with weak regulatory standards will comply with World Bank standards (like the Oscar Meyer hot dog commercials: We answer to a higher authority), that projects will include an action plan and management system for mitigating ESG risks, and that the plans will be submitted for independent review.

As one might expect, there is no agreement on the success of the EP; some bankers say the guidelines are too stringent, while some NGOs say they are too loose. On the positive side, financial institutions have noted an improvement in the quality of projects submitted, suggesting that project sponsors are incorporating ESG oversight from the start—presumably to avoid hassles with their bankers. An official of the World Bank's International Finance Corporation wrote in 2018, "...the Equator Principles have improved labor standards and environmental practices, and strengthened engagement with indigenous peoples and local communities."[4]

But there have also been egregious violations of the EPs, leading many NGOs to charge that the Principles are nothing more than a fig leaf for business-as-usual. Strategic reviews have found that the application of the EPs is inconsistent across member banks, and that it's impossible to accurately assess EP performance due to limited information from member banks. Perhaps most important, there are no consequences for signatories that fail to abide by the Principles—the whole thing is voluntary, after all. So it's not surprising that in 2019, ten EP banks wrote a letter strongly criticizing the actions of other EP banks in financing projects such as the Dakota Access Pipeline, which was condemned for its adverse impact on indigenous people.

Among the biggest offenders was the Sakhalin II oil and gas development project in Russia, which turned out to be a stern test of the EPs.

By most accounts, it seems that the EPs failed the test. Sakhalin II was the world's biggest integrated oil and gas project, and came under withering criticism for its adverse impact on rivers, forests, whales, salmon, and indigenous people. The Rainforest Action Network took out a full-page ad in the *Washington Post* criticizing the Dutch bank ABN Amro for "outstanding environmental hypocrisy" in connection to its financing of the project. In fact, ABN Amro provided $1 billion to the Russian government-controlled gas giant Gazprom, for its purchase of a majority stake in the project. Said one environmental activist, "All banks involved in the Great Game around Sakhalin want it both ways; but they can't claim to be environmental leaders while taking over the financing of one of the most ecologically destructive oil and gas projects in the world."[5]

All of the banks involved in financing Sakhalin II were EP signatories; ABN AMRO was one of the original ten founders of the Principles.

Then there's Vietnam. Activist groups charge that six EP signatories have violated the Principles through their funding of coal-fired power stations throughout the country; these violations include a lack of transparency and information and a lack of engagement with communities, especially fishing communities for whom the projects threaten their livelihoods. The projects threaten to significantly add to Vietnam's already-high levels of air pollution, which a Harvard study expects to cause almost 20,000 excess deaths by 2030. One critic comments, "The EPs as they are written are far from perfect. However, if these principles are to have any meaning, the financial institutions that commit to them must comply with them."[6]

The EPs indeed are far from perfect. But they're much better than nothing, and they certainly have had some impact. ANZ Bank, for example, reportedly withdrew from financing a $2 billion Tasmanian pulp mill project that had drawn heavy criticism for its potential to destroy high conservation value forests and local communities. The EP webpage notes that "the EPs have…helped spur the development of other responsible environmental and social management practices in the financial sector and banking industry and have supported member banks in developing their own Environmental and Social Risk Management Systems."[7]

But in the end, the EPs are still about risk mitigation, not opportunity.

Moving on: Sustainable banking opportunities

After the EPs, the next big step for banks was the realization that a sustainable approach to finance offered business opportunities, not just risk mitigation. Following the 2008 financial crisis, many banks took a hard look at their fundamental strategies, and began to consider the demands of a wider range of stakeholders, including employees, society, and environment. This is a tacit acknowledgment that ignoring ESG factors—especially the governance piece—contributed to the ferocity of the crisis, as well as a realization that firms with good ESG practices fared better than others in hard times.

This process is accelerating in the wake of the COVID-19 pandemic, which has laser-focused public opinion on issues of poverty and inequality. Netflix, for example, announced in mid-2020 that it would shift 2% (around $100 million) of its cash holdings to banks and credit unions that primarily serve Black communities, in order to improve these financial institutions' ability to offer loans to often-underserved people and businesses.

Like Netflix, bank clients and shareholders are demanding more than office recycling of their bankers; they're demanding sustainability-based lending at the core of the bank's strategy. Says one French banker, "Sustainability topics are increasingly included in conversations with clients."[8] The fact is that more than $23 trillion is now invested in sustainable assets, and bankers can either capitalize on this market opportunity or get left behind. Deutsche Bank, for example, has set up a "dedicated sustainable finance team within its capital markets division in response to the growing focus on environmental, social and governance issues among its clients." The bank sees this as a "key differentiator," a competitive advantage in appealing to investors and clients alike.[9]

ESG Lending: Old-style

In the first decade of the 21st century, major US banks began a (public) campaign to finance sustainable entrepreneurship, usually by lending money to support the building of environmentally sound buildings and enterprises. Wells Fargo committed to dedicating $1 billion over 5 years to this purpose in 2005; 2 years later, BankAmerica launched a $20 billion initiative.

Bloomberg reported in 2019, "While it's hard to imagine the world's profit-driven banks offering incentives for doing good, corporate lending tied to some measurable sustainability metric—like cutting emissions or reducing food waste—surged eight-fold in 2018 to $36.4 billion." "This is a new world for most financiers and treasury teams," said Peter Elleman, the managing director for loan markets at ABN Amro NV in London, which is now lending in this space. He said having proof of a company's social responsibility is "a good indicator of good governance, and hence likely lower credit risk."[10]

Sustainable lending is still dwarfed by traditional lending—but Bloomberg notes that "some big deals—like the $3.5 billion ESG financing San Francisco-based warehouse developer Prologis Inc. signed in January [2020]—are putting ESG on the map."[11] Largely driven by consumer demand and awareness of reputation risks, more banks are positioning themselves as responsible partners in the drive for improved ESG impact. They are not only offering more sustainable loans, but also pulling out of sectors like coal and private prisons that draw heavy public criticism.[12]

Some 130 global banks, with $47 trillion in assets, have signed onto a UN-backed framework for bringing their strategies in line with the Paris Agreement on climate change. Signatories will have to set several long-term targets, and assess the negative and positive environmental impact of their loan portfolios. As part of this commitment, banks will "need to develop new products such as green loans or mortgages…with green lending to small-and-medium-sized businesses and households key for the growth of sustainable finance." This is about more than green financing of renewable energy projects; it's about proactively working with borrowers to help them reduce their carbon footprint.[13]

By mid-2019, the global "responsible loans market" had reached $111.5 billion, a 40% increase from the previous year according to S&P Global Ratings. The report found that "a growing number of banks are using lending to encourage and promote social and environmental causes, while also making decisions to scale back or divest from certain controversial industries."[14]

It's easy to get excited about these developments—until you compare the $111.5 billion in lending to total US bank lending of $15 trillion in May 2020. And until you focus on bank lending based on social sustainability rather than just climate change, in fact, a Google search of "banks + social lending" produced only sites on peer-to-peer lending—nothing at all on banking.

The biggest hurdle to more widespread progress is probably the lack of agreement on how to objectively gauge a borrower's social responsibility. As previous chapters have pointed out, it's relatively more straightforward to tie green loans to a widely accepted metric, such as CO_2 emissions—hence the oversize market share of green versus social lending. More than a dozen organizations offer sustainability ratings on other loans, but these are not widely accepted or uniform.

Indeed, a lack of widespread guidelines leads to a lack of widespread progress. Even tying a loan to these sustainability ratings isn't foolproof, since:

> [T]he scoring methods aren't consistent. In July, U.S. think tank American Council for Capital Formation released a critical report after finding a correlation of 0.32 between the sustainability ratings of MSCI and Sustainalytics on companies in the S&P Global 1200 Index. By comparison, credit ratings of Moody's and S&P Global Ratings are 0.90 aligned, it said.[15]

Ouch.

Something new: Sustainability-linked loans

In 2017, a new style of sustainability-based lending appeared on the scene. The so-called "sustainability-linked loans," also known as positive-incentive deals, link the interest rate on a lending facility to the borrower's performance against a predetermined sustainability target. If the goal is met, the interest rate drops; if the goal is missed, the interest rate goes up.

Here's what's really innovative about this: Unlike the ESG-based lending of the past, sustainability-linked loans (SLLs) are used for general corporate purposes rather than for specific ESG-based projects. And unlike ESG-based lending, it's the pricing of the loan rather than the project itself that's tied to a sustainability target.

SLLs quickly became very popular for large corporate borrowers; in 2018 alone, corporate lending tied to some measurable sustainability metric—like cutting emissions or reducing food waste—surged eightfold to $36.4 billion, according to Bloomberg NEF.[16] SLLs could be transformative in the world of sustainable lending; after all, what borrower would turn their back on potential interest rate savings?

While bankers usually do not disclose interest rate margins, anecdotal evidence suggests that the incentive is enough to propel corporate borrowers toward meeting sustainability targets. In Europe, where ESG-linked financing in general is much more developed, "the borrower typically receives a 5 to 10 percent discount on the interest rate depending on the cost of capital. In other words, the higher the overall rate, the larger the discount."[17]

Here are some examples:

- ING made the world's first SLL in April 2017: $1.2 billion, to Dutch electronics company Philips. The company requested the SLL, according to one of its bankers:
    It was really a question from the client, 'Can we do something around our goals without having to issue a green bond?' Because they didn't have a specific use of proceeds. Then jointly we came up with this way of tying their performance to, in that case, their Sustainalytics rating. That was how the first one was born.[18]
- The first US SLL, in the amount of $1.4 billion, went to CMS Energy in mid-2018. The borrower, which is committed to eliminating its coal-powered energy production by 2040, will hopefully get a reduced interest rate if it meets certain targets related to renewable energy generation.
- Xylem Inc., a US maker of water equipment, said that it got an incentive of as much as 5 basis points on an $800 million revolving facility tied to a sustainability rating from Sustainalytics.
- London utility Thames Water borrowed £1.4 billion in a five-year facility tied to its Global Real Estate Sustainability Benchmark rating. It will enjoy a lower interest rate if it reaches its sustainability goals; any interest savings will go to its charitable fund, which raises funds for water and environmental projects.
- British housing association London & Quadrant (L&Q) borrowed £100 million from BNP Paribas, which offered L&Q a lower interest rate if it helped 600 unemployed residents find work in the loan's first year (the number rises each year after that). The borrower, which builds and rents out affordable housing in London, has indicated that the interest rate incentive is "significant."[19]

"If this catches on, it is going to be the next big investment opportunity," said Kajetan Czyż, the program director for sustainable finance at the University of Cambridge's Institute for Sustainability Leadership. "Banks need to adapt to this new suite of opportunities this shift creates."

The opportunity for borrowers to benefit from lower interest costs is obvious, but what's in it for the banks? In fact:

[B]anks that fill their loan books with so-called positive-incentive deals could be better placed to not only attract clients, like sustainability conscious millennials, but also lower funding costs. That's because loans tied to [ESG goals] usually go to companies that have track records of profitability and debt repayment.

As one banker explained, "It will make a material difference to our funding costs."[20]

Is sustainability-linked lending a real game-changer, or a fad?

In this era of heightened attention to environmental issues; to social issues of diversity, equity, and inclusion; to governance issues like transparency and cronyism, many companies would like to achieve positive rather than negative impact. This fits well with the corporate business model of, say, a clothing manufacturer (think Patagonia: repair, reuse, recycle) or home builder. But how to create and prove positive impact in their core business is less obvious for other industries, from cloud computing to Twitter.

For these companies, SLLs are a solution to a vexing problem. SLLs can provide the borrowers with a way to access discounted funding and incentives to meet sustainability metrics—without having to embark upon ESG-based products that don't fit into their core business model. Companies in *any* industry, even oil and mining, can get capital this way. "Banks are often criticized for the companies they lend to," the banker said. "But it's easy to walk away from something. It's harder to engage and [effect change]."[21]

Still, SLLs aren't for everyone. A corporate borrower must have a credible sustainability policy in place and be committed to achieving ambitious and measurable targets; it's not just a matter of recycling paper or installing low-flush toilets.

As always in the field of sustainable finance, the catch is how to quantify social impact. Bankers (and financial markets) are experts in pricing capital according to *financial* risk. So a AAA-rated company like Microsoft can borrow at a much lower interest rate than a BBB company (e.g., Marriott or Kraft-Heinz) because Microsoft is essentially risk-free.

How to match social value to interest rate margins, however, is uncharted territory. Since "all companies face different ESG challenges – even in the same industry – [then] loan incentives are useless if targets are too vague, impossible to measure, unrealistic or too easy."

The industry is basically making it up as it goes along—which is perfectly fine. Lenders thus far have utilized two different approaches to pricing SLLs, using either third-party companywide ESG ratings, or setting specific targets, such as cutting emissions. "There is no one-size-fits-all" approach, said one banker. But this means that there is no common standard either—a common problem in the impact finance world. The

Loan Market Association, a London-based industry group, published its Sustainability Linked Loan Principles in 2019 with a view to addressing some of these concerns; while this is a good first step, the principles are vague and unenforceable according to critics.[22]

A survey by Bloomberg News found that lenders' number one worry about SLLs was the "lack of ESG data," and number two was "noncomparable ESG ratings." Number four is in the same vein as the first two; "can't reflect ESG improvements in financial terms." (Numbers three and four were "KPIs [key performance indicators] may miss other risks" and "metrics may not be ambitious enough.")

Faced with these concerns, it's tempting for lenders to fall back on some kind of grade or rating given by a third-party agency. A grade has the advantage of tying together a wide range of factors, from pollution to labor rights to corruption, into one neat package: The final score. Grades are easy to understand, and easy to defend (*we* didn't decide on the grade, it's a third-party agency!).

The danger of ratings, however, is that they're still an attempt to quantify the unquantifiable. While some impacts are easy to assess and measure (e.g., air quality and water quality), others are not (quality preschool and gender equity). Ratings "mask a maze of complexity, as providers distill down potentially hundreds of data points to reach a single score."[23] Ratings also require weightings of various factors, which are essentially subjective in nature (which is more important—girls health or education?).

The alternative to ratings is linking loans to a few key performance indicators, or KPIs. For instance, French agricultural cooperative Agrial signed a €900 million loan tied to five specific goals including worker safety and the development of organic products.

Using KPIs avoids the complexity of ratings, but it also introduces new complexities in the form of devising and pricing out exactly the right goals. KPIs also offer no way to compare impact across various borrowers. While the criticism of ratings is that they reduce huge factors into one single number, the advantage is that those numbers allow lenders to compare one borrower's performance against others. KPIs don't allow the latter, but they solve the problem of the former.

Where's King Solomon when you need him?

Full steam ahead: The post-COVID-19 era

Moody's Investors Service commented in mid-2020:

> The COVID-19 pandemic will make financial firms increasingly focus on the public good, as they are required by governments to

contribute to financial stability... As banks offer loan relief to the corporate sector and households and insurers accept delays in premium payments to lessen the COVID-19-triggered economic shock, this will reduce a bank's ability to act in a purely commercial manner.

Banks may need to lower interest margins and therefore profitability for some time to come, the report suggested.

In fact, it's much more than government requirements (e.g., reduce dividends or stock buybacks) that will increasingly focus banks on ESG factors in a post-COVID-19 world. Even before COVID-19, as noted above, financial institutions were already accelerating the pace of their sustainable financing activities. Now, "the crisis has given banks an opportunity to put their campaigns on corporate purpose and stakeholder capitalism to the test,"[24] not just supporting customers but proactively improving sustainability performance.

All of that will accelerate to warp speed in the post-virus world. It will be driven by public demand for actions that improve diversity, equity, and inclusion—and by a newfound corporate zeal to support these actions (or at least be *seen* to support these actions, aka greenwashing).

Financial inclusion, of course, falls squarely within the banker's wheelhouse, and banks have jumped on this bandwagon. Some have helped provide tablets to low-income households and to train those without access to digital banking; others have developed dedicated phone lines for elderly customers, for example.

Self-serving? Sure, but why not?

The pandemic, in fact, vastly increased the value of digitization; the lesson was driven home that a lack of digital access contributes to the contagion of inequality that is consuming the United States. Everyone, for a time, *had* to do their financial and other business online—and once online, everyone will probably stay there.

And it's in both the banks' and their customers' best interest that all be empowered to go online, and deposit their savings there, and borrow money there. This is an area that especially invites impactful lending from banks; bankers can lend money at low interest rates to enable poorer customers to digitize. And digitization, in turn, practically ensures that these customers will remain with the bank once they have mastered the online process. It also helps customers engage in online business activities, which will enable them to pay back the loans and improve their life outcomes.

Islamic banking

The Islamic finance community too is increasingly interested in digital transformation of their services. "Against the backdrop of the COVID-19 pandemic, fintech will continue to play a significant role in the industry's development in the coming years by improving access to financial services and transforming Islamic social finance," suggests one observer. For example, the National Committee for Islamic Finance in Indonesia has helped develop a digital platform for disbursing Islamic social finance funds, and to help Islamic finance organizations better manage these funds and payments.

Also in Indonesia, Islamic microfinance firm Blossom Finance has begun to accept online cryptocurrency payments, which are distributed to Blossom's 87 partner microfinance institutions.

More broadly, the United Nations Development Program (UNDP) has "highlighted several sharia-compliant financing instruments that could be part of the integrated pandemic response plan including *zakat* (charity) and *sukuk* (Islamic bonds) to help countries prepare, respond, and recover from the pandemic." As Stuart Brown wrote in the *Jakarta Post*,

> The ongoing COVID-19 outbreak has prompted financial institutions across the globe to pay greater attention to environmental, social, and governance (ESG) risks to build greater resilience in their business operations and supply chains, and we believe that Islamic finance markets will see a similar trend as well.
>
> In fact, an analysis of the 6,554 companies in Refinitiv's EIKON global database shows that sharia compliance screening can do much to improve ESG performance and sharia-compliant companies—to which Islamic financial institutions will direct capital—have ESG scores that are on average 6 percent higher than for those excluded by the sharia screening process.
>
> The principal source of ESG risk facing Islamic banks is embedded in their balance sheets though the financing they provide, and it is becoming clear to financial institutions around the world that ESG risks will affect their potential profitability, portfolio risk levels and returns on capital.
>
> Not only will improving ESG risk management benefit the bottom line, the strategic shift towards responsible finance will also unlock new opportunities for Islamic banking to differentiate itself from peers and unlock new business opportunities in the post-COVID environment.[25]

Sustainability is strategy

As this chapter has described, Islamic finance is but one banking sector that is looking to unlock new opportunities in the field of ESG-focused

148 *Sustainable banking*

finance. Whether greenwashing or true blue, the outpouring of enthusiastic and loud support for a more just and equitable post-COVID-19 world will spur much faster growth in bank-based sustainable finance. Most important is the ongoing move to incorporate ESG into the core banking model. For example, *Euromoney* named HSBC the "world's best bank for sustainable finance in 2020," lauding its "commitment to developing partnerships and products that will bring finance at scale to create a more sustainable and resilient planet." HSBC was joint lead manager on the first COVID-19 bond issuance from Bank of China, Macau in early 2020, while continuing its efforts to drive the low-carbon transition; it financed the largest offshore wind deal to date in Taiwan and provided a green SLL to support the first food-grade-ready plastics recycling facility in Hong Kong.[26]

Let's all look forward to a future in which banks compete vigorously and fiercely to earn the title of "world's best bank for sustainable finance."

Notes

1 Project finance is not just the purview of banks; other sources of funding for these large projects include institutional investors and private placements. I've included it in the banking chapter because it played such a meaningful role in awakening banks to the universe of sustainable finance.
2 Beckers, F. & Stegemann, U. (November 1, 2013). A risk-management approach to a successful infrastructure project. *McKinsey*. Retrieved from: www.mckinsey.com/industries/capital-projects-and-infrastructure/our-insights/a-risk-management-approach-to-a-successful-infrastructure-project.
3 Esty, B.C. & Ferman, C. "Chad-Cameroon Petroleum Development and Pipeline Project (A) and (B)," Harvard Business School Case #202010, October 2001; revised March 2006. Retrieved from: www.hbs.edu/faculty/Pages/item.aspx?num=28573.
4 . Le Houérou, P. (September 18, 2018). Opinion: The equator principles just turned 15, we should celebrate their impact. *Devex*. Retrieved from: www.devex.com/news/opinion-the-equator-principles-just-turned-15-we-should-celebrate-their-impact-93435.
5 Pacific Environment. (2007, April 26). ABN AMRO Financing for Sakhalin II poses huge risk for potential buyers. *BankTrack*. Retrieved from: www.banktrack.org/article/abn_amro_financing_for_sakhalin_ii_poses_huge_risk_for_potential_buyers#_.
6 Market Forces. (October 11, 2018). Unprincipled: Banks Violate Equator Principles in Financing Vietnamese Coal-Fired Power Stations. Retrieved from: www.marketforces.org.au/wp-content/uploads/2018/10/EP-report.pdf.
7 The Equator Principles Association. (2020). The Equator Principles. Retrieved from: https://equator-principles.com/about/.

8 Poh, J. (March 6, 2019). Banks can't ignore the $23T market for doing good. *Bloomberg*. Retrieved from: www.bloomberg.com/news/articles/2019-03-06/banks-can-t-afford-to-ignore-the-23-trillion-market-for-doing-good.
9 Gledhill, A. (April 20, 2020). Deutsche Bank forms sustainable finance team for capital markets. *Bloomberg*. Retrieved from: www.bloomberg.com/news/articles/2020-04-20/deutsche-bank-forms-sustainable-finance-team-for-capital-markets.
10 Poh, op. cit.
11 Ibid.
12 Hrushka, A. (September 4, 2019) "'Responsible' loans jump 40% as banks take green, social stances." *Banking Dive*. Retrieved from: www.bankingdive.com/news/responsible-loans-jump-40-as-banks-take-green-social-stances/562227/.
13 Laidlaw, J. (October 8, 2019). Lenders must set clear ESG targets under new UN responsible banking framework. *S&P Global*. Retrieved from: www.spglobal.com/marketintelligence/en/newsinsights/trending/ogTMPV1VWGymqVfNOd4OQw2.
14 Hrushka, op. cit.
15 Poh, op. cit.
16 Clouse, C.J. (March 6, 2019). ESG loans broaden access to sustainability-linked financing. *GreenBiz*. Retrieved from: www.greenbiz.com/article/esg-loans-broaden-access-sustainability-linked-financing.
17 Ibid.
18 Ibid.
19 Poh, op. cit.
20 Ibid.
21 Ibid.
22 Ibid.
23 Poh, J. (November 15, 2019). Banks struggle to value good behavior. *Bloomberg*. Retrieved from: www.bloomberg.com/news/articles/2019-11-15/esg-borrowers-want-credit-for-targets-lenders-struggle-to-value.
24 Kim, B-e. (May 20, 2020). "COVID-19 will underline corporate social behavior: Moody's." *Korea Times*. Retrieved from: www.koreatimes.co.kr/www/nation/2020/05/113_289859.html.
25 Brown, S. (June 5, 2020). "How COVID-19 will reshape Islamic finance markets." *The Jakarta Post*. Retrieved from: www.thejakartapost.com/academia/2020/06/05/how-covid-19-will-reshape-islamic-finance-markets.html.
"World's Best Bank for Sustainable Finance 2020: HSBC." *Euromoney*. September 10, 2020.
26 Ibid.

9 Gender-smart investing
Are women the silver bullet?

Pre-pandemic, the development of innovative financial instruments to transform women's lives included groundbreaking initiatives from microfinance to gender lens investing to women's impact bonds. While these approaches vary in their methodology, metrics, and outcomes, they share a common commitment to investing in women, as well as the dual goals of improving women's lives and, through empowered women, improving economic and social development for all.

Most financial instruments that focus on women are focused specifically and narrowly on women's access to credit—or lack thereof—and on the development of women entrepreneurs and women-owned businesses. This approach, which is exemplified by the microfinance industry, is limited in its impact. Beyond microfinance and supporting women entrepreneurs, gender-lens investing involves creating investable financial products across different asset classes that aim to support companies and other institutions seeking to help women advance. Gender-lens investing offers the potential for truly transformational, rather than transactional, progress toward women's empowerment as well as economic and social progress.

COVID-19 hits women

The devastation wrought by COVID-19 in 2020–2021 highlights both the gender-differentiated impact of bad times like the pandemic, and the opportunity to "build back better" by focusing on the empowerment of women.

Indeed, the UN strongly recommends putting "gender equality at the center of response efforts" to the pandemic in order to avoid throwing sustainable development badly off track and to achieve the goal of building back better. The UN Secretary-General affirms:

Central to [recovery] efforts is the need to advance gender equality, address upsurges in gender-based violence, and target women in all aspects of economic recovery and stimulus plans. This will mitigate the disproportionate impacts of the pandemic on women, and is also one of the surest avenues to sustainable, rapid, and inclusive recovery for all.[1]

In many parts of the developing world, of course, gender inequality was relatively high pre-pandemic, and this has only been worsened by the COVID-19 shock. The UN underlines this with a number of critical arguments:

- Women constitute 70% of the workforce in the health and social sectors globally, so take a disproportionate amount of the risk of catching COVID-19 during the pandemic.
- The share of unpaid care and domestic work, already a disproportionate burden on women, skyrocketed due to school closures that kept hundreds of millions of children at home during the height of the pandemic.
- Women are unequally burdened with the care of elderly relatives who are more at risk of developing COVID-19-related complications.
- The crisis also has a disproportionately negative economic impact on women, who make up the majority of part-time and informal workers, generally earning lower pay.
- Since women work overwhelmingly in the informal sector, often operating in pandemic-inaccessible spaces (people's homes, public markets) and enjoying little to no access to government support, they are much more likely to be newly impoverished than men.
- Women perform markedly more unpaid labor than men in almost every country in the world.
- Women migrant workers are often nurses and domestic workers, who face higher risks of wage loss and unemployment, and limited access to health care and social protection.
- Recent evidence points to higher rates of domestic violence during the pandemic.
- According to McKinsey, women's jobs are 1.8 times more vulnerable to the crisis than men's jobs. Women also experience higher rates of workplace discrimination as employers may see women who are struggling with care obligations as less competitive and committed than male workers.
- UN Women has found that fewer women than men in some countries are receiving necessary information to deal with COVID-19,

partly because of differences in cellphone ownership, access to education and the Internet; this is especially problematic since women play a critical role in family hygiene and care.
- There is also a disproportionate impact on women's mental and emotional health, and greater challenges for women in accessing medical care.

While COVID-19 mortality is greater among men, it is clear that the socioeconomic impact of the pandemic, like that of most disasters, falls much more heavily on women than on men. This impact is even worse for women in minority and lower-income groups. An avalanche of unpaid care work is falling on the shoulders of women, such as cooking, cleaning, and caring for children and sick relatives. With children at home instead of school, with men at home instead of work, and with many sick people at home instead of hospitals, there is much more unpaid care work to be done—so the distribution is becoming more lopsided, not less.

Taking action now to advance gender equality could add $13 trillion to global GDP by 2030 compared to a gender-regressive scenario, according to McKinsey.

Innovative finance for women

Pre-pandemic, the development of innovative financial instruments to transform women's lives has included groundbreaking initiatives from microfinance to gender lens investing to women's impact bonds. While these approaches vary in their methodology, metrics, and outcomes, they share a common commitment to investing in women, as well as the dual goals of improving women's lives and, through empowered women, improving economic and social development for all.

Most financial instruments that focus on women are focused specifically and narrowly on women's access to credit—or lack thereof—and on the development of women entrepreneurs and women-owned businesses. They address these barriers to women's ability to found and scale business enterprises:

- Limited access to critical assets/services, translating into inability to scale businesses;
- Lack of knowledge and skills, compromising women's earning capacity and job mobility;
- Poor access to credit and finance, resulting in vulnerability to economic shocks;

- Absence of market linkages, containing women in the informal workforce; and
- Inefficient use of natural capital, keeping women trapped in "subsistence" livelihoods.[2]

A few statistics tell an unsettling tale: In Latin America alone, experts estimate the credit gap for women-led small- to medium-sized enterprises (SMEs) at $85 billion, while a joint IFC/McKinsey study puts the worldwide gap between the financing that women need to start and grow businesses, and what they actually receive, at up to $320 billion.[3] In developing economies, women are 20% less likely than men to have a bank account, and 17% less likely to have borrowed formally in the past year. Even if women can gain access to the banking system, lack of financial education and decision-making authority in patriarchal societies can prevent women from achieving financial success. The World Bank concludes, "On virtually every global measure, women are more economically excluded than men."[4]

Thus it is not surprising that women-focused financial innovations have largely centered on improving women's access to credit, and helping them to become successful entrepreneurs. The open question, then, is whether these innovations have proven to be truly transformational, or merely new and shiny. Is support for women entrepreneurs the most efficient and effective use of capital? Does it achieve the scale and scope necessary to become truly transformative? What more is needed?

A multiplier effect: The business case for investing in women

Why invest in women? Why develop innovative financial instruments and techniques to improve outcomes for women?

The most common argument is based upon the well-documented truth that investing in women can be a silver bullet to catalyze broader development within a family, community, region, and society.

Indeed, the emphasis on women as drivers of broader economic and social advancement largely eclipses the moral argument that providing equal education and opportunity to half the world's population is, quite simply, the right thing to do. Women's empowerment advocates seem to shy away from this values-based argument, relying instead on the "business case" for investing in women.

A joint statement from the OECD, Vital Voices, and UN Women puts forward this business case: "Financing gender equality should be seen as an investment in the future," not an expenditure,[5] as empowering women yields a high return on investment. Since women control the bulk of household spending decisions, are more loyal customers, and are more likely to take advantage of cross-selling opportunities than men, they are valuable clients.

This argument further develops the business case for advancing women's economic power as a means of unlocking growth, elevating a brand, and driving customer loyalty. A report from Veris Wealth Partners underlines this point:

> This research keeps corroborating the fact that, if we wish to create better companies and communities, it is a *requirement* that the flow of wealth shift toward lifting women and girls from poverty while also reducing gaps in women's leadership and financial status.[6]

Beyond the business case, as the above statement demonstrates, the other oft-cited argument is the broader social gains that stem from investing in women. This has been dubbed the multiplier effect, since women are known to spend more of their money on food, health care, home improvement, and schooling for children than men do.

Moreover, the UN estimates that failure to achieve the Millennium Development Goals target for gender equality and empowerment of women could reduce per capita income growth rates by 0.1–0.3 percentage points worldwide. "Research shows that almost any investment we make in women and girls will have multiplier effects on the Millennium Development Goals," a report concludes.[7]

Creating women entrepreneurs

An offshoot of the business case argument is the equally oft-cited goal of creating more women entrepreneurs and women-owned businesses. Women-owned businesses (WOBs) are expected to perform better than male-dominated businesses, so will automatically produce greater community benefits.

Sometimes, though, it seems that creating women entrepreneurs is simply a goal in and of itself, rather than a path to a larger goal. The literature almost assumes that every woman has the will and ability to run her own business—all she needs is the right opportunity. (Does that pass our sniff test?) Also, measuring progress toward creating more WOBs is relatively simple. So there is a strong institutional bias in favor of directing women-focused finance toward entrepreneurship.

The focus on WOB is based, again, on a business case: The fact that women entrepreneurs in developing countries are a powerful source of economic growth and opportunity. About one-third of all SMEs in emerging markets are owned by women, but they face a daunting credit gap. (The needs are greatest in sub-Saharan Africa and East Asia.) And yet, women-led SMEs default on payments 54% less than men; despite investing 50% less than male entrepreneurs, female entrepreneurs make about 20% more revenue.

What is an empowered woman?

The foregoing comments should demonstrate that as more and more organizations commit themselves to supporting women's empowerment, there is less and less clarity about what that really means. Does it refer to the number of women-owned businesses? Women politicians? Women head of households? Kabeer defines empowerment as "the expansion in people's ability to make strategic life choices in a context where this ability was previously denied to them."[8] This is helpful as a broad guideline, but still fails to provide an adequate view of what it means to empower women. The lack of clarity is meaningful, as it perhaps contributes to the narrow view of defining empowered women as business owners that pervades this entire sector.

Innovative finance for women: Microfinance

Remember Sufiya Begum from Chapter 5. Sufiya's tale is a metaphor for the debate over microfinance that rages today—for all the volume of research and writing on the topic, for all the millions upon millions of dollars lent and repaid, nobody really knows with any certainty what the global impact of microfinance has been on women, or is likely to be.

Microfinance—and specifically, microlending—was the first and remains the most visible example of wide-scale investment in women in developing countries. There is no doubt that microfinance was truly innovative; the notion that banks could lend small amounts of money to poor, unbanked women—and make money doing so!—was so revolutionary as to be laughable when the industry was born. More than that, Yunus and others expected microfinance to drive a breathtaking, worldwide transformation for both women and societies (remember that Mohammed Yunus hoped to relegate poverty to museums by 2030).

Obviously, that goal is unlikely to be met. But, four decades into the microfinance revolution, has microfinance transformed the lives of women and, through them, transformed societies? While Chapter 5 explored the role of microfinance in addressing poverty, here we will think about microfinance and women.

Does Microfinance Empower Women?

Juan Somavia, ILO Director–General: "Microcredit plays a critical role in empowering women, helps deliver newfound respect, independence, and participation for women in their communities and in their households."[9]

Microcredit Summit Campaign Report, 2000: "Microcredit is about much more than access to money. It is about women gaining control over the means to make a living. It is about women lifting themselves out of poverty and vulnerability. It is about women achieving economic and political empowerment within their homes, their villages, their countries."[10]

ILO Report: "Microfinance helps empower women from poor households…Microfinance services lead to women's empowerment by positively influencing women's decision-making power and enhancing their overall socioeconomic status…microfinance has the potential to make a significant contribution to gender equality and promote sustainable livelihoods and better working conditions for women."[11]

Microfinance begins and ends with women. The notion of bettering women's lives and generating broader social benefits through women, is one of the basic tenets of microfinance. Some 70% of the world's poor are female, but women are almost always at a disadvantage when seeking access to credit and other financial services. Commercial banks traditionally focus on men and formal businesses, sidelining women who make up a large and growing segment of the informal economy.

As Chapter 5 demonstrated, microfinance completely upends this tradition. From its beginnings in South Asia and Latin America in the 1970s, microfinance has targeted women borrowers; at most microfinance institutions (MFIs), women comprise 85%–100% of the clientele. Over the past few decades, donor governments, agencies, and development practitioners have lauded microfinance as a strategy capable of empowering women – and through them, society.

The actual outcome of nearly five decades of microfinance with regard to women's empowerment, however, is far from clear. The first challenge, of course, is how to identify and measure so nebulous a goal as "women's empowerment." Researchers have sought to capture outcomes by looking at various dimensions, such as microfinance's impact on women's decision-making power, self-confidence, status at home, involvement in the community, political empowerment, and rights. Others weigh family relationships and the incidence of domestic violence.

The evidence, discouragingly, is mixed. Studies show that microfinance does indeed have a positive impact on some of these dimensions of women's empowerment. But there is also evidence that microfinance throws up some new challenges for women; that it can be ineffective in achieving the above goals; and that its overall potential for improving women's lives is limited.

Moreover, common sense suggests that simply handing money to women with no experience of handling it, and giving them access to financial resources, creates a new set of challenges and burdens for the borrowers. It is increasingly clear that access to small amounts of money is not enough. In fact, there are multiple reasons as to why microfinance is proving an uncertain path to women's empowerment:

Patriarchy is a powerful constraint

Most poor women still function within a highly patriarchal society. This culture constrains women's power to bargain and make decisions on economic issues within the household, as well as their ability to control the money borrowed and build a network to enhance their chances of business success.

As noted in Chapter 5, Lamia Karim concurs that while women are the official borrowers from MFIs, men often have use of the money. According to her research, some 95% of women borrowers hand over the proceeds of their loans to husbands or other males. Only if a woman is a widow or has a sick or weak husband, Karim believes, does the woman actually retain control over her money.

Karim bolsters this argument with an anecdote:

> An elderly widow told me that on the day she was returning home from the Grameen Bank with her loan, her nephew demanded that she hand it over to him. He said, "Aunt, I know that you received a loan from the Grameen Bank today. I have need of money for my business, and as my aunt, it is your duty to give it to me." She explained that as a widow and as an aunt, it was her familial obligation to help her nephew. If she disagreed, the family would pressure her to relent.[12]

Karim is not alone in her conclusions; groundbreaking research supported by the World Bank in Pakistan found that more than two-thirds of women microfinance borrowers required a male relative's permission in order to qualify for any kind of loan. Another study showed that 40%–70% of the microfinance loans disbursed to women were used by their husbands, and that household tensions increased following the first microfinance borrowing.

Even when they use the funds for their own purposes, women's choice of activities and their ability to increase incomes are seriously constrained by gender barriers. Another researcher concluded that [women's] "empowerment cannot be assumed to be an automatic outcome of microfinance programs, whether designed for financial sustainability or poverty targeting."[13]

Microfinance borrowing can exploit and undermine women

In the microfinance world, women alone bear the responsibility for repaying the loans—although the benefits of the loan often accrue to men and other household members. This causes higher levels of stress, especially since women (predictably) still bear full responsibility for their household chores regardless of their business-related tasks. As a result, microfinance loans often fail to pull women out of poverty; in fact, the women frequently borrow from other sources to pay back the initial loans, leading to a vicious cycle of rising indebtedness. This reflects, in part, the dangers of bringing poor and vulnerable women into the financial marketplace without adequate safeguards and protections.

Karim underlines the above point by noting that the typically 95%-plus repayment rates cited by MFIs fail to distinguish between loans that are willingly repaid, and those that are coercively repaid. She argues that the economic shaming of women is a form of quasi-collateral; when loan defaults occur, the MFI uses women's groups to shame the defaulter and her family into repayment at any cost. In communities where rural life is based on women's honor, the power of this economic shaming cannot be underestimated.[14]

Is microfinance effective in reducing poverty among women?

How effective is microfinance in achieving its primary objective of poverty reduction for women? There is still a mainstream assumption among development circles that microfinance does indeed reduce poverty, improve women's socioeconomic status, and improve social indicators such as health and education. As one commentator noted, "optimism about the implicit empowerment potential of credit and savings pervades most donor states on microfinance."[15]

But is this optimism justified? A recent issue of the prestigious *American Economic Journal: Applied Economics* kicked off a firestorm by publishing a set of independent studies that found that microlending usually fails to raise incomes. The report combined randomized control trials—the gold standard for social science research—and was backed by scholars at major international universities. It put together six studies that each independently tried to measure how the lives of microloan recipients had changed in countries such as Mexico, Mongolia, and India between 2003 and 2012. Although microloans did give borrowers better access to credit, the studies found no evidence of higher incomes or consumption. Perhaps most discouraging, they also found no evidence of more empowered women or better-educated children. One even suggested that the microloans may have encouraged families to remove children from school in order to work.

"Bringing these together really has shifted the conversation," said Timothy Ogden, managing director of the Financial Access Initiative, a New York University research center. "There are a lot of people that were unaware" that microfinance fails to lift many people out of poverty.

"This is kind of a defining moment," Abhijit Banerjee, an economics professor at the Massachusetts Institute of Technology who co-wrote one of the studies, said at a World Bank conference. "The big question that we would like to answer is what is the right product [for the poor] to have? What is missing?"[16]

Looking forward: Microfinance, not microlending

While these and other studies demonstrate that *microlending* is an uneven and often ineffective tool for improving the lot of women, they also point the way to more effective future strategies.

Women's World Banking (WWB), a leading organization that works closely with a global network of MFIs to create new credit, savings, and insurance products specifically designed for women, is already pointing to the future in this regard. A senior official of WWB, tellingly, said that "we don't talk about microfinance much anymore—the issues are so much more now." For example, WWB is working with a large commercial bank in Nigeria to provide banking services for low-income women who run open-air stalls and cannot take the time to wait in line at a branch. The goal is to "bring the bank to them," and the program has been so successful that the bank is investing millions more in what it now sees as a growth opportunity.

Microinsurance also has "tremendous potential," according to WWB, which is developing "a broad suite of insurance products."[17] Risk management for the poor, including insurance and savings services to safeguard people against death, illness, natural disasters, poor crops, and other setbacks, is the new, and infinitely more promising, frontier for MFIs.

Beyond microfinance: Supporting women entrepreneurs

As noted above, the primary goal of innovative finance for women in the past five decades has been to close the gap in women's access to finance, both in the developed and developing worlds. Microfinance is the most widespread and obvious manifestation of this approach, and has partly compensated for women's poor access to finance—but microfinance is not enough. In particular, women often are unable to scale up from microfinance to the larger individual or business loans needed to support entrepreneurship. A senior IFC official noted in a recent interview that "because microfinance is so prevalent, there is a gaping hole in financial services for slightly larger women-owned enterprises."[18]

Once again, advocates rely heavily on the "business case" to justify supporting women entrepreneurs, pointing out that many of the sectors with the greatest promise of economic growth in poor countries rely heavily on women. But while there are about 8–10 million formal women-owned SMEs in developing countries (around 35% of all SMEs), the average growth rate of women-owned businesses is significantly lower than for men-owned businesses. The usual suspects can be lined up to explain this difference:

- Regulatory issues;
- Lack of access to finance;
- Relatively low rates of business education or work experience;
- Risk aversion;
- Tendency of women-owned businesses to cluster in low-growth sectors;
- Burden of household management.

Not only are women entrepreneurs less likely to take out a loan, but terms of borrowing tend to be more onerous. Many country studies indicate that women entrepreneurs are more likely to face higher interest rates, be required to provide higher levels of collateral, and have shorter-term loans. Nonfinancial barriers also play a role; in many countries, for example, women may not enter into contracts in their own name or control property within marriage.[19]

Innovative finance is tackling these barriers in various ways. In spring 2014, for example, Bank of America announced that it would invest $10 million in Calvert Foundation for loans to support women in developing countries in Latin America, Asia, Africa, and Eastern Europe. The funds would be used to connect women-led SMEs with finance, and provide access to services and products for women.

Goldman Sachs and 10,000 women

In 2007, investment banking behemoth Goldman Sachs committed $100 million to its 10,000 Women initiative based, in part, on research demonstrating the high return on investment in women due to the multiplier effect of empowered women. The program, which delivers business education and other skills training in partnership with local institutions, met its goal of reaching 10,000 women in 2015 and has renewed its commitment. This is a philanthropic program, however, not a form of innovative finance. And it is focused on developing women entrepreneurs, which is where the bank believes it can have the greatest impact.

> **Meet the women: *10,000 women***
>
> Hyderabad, India: Varsha has two brands, one focusing on customized fashion design and the other called "Jus Blouses," which creates handcrafted blouses accompanied by saris. She says that:
>
>> 10,000 Women has taught me to implement new ideas quickly, to get ahead of competitors, to streamline my finances, and to make decisions that will quickly increase the profitability of my firm. Since graduating from 10,000 Women, I have increased my revenue by 200% and have hired 24 new employees. I have grown my business by entering a nice market and starting a new brand…I have also streamlined my business and developed a new strategy.
>
> Going forward, Varsha plans to open two new branches and to franchise her brand in other cities.
>
> Cairo, Egypt: When Nora took over running her late husband's printing and supply business following his death, she had to "learn the printing business from the bottom up. I was unaware of the financial problems the business was facing when I first took over and I had to work with suppliers and debtors to rebuild confidence in the business"—all while raising her two sons as well. Matters

only worsened after the Egyptian revolution in 2011, as clients were unable to pay bills and currency devaluation raised costs. Nora says that 10,000 Women gave her confidence, taught her to understand the business's finances, and identify new markets, which has been especially valuable in the economic downturn. "Also," she adds, "many 10,000 Women graduates are now my clients."

Belo Horizonte, Brazil: When Rosana started a business in 2002 that designs, manufactures, and sells stainless steel and Corian products, she had minimal business skills. She was the youngest of nine children, from a poor rural area whose father was an illiterate farmworker. "I joined 10,000 Women hoping to grow my business and increase my management skills," she explains. "Prior to the program, I managed through intuition alone." Since graduating from 10,000 Women, Rosana decided to diversify her product line, improved her financial and marketing management, and increased her workforce. The program also "increased my desire to give back to my family and my community…My employees are all from poor communities near my manufacturing facility," and she provides them with breakfast and lunch every day. "My dream," she concludes, "is to start a school in the area."

Source: www.goldmansachs.com/citizenship/10000women/meet-the-women-profiles/

IFC: Banking on women

The World Bank's International Finance Corporation (FC) launched its Banking on Women (BOW) program in 2010 to provide funds for on-lending to women entrepreneurs, and for advisory services to help commercial bankers serve women clientele in developing countries. IFC is the private sector arm of the World Bank, and its mission is to invest in private sector companies to spur private sector development.

Accordingly, BOW invests in banks on a commercial basis. All investments are intended to be profitable, as well as socially beneficial—a perfect example of impact investing at its best. "We expect a market rate of return on our investments," says a senior official. And the financial institutions that BOW invests in see this as a market opportunity, not an example of corporate social responsibility or charity—"this is the key differentiating factor, because this is sustainable," the official concludes.[20]

Gender-smart investing 163

In a sense, then, BOW and other programs to finance women entrepreneurs are a response to market failure—the failure of mainstream financial institutions to recognize the market opportunity of women. The target population of the BOW program is women-owned small to medium enterprises, possibly including women who have "graduated" from microfinance. BOW's guiding principle is that it provides market-level funding where markets have failed to provide this funding on their own.

BOW took another step toward innovative finance with the 2013 launch of a $165 million "women's bonds" program, the first debt sale by the World Bank specifically aimed at raising money for businesses owned or run by women in emerging markets. The IFC issued the five-year, triple-A rated bond to Japanese investors, and it was distributed by Daiwa Securities. (According to the IFC, Japanese retail and institutional investors—especially women investors—are particularly well-disposed toward innovative, low-risk financial instruments focused on social issues.) The funds will be used for local banks and financial intermediaries in developing countries, which are required to on-lend to businesses in which women are majority owners, or own at least one-fifth of the company and hold senior leadership positions.

BOW's website explains:

> [T]he program has developed a track record which includes 16 investment projects, ranging from long term loans to instruments such as risk sharing facilities that help share the risk financial institutions undertake when assuming greater exposure in new or riskier markets, amounting to almost US$700 million in Africa, Latin America and the Caribbean, East Asia and the Pacific, and East and Central Europe. In addition, IFC issued the first-ever Banking on Women Bond in 2013 that raised US$165 million to be invested in projects that will support women entrepreneurs in developing countries.[21]

IFC + Goldman Sachs

In 2014, the IFC joined forces with Goldman Sachs to create the "first-ever global finance facility dedicated exclusively to women-owned SMEs that will enable approximately 100,000 women to access capital." The Women Entrepreneurs Opportunity Facility will be seeded by Goldman and IFC, and seeks to raise up to $600 million in capital from other public and private co-investors.

Goldman's seed capital funding of about $50 million is in the form of a philanthropic donation through its Foundation, which will fund capacity building support for banks and women borrowers.[22] That makes this facility an example of "blended finance," in which seed funding comes from philanthropic rather than investment capital. Founders of this facility hope to crowd in private investment alongside their seed capital. Goldman officials explain that the goal is to get money to women entrepreneurs and to illustrate the bankability of them as a market. One official commented that $600 million obviously will not solve a $300 billion credit gap—but the demonstration effect is key given Goldman's reputation.

IDB and other institutions

Similarly, in 2012 the Multilateral Investment Facility (MIF) of the Inter-American Development Bank (IDB) launched the Women's Economic Empowerment Initiative (WEempower), which targets women entrepreneurs in Latin America and the Caribbean. The initiative deploys two types of tools to maximize IDB support for women-led SMEs:

- Loans, partial credit guarantees, or risk-sharing mechanisms to encourage lending by local banks in this sector;
- Technical assistance for banks that want to target women-led small and medium enterprises as a profitable sector.

Measuring impact or counting heads?

Other organizations—bilateral, multilateral, and NGOs—have launched similar programs to support women's entrepreneurship in developing countries. These range from very small and local to larger and multi-country initiatives. All share the rather narrow vision, however, of empowering women through entrepreneurship, and all are largely in the form of philanthropic rather than commercial capital.

Perhaps most striking, all lack a rigorous approach to impact measurement. Despite pouring billions of dollars into financial services for women, and particularly women entrepreneurs, no one really knows what impact this has on women, families, and their communities.

One BOW official commented, "impact measurement and feedback loops are the most important and trickiest part of our work."

So they resort to counting. BOW regularly measures indices for the banks in which they invest, such as the increase in a bank's portfolio of financial services to women entrepreneurs; number of loans and customers within that portfolio; level of nonperforming loans to women and their companies; and overall health of the financial institution.

Bank officials are really struggling, though, with the question of how to understand the holistic impact of women's improved access to finance. Does this really produce more growth? More employment? More financial stability? And this is just the business side of it; the broader social impact is an even bigger step. If a woman is a successful business owner, are her children in school more? Eating better? Enjoying better health? These questions are deeply interesting but also deeply difficult. "The more and more we try to measure them, the more and more those measurements look like estimates," says the bank official.[23]

Joy Anderson and Suzanne Biegel worry a great deal about this substitution of "counting" for more sophisticated and challenging analysis. As they write:

> Often, "thinking about gender" just means counting women and girls. We ask: How many women on a board, how many female entrepreneurs, how many girls in the school? But counting only gets you so far. Counting only lets you operate in whole numbers, rather than more nuanced calculations. We need to do more sophisticated math. Gender is a dynamic concept that defines norms, behaviors, identities and how those are (or are not) valued in a culture. Gender analysis, like financial analysis, assesses how value is constructed and assigned.[24]

Thus, Anderson suggests moving beyond just counting women-led businesses to a broader, more sophisticated approach that involves aligning the value of gender with the right asset class. For example, she asks, which parties in the financial system value reducing public violence against women? The most likely answer is the transportation and hospitality industries; they have the most to lose if public violence against women spikes (see: India). Accordingly, those industries have a strong financial incentive to support anti-violence initiatives, which are also, of course, of great benefit to women and society.[25]

Gender-lens investing

Moving on from microfinance and entrepreneurship, in the past decade or so women's advocates have advanced the notion of gender-lens investing (GLI)—an approach that espouses the same goals as microfinance, but deploys different tools. Simply, GLI involves creating investable financial products across different asset classes that aim to support companies and other institutions seeking to help women advance. In addition to standard financial metrics, these investment managers approach the investment process with a gender lens as well.[26]

A 2013 paper by Veris Wealth Partners sets out the business case for investing with a gender lens, arguing that investment in companies or organizations that seek to advance women can be a smart business strategy. "Using a gender lens is transformational," the authors argue, "perhaps as much so for the investors as for the recipients of their capital." The article suggests that the gender lens approach gives investors the opportunity to maximize financial gains when companies actively promote women as managers and board members; and to catalyze social gains when women gain access to education, jobs, and capital.[27] This is, of course, a variation on the themes discussed at the beginning of this chapter—investing in women is good for business, and for society.

The concept was further advanced with the Fall 2014 edition of the *Stanford Social Innovation Review*, in which authors Sarah Kaplan and Jackie VanderBrug wrote:

> A movement focusing on the nexus of gender and investment is emerging. This movement, which encourages the use of capital to deliver financial returns and improve the lives of women and girls and their communities, is known as "investing with a gender lens."[28]

GLI, of course, is not limited to the developing world; indeed, substantial evidence indicates that scarce capital for women is not confined to developing countries. An HBS study shows that US venture capitalists far prefer investing in men (and attractive men, at that). "Women-led businesses probably only receive between 5% and 10% of all the VC that's allocated to startups in their very earliest growth phases," said one researcher[29].

So much for meritocracy!

In the developing world, these barriers are even more daunting when combined with poorer levels of education, health, political status, and decision-making ability for women. This has led to a growing number of women-centered impact investment initiatives in the developing world under the umbrella of GLI. GLI encourages better gender-based outcomes by increasing access to finance and other resources for women-run enterprises; encourages organizational policies and practices that advance gender equality; and/or provides products or services for women and girls. As said by a USAID official, "The field of GLI believes in the power of investments to generate large-scale social and financial returns when gender analysis is integrated into financial analysis and decision-making."[30]

GLI can include innovative financial instruments, or a re-direction of existing financial instruments. Examples include mutual funds that promote women in leadership positions or offer loans and other financial services to MFIs, women's bonds, and sector-based funds such as Root Capital's Women in Agriculture initiative.

Examples of GLI: Equities, bonds, and notes

In this category, a sampling of GLI initiatives includes:

- Pax Elevate Global Women's Index Fund, which invests in companies that are committed to gender diversity on Boards and in management, and that advance programs to elevate women in the workplace;
- US Trust Women and Girls Equity Strategy, which allows investors to apply a gender lens to US equity and fixed income investment;
- Morgan Stanley Parity Portfolio, a separately managed account for high net worth individuals (HNWIs) and institutional investors that focuses on increasing female Board representation; and
- Barclays Women in Leadership Total Return Index, which is comprised of companies with a female CEO, or companies where women make up at least one-fourth of the Board.

Examples of GLI: Calvert WIN-WIN Initiative

Beginning with a pilot in 2012, Calvert created the Women Investing in Women Initiative (WIN-WIN). The first fund directed 75% of its investments to women in the US and 25% in developing countries, while the second fund (in September 2014) committed to lend an additional $20 million to organizations that develop and distribute clean energy technology. This commitment reflects the danger to women's health and advancement posed by indoor air pollution in the developing world. Open-fire cooking, perilous journeys to collect firewood, and the lack of electricity—all of which have an outsized impact on women—can be mitigated through providing access to clean cookstoves, solar lighting, and other clean energy products.

Examples of GLI: Women's Livelihood Bond (WLB)

Singapore-based Impact Investment Exchange (IIX) issued in mid-2020 its third Women's Livelihood Bond (WLB3), a series of gender-linked bonds aimed at creating sustainable livelihoods for more than 3 million women in developing Asia. WLB3, specifically, will back enterprises in India, Indonesia, Cambodia, and the Philippines to support women in recovering from the economic effects of the pandemic.

While the WLB series is smallish—the total raised will be $150 million—it is also groundbreaking, as the first issuance was also the first impact investing instrument to be publicly listed, on the Singapore Exchange.

And bond proceeds go well beyond the usual (read: uninspired) theme of enabling women entrepreneurs. Indeed, beneficiaries of the bond include:

- Solshare Bangladesh, providing 19,000 households with access to electricity;
- ERC Eye Care India, providing nearly 100,000 patients (67% women) with eye surgery and treatment; and
- SAMIC Cambodia, providing underserved borrowers (80% women) with funds to build latrines and other water-related facilities in their homes to reduce the risk of disease.

Examples of GLI: Root capital Women in Agriculture Initiative

The Women in Agriculture Initiative (WAI) seeks to improve opportunities for women in agriculture by supporting small and growing businesses with access to credit and financial training, and by promoting gender-inclusive practices. In 2019 Root lent $21 million to gender-inclusive businesses, equal to 42% of total disbursements, and supported the incomes of 271,000 women farmers. The goal is to improve the economic potential of women in agriculture, from which most of the world's poor women derive the bulk of their income.

Women in agriculture snapshot: Musasa and Marie

Like many women [in Rwanda], Marie Bedabasingwa, now 60 years old, lost her husband and her eldest son in 1994. The reconstruction process after the genocide called on Rwandan women to play a greater role, and Marie and others were able to rebuild their farms and families through participation in coffee cooperatives like Musasa [Root Capital's first client in Africa].

Today, in addition to coffee, Marie raises rabbits and goats and grows bananas, beans, maize and sweet potatoes. But she's most delighted by her dairy cows. Marie received two free cows through Musasa by participating in agronomic trainings and being identified as a "lead farmer," meeting the cooperative's criteria for best on-farm

> practices...As Marie sells milk, she will earn additional income and contribute to boosting food security in the community...
> Marie reckons she'll be able to deliver 20 liters of milk per day per cow to Musasa's new chilling plant and, as a result, earn 150 to 200 Rwandan francs per liter, or roughly $10 a day. The extra income will help her continue to pay school fees for five children, including her granddaughter, whose parents—Marie's daughter and son-in-law—were both tragically killed during resurgence attacks across the Congolese border during the dark years of post-genocide instability.
>
> Source: Root Capital Women in Agriculture Initiative, Annual Report 2014

As Root points out, women "produce more than 50% of the world's food but enjoy significantly lower rates of property ownership than their male counterparts...women do 80% of farm work in sub-Saharan Africa but receive less than 10% of small farm credit available to smallholders."[31]

As in the case of microfinance and other women-focused financial initiatives, this too rests on the premise that empowered women will improve society. Tjada McKenna wrote recently in *The Guardian*:

> If we're going to end hunger in our lifetimes, we need to empower women. The statistics are well-known. Women make up half of the agricultural labour force in many developing countries, but barriers to credit, inputs and extension services, as well as land ownership and rights, limit their production.
>
> We already know that if women had equal access to productive resources, they could increase their yields and feed more hungry people in the world. And women are more likely to reinvest their income back into their families to improve education, nutrition and health. When women flourish, families and communities do too.[32]

While this is no doubt both compelling and valid, it is worrisome that development practitioners still feel the need to justify women-focused finance by espousing the "business case." It also underscores, once again, the focus on using finance to enable women to become producers and business owners/managers, rather than on other aspects of women's development.

Scope, scale, and impact: When does innovation become transformation?

As this chapter demonstrates, innovative financial techniques from microfinance to women's bonds have been developed and deployed in the last half-century in the name of women's empowerment. There is no doubt that many of these techniques represent financial innovation, and microfinance has even achieved significant scale. But innovation for innovation's sake is not particularly useful. The more important question remains: Have these innovations demonstrated the ability, or at least the potential, to be actually transformational in the lives of women and their broader community?

The long-term outcomes of the above initiatives in microfinance, entrepreneurship, and GLI are yet to be determined. However, they suffer from three fundamental weaknesses. The first is related to **scope:** They assume that supporting women entrepreneurs is critically important to women's empowerment, and thus worthy of the highest levels of attention.

The second weakness is related to **scale:** All of these initiatives, with the obvious exception of microfinance, suffer from a notable lack of scale. The global microfinance market is projected to reach $314 billion by 2024; by any standards, the industry has reached a size large enough to produce real impact. But even so, the global women's credit gap is still estimated at up to $320 billion. And apart from microfinance, it is difficult to see how financing initiatives in the tens (or even hundreds) of millions can address the problem. Thus far only microfinance has been able to scale up from innovative to widespread.

And the third question circles around **impact**, which is related to the first two. Even if an innovation reaches scale, like microfinance, how do we measure its impact? How do we ensure that this innovation is the best use of scarce financial and human resources?

As discussed above, despite its scale there is significant evidence that microfinance has not yet proven transformational, largely because of its emphasis on lending rather than savings and insurance. As for scope, this remains narrow. A Google search for "financing women's development," for instance, immediately zeroes in on supporting women-owned businesses; the newcomer could be excused for assuming that women-owned businesses are the only important path to women's development. These are some of the top ten Google hits on women's development:

- Women-owned businesses/US small business administration;
- Microfinance program-women's business development;

- Community capital development/helping women and minority entrepreneurs;
- Office of Women's Business Ownership;
- Strengthening access to finance for women-owned SMEs;
- Expanding women's access to financial services.

This institutional emphasis on directing innovative finance to women entrepreneurs, however, suffers from a lack of critical introspection, and diverts attention—and funding—away from other avenues. Directing the bulk of innovative women-focused finance to women entrepreneurs threatens to exclude women who lack the will and/or capacity to be enterprise managers. Further, this narrow focus diverts attention away from developing innovative financial techniques to improve women's life outcomes by other means, notably education.

As Jeff Skoll remarked at the Skoll World Forum in April 2015, "If there's a silver bullet to global development, it's girls' education." Funding women entrepreneurs is, to say the least, a rather indirect path to fostering girls' education.

Indeed, the UN Millennium Development Goals on women include a commitment to addressing:

> [U]nderlying structural constraints to achieving gender equality, with strong targets on ending all forms of discrimination against women, ending violence against women and girls, and harmful practices such as early, child and forced marriage, recognition of women's unpaid care work, and lack of access to sexual and reproductive health.

Nonetheless, innovative finance for women continues to focus tightly on credit and entrepreneurship—while persistent and wide funding gaps remain in priority areas such as education, maternal health, women's economic rights, and violence against women and girls. In these areas, funding remains largely limited to traditional grant funding, and financial innovations are virtually nonexistent.

In their thought-provoking article, Kaplan and VanderBrug suggest three ways in which gender-lens investing can improve financial and social welfare for women: By providing access to capital, promoting workplace equity, and creating products and services that improve the lives of women and children.[33] As this chapter suggests, though, innovative finance has largely focused on promoting women's access to capital. Very small sums of capital have been deployed, through GLI funds, to promote workplace equity. As for "products and services," once again most of this work has been carried out in the realm of financial services. The exception to this rule—investment in clean cookstoves—is fronted by the Global Alliance for Clean Cookstoves, which relies primarily on traditional donor government funding rather than innovative finance. And while significant amounts of capital have flowed into cookstove funding, outcomes with regard to actual impact on women have been discouraging.

The laser focus on financial access and services may stem from the widespread use of the "business case" argument to support investing in women. It is curious—and unsettling—that lifting women and girls from poverty is not in itself a strong enough argument for investing in women. Rather, the "business case" argument stresses the ability of empowered women to create better companies and communities. When women flourish, companies and communities do too.

It may also stem from the relative ease of focusing on financial inclusion. Banks are already set up, points out an IFC official, while financing access to education is much less straightforward and returns are lower and more difficult to define. In that sense, providing access to credit for women is the low-hanging fruit of women's development.

Finally, it reflects the difficulty of measurement—and, thus, the tendency to focus on what can be quantified with relative ease.

Thus, three key factors have, to date, severely constrained the transformational impact of innovative finance for women's development:

- Lack of scale, with the exception of microlending—which has itself fallen well short of its original goals;
- Lack of scope, reflecting the emphasis on the "business case" for investing in women and the resultant emphasis on fostering women's entrepreneurship; and
- Lack of hard evidence on impact.

Almost certainly, a more values-based argument would support increased flows of investment for other aspects of women's development than financial inclusion and entrepreneurship.

Take education, for example: At current rates of progress, according to UNICEF, girls from the poorest households in sub-Saharan Africa will not achieve universal lower-secondary school education until 2111, almost a century from now.[34]

Or women's health: MDG5—which relates to reducing maternal deaths and achieving universal access to reproductive health—has not made sufficient progress and is the most underfunded of all the health MDGs. Some 220 million women in developing countries cannot get modern contraceptives; 800 women die each day because of lack of access to quality care in childbirth; and pregnancy and childbirth-related deaths are one of the leading causes of death for teenage girls.

And violence against women and girls "is a global health pandemic," which has worsened along with the COVID-19 pandemic.

> One in three girls in developing countries will be married as a child bride – more than 25,000 daily. This is of particular concern as a girl under the age of 15 is five times more likely to die in childbirth than a woman in her twenties.

Violence against women brings high costs; one estimate of lost productivity from domestic violence puts the loss at 1.2%–2% of the gross domestic product (GDP) annually. Also, "the damaging effects of child, early and forced marriage are well documented. It harms health, halts education, destroys opportunity and enslaves young women in a life of poverty, and it limits the development of entire communities."[35]

There is clear agreement among leading institutions such as the G8 and UN Women on what can be done to stem the tide of violence: A judicious mixture of prevention, protection, prosecution, and provision of services to survivors. But this all takes money—and "initiatives to address gender-based violence are chronically underfunded."

It also takes a basic commitment to gender equality that goes far beyond counting the number of women-owned businesses. "The root cause of violence against women is gender inequality—an institutionalized belief that women are inferior to men,"[36] and that men will go unpunished for this particular crime.

One relatively inexpensive beacon of hope in this arena is mobile innovation. The field of mobile health has taken great leaps forward in recent years. Mobile technology, for example, enables pregnant women who lack access to health care providers to receive information on their phones. "From alleviating poverty to expanding educational opportunities to improving health, mobile technologies can help transform the lives of billions, and particularly the lives of women and girls."[37]

But education is the silver bullet. As Jeff Skoll says, "The fight to achieve global gender equality in education is one of the most incredible opportunities sitting in our laps right now." If all agree that girls' education is both a huge challenge and a shining opportunity, then there is an urgent need for innovative finance to develop the scope and scale needed to fund it. This is not just a call for more philanthropy to flow to this sector, which is not going to happen in today's constrained environment for governments, aid organizations, and philanthropies. (At present,

US-based foundations spend just 1% of their development resources on basic education in poor countries.)

In fact, there is plenty of potential funding available—in the form of trillions of investment dollars in the hands of investors with a demonstrated interest in achieving both financial and social value. If these impact investors choose to channel some of their wealth toward women's health or education, the sector could be awash with funds. The scarcity is not a lack of dollars; it is the lack of viable financial instruments to enable investors to invest their dollars in the social sector. Fixed-income instruments in this area are making progress—but these instruments can be complex (as Joy Anderson notes, "you tend to lose impact investors at the world 'complex'"), with uncertain risk/return profiles.

This leaves a gaping hole; the demand for real and transformative financial innovation in this area is massive. Where is the Muhammad Yunus or Bill Gates of girls' education? When will finance for women move beyond the narrow focus on entrepreneurship to enable progress in health, education, and real gender equality?

To paraphrase President George Bush, it's the vision thing.

Notes

1 Antonio Guterres. "Put women and girls at the center of efforts to recover from COVID-19." (April 9, 2020). United Nations. Retrieved from: www.un.org/en/un-coronavirus-communications-team/put-women-and-girls-centre-efforts-recover-covid-19.
2 http://asiaiix.com/commitment-womens-impact-bond/.
3 IFC Advisory Services. (2013). "Closing the Credit Gap for Formal and Informal Micro, Small, and Medium Enterprises." Retrieved from: www.ifc.org.
4 World Bank, "Expanding Women's Access to Financial Services," February 26, 2014. Retrieved from: www.worldbank.org/en/results/2013/04/01/banking-on-women-extending-womens-access-to-financial-services.
5 OECD, Vital Voices, and UN Women, Roundtable on Financing Gender Equality and Women's Empowerment Summary, October 14, 2014. Retrieved from: www.oecd.org.
6 Veris Wealth Partners, "Women, Wealth and Impact: Investing With A Gender Lens," November 2013. Retrieved from: www.veriswp.com.
7 MDG Achievement Fund (October 2013). "Gender Equality and Women's Empowerment." Retrieved from: http://mdgfund.org/sites/default/files/Gender%20Equality%20and%20Women's%20Empowerment%20-%20Development%20Results%20Report.pdf.
8 Naila Kabeer. (1999). "Resources, Agency, Achievements: Reflections on the Measurement of Women's Empowerment." University of Toronto, Retrieved from: www.utsc.utoronto.ca.

9 "Small change, Big changes: Women and Microfinance," International Labor Office, Geneva. Retrieved from www.ilo.org/wcmsp5/groups/public/@dgreports/@gender/documents/meetingdocument/wcms_091581.pdf.
10 Vani S. Kulkarni (2011). "Women's empowerment and microfinance: An Asian perspective study," International Fund for Agricultural Development. Retrieved from: www.ifad.org.
11 International Labor Office.
12 Lamia Karim (2011). *Microfinance and its Discontents: Women in Debt in Bangladesh*, University of Minnesota Press, p. xvi.
13 Linda Mayoux, "Micro-finance and the empowerment of women: A review of the key issues," International Labour Organization, p. 4.
14 Karim, p. xviii.
15 Mayoux, p. 3.
16 Eric Bellman (March 17, 2015). "Calls Grow for a New Microloans Model," The *Wall Street Journal*, Retrieved from: www.wsj.com/articles/calls-grow-for-a-new-microloans-model-1426627810?mod=e2tw.
17 Interview with senior Women's World Banking official in New York, April 2015.
18 Interview with senior official of IFC's Banking on Women initiative, April 2015.
19 "Strengthening Access to Finance for Women-Owned SMEs in Developing Countries," Global Partnership for Financial Inclusion, IFC, 2011.
20 Banking on Women interview.
21 IFC Banking on Women website. Retrieved from: www.ifc.org/wps/wcm/connect/Industry_EXT_Content/IFC_External_Corporate_Site/Industries/Financial+Markets/MSME+Finance/Banking+on+Women/.
22 "Goldman Sachs 10,000 Women, IFC to Raise Up To $600 Million to Support Women Entrepreneurs." Retrieved from: www.goldmansachs.com/citizenship/10000women/news-and-events/10000women-ifc.html.
23 Banking on Women interview.
24 Joy Anderson and Suzanne Biegel, "ReValue Gender: How to upgrade your due diligence with a gender lens (2.0)," 11/15/14, unpublished paper.
25 Interview with Joy Anderson, Criterion Institute, June 2015.
26 "Investing to Advance Women: A Guide for Individual and Institutional Investors," US Forum for Sustainable and Responsible Investment, USSIF Foundation, Washington, D.C.
27 Veris, p. 1.
28 Sarah Kaplan and Jackie VanderBrug (Fall 2014). "The rise of gender capitalism," *Stanford Social Innovation Review*.
29 "A New Bond Aims To Save Women's Lives in Developing Nations," *Forbes*, September 28, 2014. Retrieved from: www.forbes.com/sites/annefield/2014/09/28/a-new-bond-aims-to-transform-womens-lives/.
30 USAID Gender Lens Investing Activity. Retrieved from: www.usaid.gov/sites/default/files/documents/1861/Asia_Gender_Lens_Investing.pdf.
31 Root Capital Women in Agriculture Initiative website. Retrieved from: www.rootcapital.org/support-us/women-agriculture-initiative.

32 Tjada McKenna, "How can we empower women in agriculture to end hunger?" *The Guardian,* March 18, 2015. Retrieved from: www.theguardian.com.
33 Kaplan and VanderBurg.
34 Rick Gladstone, "Unicef report describes grim trends for the poorest," *The New York Times,* June 22, 2015. Retrieved from: www.nytimes.com/2015/06/23/world/americas/poor-children-still-at-risk-despite-progress-unicef-warns.html.
35 John Baird, "Ending Child Marrriage," and Jill Sheffield and Katia Iversen, "A Dream of Progress for Girls and Women," and Phumzile Mlambo Ngcuka, "Increased financing needed to end the global pandemic of violence against women," in "Financing the Future of Global Health," *Global Health and Diplomacy.* Retrieved from: www.GHDNews.com.
36 Mlambo-Ngcuka.
37 Kathy Calvin, "Seizing the Mobile Opportunity for Women and Girls," in *Financing the Future of Global Health.*

10 The way forward

Awakening to the misery wrought by COVID-19 and new evidence of the perils of inequality, all participants in financial markets share a serious determination to build back better. By harnessing the power of financial institutions, equity markets, and bond markets—as well as government and philanthropy as enablers—this moment in time is a golden opportunity for disruptive innovation.

Bankers and bears

There's an old story about two bankers who chartered a plane with a pilot to drop them off in the wilds of Alaska for a week of elk hunting, just as they had done the year before. When the pilot returned with the plane to pick them up, the bankers were excited because each of them had bagged an elk. The pilot regretfully explained, "Unfortunately, our plane can only fly with the weight of one elk. You'll have to leave the other one behind."

But the bankers insisted on taking both their prizes home, so the plane took off with both elk. About 15 minutes into the flight the engine started to sputter, and within seconds they were crash landing. Staggering out of the wreckage, one banker said to the other, "Do you have any idea where we are?" And the second banker replied, "Yes! We're about a mile east of where we crash landed last year."

Then there's Sir Winston Churchill: Those who fail to learn from history are doomed to repeat it.

And Albert Einstein: Insanity is doing the same thing over and over again, and expecting different results.

That's the central theme of this book: The impact revolution is about doing things *differently*.

A crisis is a terrible thing to waste

We learn a lot from disasters. When an airplane crashes, investigators investigate doggedly until they figure out what brought the plane down, and how to fix the problem so that it doesn't happen again (see Boeing 737 MAX). When a space shuttle explodes, experts determine how to make it better and stronger and safer for the next flight. When an earthquake shatters buildings and people, we (hopefully) learn to build earthquake-proof buildings before the next disaster. And so on.

In just the first two decades of the 21st century, we have seen crises galore: 9/11 kicked off the new century, then Hurricane Katrina, the financial crash of 2008–2010, and the COVID-19 pandemic of 2020–2021.

What has this litany of disasters exposed?

- We've learned that the world is rife with inequality—in health care, and access to jobs, education, clean water, and a stable food supply—and that inequality is a silent killer.
- We've learned that financial markets and governments and people are remarkably resistant to change: Even after massive shocks to the system, governments dismantle financial regulations, homes are rebuilt in the exact same places that were just devastated by natural disasters, and people refuse to adapt to something as simple as wearing masks to save lives.
- We've learned that doing the same thing over and over again isn't just insanity, it's catastrophic.

There's a lot of bad news in the world today. According to UNICEF, the world's poorest children face a grim fate; millions will face preventable deaths, diseases, stunted growth and illiteracy. From 2000 to 2015, there was significant progress in terms of reducing poverty and other ills in developing countries—but the COVID-19 pandemic has reversed many of these gains, and its pernicious effects will not evaporate quickly.

We know that education—especially girls' education—is the silver bullet in development. Nonetheless, the UN special envoy for global education lamented in 2015:

> We have a long way to go. While over 40 million more children are in school today than in 2000, 58 million primary-age and 63 million secondary-age children remain out of school, with about half of the world's out-of-school primary-age children in conflict- and crisis-affected countries. Indeed, there are more child refugees than at any time since World War II. Girls face a particularly difficult challenge,

because they must struggle to gain the right to an education, even as the fight against child marriage, child labor, and the trafficking of women and girls is yet to be won.[1]

And this was 5 years before COVID-19 sent hundreds of millions of children home for school during worldwide lockdowns, some never to return (research indicates that girls are much less likely to return to school than boys).

Build back better

In this grim environment, it is essential to build back better as the world slowly recovers from the devastation of the COVID-19 pandemic. And the good news is that we have learned from this crisis:

> A young man once asked a rich old man how he made his money. The old guy said, "Well, son, it was 1932. The depth of the Great Recession. I was down to my last nickel."
>
> "I invested that nickel in an apple. I spent the entire day polishing the apple, and at the end of the day, I sold that apple for ten cents."
>
> "The next morning, I invested that dime in two apples. I spent the entire day polishing them and sold them at 5:00 PM for twenty cents. I continued this system for a month, by the end of which I'd accumulated a fortune of $1.37."
>
> Awed, the boy asked, "And that's how you built an empire?"
>
> "Heck, no!" the man replied. "Then my wife's father died and left us a million dollars."

That's what the financial world has become: It's all about lucky money, non-productive investments (Bitcoin, anyone?), shifting money, and quick money. Wall Street triggered the Great Recession of 2008–2010 by taking on excessive risk, essentially gambling rather than doing its job.

Innovative finance is all about turning this greed into good. It's a response to market and policy failures; microfinance and gender lens investing, for example, arose from the failure of the mainstream financial community to recognize the opportunity of financing women—both as potential customers and as drivers of development. These are *disruptive innovations*, which shake up the financial world and have the potential to stimulate dramatic growth.

Still, even financial actors that fall into our category of innovative finance, tend to exhibit a herd mentality and clump around certain pet projects (e.g., financing women entrepreneurs). This is related to two factors:

- The oversized and idiosyncratic influence of individuals whose personal views come to dominate the conversation and set priorities for the whole field.
- The emphasis on being able to measure everything.

Bill Gates, for instance, single-handedly focused the world's attention on health care in Africa, especially with regard to vaccines. Health and vaccines lend themselves to easy measurement—in a sense, it's low-hanging fruit. This is undoubtedly a worthy endeavor, but in a world of severely limited resources, are we absolutely sure that vaccines are more important than education?

This also illustrates the disproportionate influence of a champion like Bill Gates, who has the ability to shape the public discussion and to eclipse public organizations through sheer wallet size. Mohammed Yunus is another such example, as the father of microfinance; so too is Sir Ronald Cohen, the father of impact investing.

These champions are powerful and well-intentioned, but are they leading us in the right directions? And is it dangerous to center such power in a few private, unelected individuals, thus sidelining sovereign, democratically elected governments and well-governed international institutions?

The lack of a Bill Gates of Muhammad Yunus to champion girls' education underlines the danger of relying on these all-powerful, ungovernable individuals. Somehow, education has not emerged as one of these pet projects; it has not gained a formidable godfather. Thus far, even innovative finance has gone for relatively easy, short-term measurable goals—even though education is the silver bullet. So annual aid for primary education amounts to just $11 per child in the Democratic Republic of the Congo; $5 per child in Chad; and $4 per child in Nigeria, the most populous country in Africa.

The way forward: Greed gone good

This book outlines an innovative financial markets approach to addressing these needs. In order to build back better from the COVID-19 pandemic, it will be necessary to crowd in private capital; public and philanthropic funds fall far short of the total needed to achieve, or even make progress toward, the Sustainable Development Goals.

And there's really good news on this front. Awakening to the misery wrought by COVID-19 and new evidence of the perils of inequality, all participants in financial markets share a serious determination to build back better. By harnessing the power of financial institutions, equity markets, and bond markets—as well as government and philanthropy as enablers—this moment in time is a golden opportunity for disruptive innovation.

Note

1 Brown, G. (June 27, 2015). "New Ways to Finance Education." Retrieved from: www.project-syndicate.org/commentary/new-ways-finance-education-by-gordon-brown-2015-06?barrier=accesspaylog.

Index

1% for the Planet 58n33

ABN Amro 139, 141
Accenture 72
accountability 75, 88
Acumen Fund 100
additionality principle 107
Afghanistan 3, 42
African Development Bank 46
age factors: investors 47, 59–60, 63, 64, 101, 103; sustainability-linked loans 144
Agrial 145
aid 1, 2–4, 107–8
Akula, Vikram 85, 86, 93–4
Albania 3
Alibaba 97
AllLife 99, 103
Amana Funds 72
Amazon 45, 96, 97, 109, 113
American Council for Capital Formation 142
American Economic Journal: Applied Economics 158–9
American Enterprise Institute 15
Anderson, Joy 165, 174
Andersson, Mats 39–40, 48
Annan, Kofi 47
ANZ Bank 139
Apax Partners 97
Apple 9, 14, 97, 105, 116
Arab Spring 17
Argentina 16
Armenia 3
Arthur Andersen 28

Asian Development Bank 115
Australia 14, 69, 139
authoritarianism 4–5
Ave Maria Mutual Funds 72

Bahrain 13
Bahrat Financial Inclusion *see* SKS Microfinance
Bain Capital 69, 72–3, 74
Banco Compartamos 85, 92–3, 94
Banco Sol 85
Banerjee, Abhijit 159
Bangladesh: gender-lens investing 168; microfinance 78–81, 87, 89; poverty 41
BankAmerica 109–10, 141
banking *see* sustainable banking
Bank of America 46, 160–1
Bank of America Merrill Lynch 116
Bank of China 148
Barclays Women in Leadership Total Return Index 167
Barings Bank 31–2
Barra, Mary 35
B Corporations 53, 55, 58n32
Bedabasingwa, Marie 168–9
Begum, Sufiya 78–9, 85–6, 87, 155
Belarus 3
Belgium 13
Biegel, Suzanne 165
Bill and Melinda Gates Foundation 65, 107
Black Lives Matter 61
BlackRock 66, 74–6, 110, 115

Blackstone Group 74
Bloomberg 141, 142, 145
Blossom Finance 147
blue bonds 114–15
BNP Paribas 128, 143
Boesky, Ivan 25, 37nn1–2
Bolivia 85
Bombas 54–5, 96, 102
bonds 112; Diaspora 112, 122–3; disaster 112, 121–2; vs. equity 112–13; future 131–2, 181; gender-lens investment 167–8; historical and market context 113–21; pay-for-success instruments 123–5; retail investors 61; Sustainable Development Goals 129; women's 150, 152, 163; *see also* COVID-19 Social Bonds; Green Bonds; Social Bonds
Bosnia and Herzegovina 3, 86
Brazil 14, 108, 136, 162
Brown, Stuart 147
Buffett, Warren 27
Bulgaria 3
Burkina Faso 83
Bush, George H.W. 29
Business and Sustainable Development Commission 131
buy-one-give-one model 54–5

Calvert Impact Capital/Calvert Foundation 62, 161, 167
Cambodia 167, 168
Cambridge Associates 65
Cameroon 49–50, 136–8
Canada 14
capitalism: affirmation 1, 6; channeling into good 40–2; failure 1, 4, 6; globalization 10; perversion of 24–37; reformation 1, 6
Castro, Fidel 12
catastrophe (cat/disaster) bonds 112, 121–2
CEO magazine 29
Cerulli Associates 63
CFO magazine 29
Chad 136–8, 180
charity *see* philanthropy
Cheney, Dick 29
child mortality rate 41
child poverty 178

Children's Investment Fund Foundation 125
Chile 14
China: COVID-19 Social Bonds 46; economic growth 48; electric vehicles 70; foreign direct investment 17; free markets 6; globalization impact 13–14, 16, 17, 19; Green Bonds 116; high net worth individuals 63; inequality 16, 17; market economy transition 12; poverty 41; and the US, relations between 11–12, 18; and the US, trade war between 18; world trade trends 18
Chouinard, Yvon 53, 58n33
Churchill, Sir Winston 6, 18, 177
Cisco 72
Citibank 51
climate change 5; BlackRock and Larry Fink 74, 75; bonds 131; business awareness of 54; disaster bonds 121; equity markets 96, 97, 102; family-based impact investors 64; Green Bonds 119, 121; Paris Agreement 141; and poverty 42; retail investors 61, 62; risks 39; Seychelles 114; Social Bonds 126, 127; sustainable banking 141; time horizon 113; venture capital and private equity firms 68, 69, 73, 74
Clinton, Bill 29
CMS Energy 143
Coca Cola 14
Cohen, Sir Ronald 96, 97, 100, 109, 180
Colombia Sportswear 53
commercials 51
communism 11
Community Capital Management Inc. 62
conflicts 42
cookstoves 83–4, 96, 108, 167, 172
corporate impact 109–11
corporate social responsibility (CSR) 109–10, 118
corruption 103, 105, 123, 135, 137
COVID-19: BlackRock 74, 75; bond market, impact on 131, 132; bonds *see* COVID-19 Social Bonds; commercials 51; Diaspora bonds 123; domestic violence 151, 173; Dow Jones Index 40; economic impact 43, 126; education impact 17, 127,

184 Index

179; electricity, importance of 49; equity markets 101; ethnicity issues 42; faith-based investors 71, 72; future 177–81; globalization impact 8, 11, 17, 18–19; India 44–5; inequality 1, 5, 8, 11, 17, 61, 118, 140, 150–2, 181; investment boost 64; investment returns 60; microfinance 93; poverty 8, 41, 118, 140, 178; Social Bonds 59; social impact 126–7, 128, 131; sustainable banking 134, 140, 145–7, 148; Sustainable Development Goals 43, 45, 46–7, 127; urgency of ESG investing 2; US accusations against China 18; vaccine 19; Venezuela 43–4; venture capital and private equity firms 74; women, impact on 150–2, 167, 173; workers remittances 56n18
COVID-19 Social Bonds 45–6, 47, 61, 112, 113, 117–20; Islamic investors 71; market growth opportunities 130; need for 126, 128; retail investors 61; sustainable banking 148
CREO 65
cryptocurrency 147
Cuba 6, 11, 12, 14
Czech Republic 3
Czyż, Kajetan 143

Danone 110
Deby, Idriss 136–7
democracy 6, 88
Democratic Republic of Congo 41, 108, 180
derivatives market 31, 32
Deutsche Bank 116, 140
development impact bonds (DIBs) 123–5
Dial 1298 for Ambulance 99, 103
Diaspora bonds 112, 122–3
digital divide 126–7, 146
disaster (catastrophe/cat) bonds 112, 121–2
d. light 102
domestic violence 151, 156, 173
Dow Jones Index 40, 100
Dow Jones Sustainability Index 51
Drexel Burnham Lambert 25
Dubai 90
Duer, William 30, 31

Ebola crisis 129
economic growth 14
economic nationalism 11, 12, 19
education: COVID-19 impact 17, 127, 179; financing access to 172; gender issues 13, 41, 48, 124–5, 171–4, 178–9, 180; India's Educate Girls Development Impact Bond 124–5; microfinance 82, 83, 84, 87, 90, 103, 159; Social Bonds 126
Egypt 17, 135, 161–2
Einstein, Albert 6, 177
electricity 49–50, 167, 168
Elleman, Peter 141
Enron 5, 24–30, 31, 32, 39, 48
Environmental Defense Fund 137
Environmental Finance 116
Envision Healthcare 100
Equator Principles (EPs) 134, 138–40
equity markets 96–7, 180; vs. bonds 112–13; firm sample 102; future 181; gender-lens investing 167; light-bulb moments 99–101; nature of impact investing 98–9; promise of impact investing 97–8; questions to resolve 106–8; reality 102–6; traditional companies 109–11
ERC Eye Care India 168
Estonia 13, 14
ethical issues: bonds 128; Enron's suspension of its code of ethics 28; General Motors 35; investment returns 51; investors 60; microfinance 78, 87
Ethiopia 41, 123
ethnicity issues 42, 110
Etsy 96, 102
European Investment Bank 115
European Union, and Brexit 5, 10, 11, 18
Eurozone 18
exchange-traded funds (ETFs) 62, 75
Exxon Mobil 15
Exxon Valdez 136

Facebook 97
faith-based investors 70–2
faith-washing 72
family offices 63–5
Fastow, Andy 26–7, 28, 29

F.B. Heron Foundation 66
Fiat Chrysler 109
Fiji 115
Financial Access Initiative 159
financial advisors 61, 130
financial crisis (2007–2010) 1, 5, 48, 178; blind faith in technology 5; Bosnia 86; causes 179; fines and legal fees 39; perversion of capitalism 31–2; risk management 101; sustainable banking 140
financial inclusion 91, 146, 172
financial literacy 90
financial models, power of 12–13
FINCA 83–4
Fink, Larry 74, 75
Folksam 129
food security/insecurity 42
Ford Foundation 66
Ford Motors 15, 109
foreign aid 1, 2–4, 107–8
foreign direct investment 17, 19
Fortune magazine 29
Forum for Sustainable and Responsible Investment 60
foundation investors 65–6
France 5, 68, 116, 135
Francis, Pope 72
free markets: benefits 19; blind faith in 6, 12; China 6; flaws 18; globalization impact 10, 11, 12, 13
Friedman, Thomas 5, 8

G8 173
Gates, Bill 41, 174 180
Gates, Melinda 41
Gavi, the Vaccine Alliance 129
Gazprom 139
gender issues: COVID-19 17; corporate impact 110; education 13, 41, 48, 124–5, 171–4, 178–9, 180; labor markets 42; poverty 41, 154, 156–9; *see also* women
gender-lens investing (GLI) 150, 152, 165–9, 170, 171, 179
Genentech 97
General Electric 15, 51, 105
General Mills 72
General Motors (GM) 34–5, 109
Generation X 101

Gentera 92–3
gig workers 126
Gini index 16
Global Alliance for Clean Cookstoves 172
Global Health Security Index 43, 44
Global Impact Investing Network (GIIN) 2, 100, 104
globalization: attitudes towards 10–11; blind faith in 5, 12; future 18–20; impact 8–20; inequality 1, 5; losers 15–17; nature of 9–10; winners 12–15
Global Real Estate Sustainability Benchmark 143
Goldberg, Randy 54
Goldman Sachs 66–7, 110, 116, 161–2, 163–4
Google 97, 105
Grameen Bank 79–83, 84, 87, 88, 91, 157
Grameen Healthcare 89
Great Depression 1
Green Bonds 46, 112, 114–17, 119, 130; ICMA Principles 114; vs. Social Bonds 120–1
greenwashing 52, 121; investors' concerns 61; Social Bonds 130; sustainable banking 146, 148
Guatemala 93

Habitat for Humanity 138
Haiti 4, 56n18, 107–8, 123
Harding, Warren 30
Harvard Business School 29, 51
Harvard Law School 67
HBS 166
Heath, David 54
Heinemann, Tom 86
high net worth individuals (HNWIs): equity markets 100; gender-lens investing 167; globalization impact 14, 16, 19; investments 62–5
Honest Tea 96, 102
Hong Kong 14, 148
HSBC 148

IBM 15
Ikea 51
illiteracy 79, 81, 90, 124
impact investing *see* equity markets

186 Index

Impact Investment Exchange (IIX) 167
Impact Multiple of Money (IMM) 73
Impact Shares 62
Inyenyeri 108
index funds 62
Index of Economic Freedom 14
India: COVID-19 44–5; Dial 1298 for Ambulance 99–100; Diaspora bonds 123; economic growth 48; Educate Girls Development Impact Bond 124–5; education 48, 124–5; Enron 29; equity markets 96, 99–100, 108; gender-lens investing 167, 168; globalization impact 13–14, 16; inequality 16; microfinance 85, 86, 87, 91, 93–4, 159; pollution-related deaths 39; poverty 41; project finance 136; public violence against women 165; women entrepreneurs 161
Indonesia 71, 115–16, 147, 167
inequality 1, 6; Black Lives Matter movement 61; business awareness of 54; COVID-19 1, 5, 8, 11, 17, 61, 118, 140, 150–2, 181; digital divide 126–7, 146; globalization impact 8, 16–20; venture capital and private equity firms 73; women's role in reducing 81
informal economy 126, 151, 153
information technology: COVID-19 impact 146; democratization 9; digital divide 126–7; globalization impact 9, 19
ING 32, 143
institutional investors 66–8, 74–6; equity markets 100; microfinance 89; project finance 148n1
insurance products: and disaster bonds 121, 122; life insurance for life-threatening disease sufferers 99; microfinance institutions 82, 84, 90, 93, 159–60
Intel 15
Inter-American Development Bank (IDB) 164
International Capital Market Association (ICMA) 112, 114, 119–20, 130, 132
International Development Association (IDA) 49
International Finance Corporation (IFC): Banking on Women (BOW) program 162–3, 164; Cameroon's Nachtigal Hydropower Project 50; project finance 137, 138; women entrepreneurs 160, 162–4; Women Entrepreneurs Opportunity facility 163–4; women-focused financial innovations 153
International Finance Facility for Immunization 129
International Monetary Fund (IMF) 3, 13, 43, 44, 126
investors: bonds 128–9; case studies 72–6; connecting to development 47–9; equity markets 98, 100–1, 103; faith-based 70–2; foundation 65–6; growth of sustainable investing 59–60; high net worth individuals and family offices 62–5; institutional 66–8, 74–6, 89, 100; retail 60–2, 82; returns *see* returns; Social Bonds 132; venture capital and private equity firms 68–70, 72–4
Iran 16
Ireland 13, 14, 15
Islamic banking 146–7
Islamic investors 71–2
Islamic law 116
Israel 72, 123

Jain, Naresh 99
Japan 10, 68, 135, 163
JLens 72
John, Daymond 55
J.P. Morgan 100, 102, 116
J.P. Morgan Chase 51
Judeo-Christian faith-based investors 72
junk bonds 24, 25, 31

Kabeer, Naila 155
Kandiel, Sophie 83
Kaplan, Sarah 166, 171
Karim, Lamia 88, 105, 157, 158
Kenya 16, 48, 96, 123
Keynes, John Maynard 4, 6
Khosh, Vinod 85
Kiva 82, 89
KKR 69, 72–4
Kosovo 3
Kraft-Heinz 144
Krishna, Ravi 99
Krygyzstan 56n18

Lagarde, Christine 19
Lay, Kenneth 26, 27, 28, 29
Leapfrog Investments 99
Leeson, Nick 31–2, 39
liberalism 11
life insurance for life-threatening disease sufferers 99
literacy 79, 81, 90, 124
Loan Market Association 145
London & Quadrant (L&Q) 143
Luxembourg 13

Macedonia 3
Maduro, Nicolás 44
Malawi 121
Malaysia 16, 71, 82
Mangal, Sweta 99
Marcario, Rose 53, 58n34
Margaret A. Cargill Foundation 83
Marriott 72, 144
Marxism 11, 12
masters of business administration (MBA) programs 2
maternal mortality rate 41, 42
Mather, Shaffi 99
McDonalds 9, 15
McKenna, Tjada 169
McKinsey 136, 151, 152, 153
Meriton, Vincent 115
Mexico: disaster bonds 121–2; foreign aid 2–3; globalization impact 12, 15, 17; microfinance 85, 92–3, 159; and the US, relations between 17
microfinance 78, 179; case studies 92–4; equity markets 101, 102, 103, 104; impact 85–9; Islamic investors 71; lessons 89–92, 108; profitability 82, 84–5, 87, 89, 91–4, 103, 106; spread 82–5; sustainable banking 147; women 80–2, 84, 86–91, 93, 104, 150, 152, 155–60, 170, 172, 179; Yunus 78–82
Microsoft 15, 72, 144
Milanovic, Branko 14, 16
Milken, Michael 24, 25
millennials: equity markets 101, 103; investors 47, 59–60, 64; sustainability-linked loans 144
Millennium Development Goals (MDGs) 40–1, 42; gender equality 154, 171; women's health 172–3
mission drift: equity markets 104; microfinance institutions 78, 87, 104
Mission Investors Exchange (MIE) 66
MIT, Poverty Action Lab 89
Mitsubishi UFJ Financial Group Inc. 61
mobile technology 173
Moldova 3
Mongolia 122, 159
Montenegro 3
Moody's 44, 142, 145–6
Morgan, J.P. 30
Morgan Stanley 51, 167
Morocco 86
MSCI 142
Multilateral Investment Guarantee Agency (MIGA) 50
multinational corporations (MNCs): globalization impact 14, 15, 16; microfinance 89
Musasa 168–9

Nakintu, Jane 83–4
Nasdaq 110
Netflix 140
Netherlands 13, 116
New Zealand 14
Nicaragua 86
Nigeria 41, 123, 159, 180
Nike 53
nongovernmental organizations (NGOs): microfinance 89; project finance 137, 138; women entrepreneurs 164
Nordic-Baltic Blue Bond 115
Nordic Investment Bank 115
North Korea 6, 11, 14
Norway 3
Nuveen 62

Obama, Barack 12, 20
Occupy movement 11
official development aid 46–7, 127
Ogden, Timothy 159
Organisation des Églises Évangéliques 83
Organisation for Economic Co-operation and Development (OECD) 48, 153
Oxfam 3

188 Index

Pakistan 86, 157
Paris Agreement on climate change 141
Patagonia, Inc. 52–4, 55, 96, 102, 144
patriarchy 157–8
Pax Elevate Global Women's Index Fund 167
pay-for-success (PFS) instruments 112, 123–5
pensions, microfinance institutions 82, 84
Peru 17, 93, 96
Pfizer 46
Pfund, Nancy 64
philanthropy: banks 138; bonds 131; capital market 49; development impact bonds 124; Dial 1298 for Ambulance 100; and disaster bonds 122; family offices 64; foundation investors 65–6; future 181; girls' education 173; and impact investing, difference between 96, 98, 107, 109–10; India's Educate Girls Development Impact Bond 125; microfinance 88, 89; pay-for-success instruments 124, 125; Social Bonds 112, 131; Sustainable Development Goals 46; women entrepreneurs 161, 163–4
Philippines 82, 117–18, 121, 122, 167
Philips 143
Poland 3
positive incentive deals *see* sustainability-linked loans
poverty: blind faith in free markets 6; Cameroon 49; Chad–Cameroon pipeline 137; children 178; and climate change 42; COVID-19 8, 41, 118, 140, 178; digitization 146; equity markets 96, 102, 107–8; foreign aid 2–4; globalization impact 8, 11, 13–15, 17–20; India 44–5; Islamic investors 71; microfinance 78–91, 93–4, 104, 155–9; Millennium Development Goals 41; natural disasters 122; Philippines 118; project finance 136; sustainable banking 146; Sustainable Development Goals 46; vaccine bonds 129; Venezuela 43; women 154, 156–9; women's role in reducing 81

Principles for Responsible Investment (PRI) 52, 69, 73
private equity firms 68–70, 72–4
Private Equity International (PEI) 69
Procter & Gamble 110
profitability 1, 6; Bombas 54–5; changing business models 54; Enron 24, 26; equity markets 106–7; globalization 9; impact investments 40; microfinance institutions 82, 84–5, 87, 89, 91–4, 103, 106; Patagonia 53; sustainability-linked loans 144; sustainable banking 146; women entrepreneurs 162
project finance (PF) 134–40
Prologis Inc. 141
Prudential 110
PwC 63–4, 69, 102

Rainforest Action Network 139
RBC Capital Markets 61
red-lined communities 52, 57–8n31
retail investors 60–2, 82
returns 50–1, 60–1; BlackRock 75; bonds 129; equity markets 100, 106–7; high net worth individuals and family offices 64; institutional investors 75; Social Bonds 130; socially responsible investment 98; venture capital and private equity firms 68
Reynolds, Eric 108
rich people *see* high net worth individuals
risk issues 38–9, 40; connecting capital markets to development 49; disaster bonds 122; equity markets 100, 101, 103, 105, 106; microfinance institutions 90, 92; project finance 135; sustainability-linked loans 144; sustainable banking 134, 138, 140, 141, 147; sustainable funds 51; venture capital and private equity firms 68, 69, 70
Rockefeller Foundation 49, 66
Rodrik, Dani 18
Rohatyn, Felix 32
Root Capital 167, 168–9
Royal Dutch Shell 96

Index 189

Russia 139
Rwanda 96, 108, 123, 168–9

S&P 500: 101
S&P Global 1200 Index 142
S&P Global Broad Market Index 51
S&P Global Clean Energy Index 101
S&P Global Ratings 141, 142
Sacheti, Manish 99
SAMIC Cambodia 168
savings products, microfinance institutions 82, 84, 90, 93, 159–60
Scharf, Charles 36–7
Schiller, Ben 99–100
Serbia 3
Seychelles 114–15
Shark Tank 55
Singapore 13, 14
sin stocks 50, 51, 71
Skilling, Jeff 24–7, 28, 29
Skoll, Jeff 171, 173
SKS Microfinance 85, 86, 93–4
Sloan, Tim 36, 37
Social Bonds 46, 112, 114, 117; COVID-19 *see* COVID-19 Social Bonds; future 131, 132; vs. Green Bonds 120–1; ICMA Principles 114, 119–20; market growth 2, 129–31; need for 126–8
social impact bonds (SIBs) 123–4, 125
socialism 6, 11
socially responsible investment (SRI) 98, 107
social washing 61, 130, 132
Solshare Bangladesh 168
Somalia 13
Somavia, Juan 156
South Africa 99, 103
South Sudan 42
Soviet Union 3, 6, 9
Spectrem Group 101
Starbucks 72, 116–17
State Street Global Advisors 110
Stiglitz, Joseph 18
Stumpf, John 36, 37
sub-Saharan Africa 48, 50, 169
Sustainability Accounting Standards Board 130
Sustainability Bonds 112, 114

sustainability-linked bonds (SLBs) 123–4
sustainability-linked loans (SLLs) 142–5, 148
sustainable banking 134; opportunities 140–5; post-COVID-19 era 145–7, 148; project finance 134–40; as strategy 147–8
sustainable development 39–40, 47–50
Sustainable Development Goals (SDGs) 38; bonds 112, 118, 129, 131, 132; capital markets 49; funding 42–8, 126, 127, 180; Islamic investors 72; language 63; venture capital and private equity firms 73
Sustainable Ventures 61
Sustainalytics 142, 143
Switzerland 14
Syria 42

Taibbi, Matt 77n24
Taiwan 148
Tanzania 16
technology: blind faith in 5; democratization 9; globalization impact 19; power of 12, 13; revolution 97–8; venture capital and private equity firms 70; *see also* information technology
Tesla 109, 113
Thailand 17
Thames Water 143
Thomson Reuters 136
Timberland 53
Tin Shed Ventures 52
TOMS Shoes 54, 102
tourism 126
Toyota 9
TPG 69, 72–3, 74
track records: equity markets 103–4, 107; pay-for-success instruments 125
trade volumes 18
Trans Pacific Partnership 18
transparency: Fink's call for 75; General Motors 35; lack of, and investors 59, 60; project finance 139; retail investors 62; Social Bonds 128
Trump, Donald 5, 11, 12, 18, 39
Turkmenistan 13, 16
Twitter 144

Uber 9, 97
UBS 64
UBS Optimus Foundation 125
Ukraine 3
under-5 mortality rate 13
undernutrition 13
UNICEF 172, 178
United Arab Emirates 13, 14
United Kingdom: Brexit 5, 10, 11, 18; Chunnel 135; COVID-19 17; globalization attitudes 10–11, 16; social impact bonds 125; sustainability-linked loans 143
United Nations (UN): Development Program (UNDP) 147; gender equality 150–2, 153, 154; girls' education 178–9; globalization impact 13, 15; Paris Agreement on climate change 141; peacekeepers in Haiti 4; poverty levels 42; Principles for Responsible Investment 52, 69, 73; UN Women 151, 153, 173; *see also* Millennium Development Goals; Sustainable Development Goals
United States: 9/11 terrorist attacks 5, 178; Agency for International Development (USAID) 3, 4, 166; black communities 5; bonds 113; Boston Big Dig 135; capital market 48; and China, relations between 11–12, 18; and China, trade war between 18; circuit-breakers 40, 55n2; Clean Air Act (1970) 37n7; climate change 39; corporate impact 110; COVID-19 5, 17, 40; COVID-19 Social Bonds 46; Dakota Access Pipeline 139; Department of Labor 77n34; disaster bonds 121; Enron 24–30; Environmental Protection Agency (EPA) 33–4; financial advisors 61; financial crisis 15; financial markets, greed in 30–2; foreign aid 2–3, 4; foreign direct investment 17; foundation investors 66; General Motors 34–5; globalization attitudes 10–11, 12, 16; globalization impact 14–15, 16, 19; Green Bonds 115, 116; high net worth individuals 63; high-tech industry 70; Hurricane Katrina 1, 5, 178; inequality 16, 146; institutional investors 68; Judeo-Christian faith-based investors 72; and Mexico, relations between 17; natural disasters 1, 5, 121, 122, 178; Panic (1792) 30; philanthropy 174; red-lined communities 58n31; retail investors 60; sustainability-linked loans 143; sustainable banking 140–1; Teapot Dome scandal 30–1; Trans Pacific Partnership withdrawal 18; Trump's election 5, 11; Trust Women and Girls Equity Strategy 167; venture capital 166; Volkswagen 33–4; Wells Fargo 35–7; women's control of personal wealth 47–8; world trade trends 18
Uruguay 121
Uzbekistan 13

vaccine bonds 129
VanderBrug, Jackie 166, 171
Venezuela 14, 43–4, 47
venture capital (VC) 52, 68–70, 72–4, 96–8, 166
Veolia 89
Veris Wealth Partners 154, 166
V.F. Corporation 53
Vietnam 12, 139
VitalVoices 153
Volkswagen 24, 33–4

Wall Street Journal 62
Walmart 15
Washington, George 30
Watkins, Sherron 27
Waze 9
wealthy people *see* high net worth individuals
Wells Fargo 24, 33, 35–7, 140–1
women: business case for investing in 153–5; COVID-19 impact 150–2; as drivers of economic and social advancement 81, 153, 154, 169, 172; empowerment 150, 152–61, 164, 169–70, 172; entrepreneurs 154–5, 160–5, 170–1, 172, 180; equity markets 101, 103; gender-lens investing 150, 152, 165–9, 170, 171, 179; innovative finance for 152–3; innovative vs. transformative finance

170–4; investors 47–8, 60, 64, 69; microfinance 80–2, 84, 86–91, 93, 104, 150, 152, 155–60, 170, 172, 179; private equity firms 69
Women Entrepreneurs Opportunity facility 163–4
Women in Agriculture Initiative (WAI) 167, 168–9
Women Investing in Women Initiative (WIN-WIN) 167
women-owned businesses (WOBs) 154–5, 160, 170
Women's Economic Empowerment Initiative (WEempower) 164
women's impact bonds 150, 152, 163
Women's Livelihood Bond (WLB) 167–8
Women's World Banking (WWB) 159
Workday 97
workers remittances 46–7, 56n18
World Bank: blue bonds 115; bonds 113, 129; Cameroon's Nachtigal Hydropower Project 50; COVID-19 impact 17; COVID-19 Social Bond 46; disaster bonds 121; electricity, access to 49; financial inclusion 91; foreign aid 3; gender inequality 153; globalization impact 13; Green Bonds 115; Islamic investors 72; microfinance 82, 157; poverty levels 41; project finance 137, 138; Sustainable Development Goals 49; women entrepreneurs 162–3; *see also* International Finance Corporation
WorldCom 24, 33
World Trade Organization (WTO) 18

Xylem Inc. 143

Yunus, Muhammad 78–82, 85, 87, 94, 155, 174, 180

Zipcar 96, 102

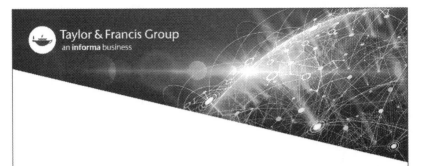